The Work Alternative

DEMETRA SMITH NIGHTINGALE
ROBERT H. HAVEMAN
Editors

The Work Alternative

Welfare Reform and the Realities of the Job Market

THE URBAN INSTITUTE PRESS
Washington, D.C.

THE URBAN INSTITUTE PRESS
2100 M Street, N.W.
Washington, D.C. 20037

The Work Alternative: Welfare Reform and the Realities of the Job Market/Demetra Smith Nightingale and Robert H. Haveman, editors.

Includes bibliographical references and index.

1.   Welfare recipients—Employment—United States.   2.   Labor market—United States.   I.   Nightingale, Demetra Smith.   II.   Haveman, Robert H.

HV91.W627   1994   94-38392
362.5′84—dc20   CIP

ISBN 0-87766-623-7 (cloth, alk. paper)

Printed in the United States of America.

Distributed by:
            National Book Network
4720 Boston Way   3 Henrietta Street
Lanham, MD 20706   London   WC2E 8LU   ENGLAND

THE URBAN INSTITUTE is a nonprofit policy research and educational organization established in Washington, D.C., in 1968. Its staff investigates the social and economic problems confronting the nation and public and private means to alleviate them. The Institute disseminates significant findings of its research through the publications program of its Press. The goals of the Institute are to sharpen thinking about societal problems and efforts to solve them, improve government decisions and performance, and increase citizen awareness of important policy choices.

Through work that ranges from broad conceptual studies to administrative and technical assistance, Institute researchers contribute to the stock of knowledge available to guide decision making in the public interest.

Conclusions or opinions expressed in Institute publications are those of the authors and do not necessarily reflect the views of staff members, officers or trustees of the Institute, advisory groups, or any organizations that provide financial support to the Institute.

ACKNOWLEDGMENTS

This book and the conference on which it is based benefited from the participation of many individuals. Intellectual and financial support was provided by officials at four foundations. James Hyman of the Annie E. Casey Foundation was actively involved throughout the project and we are indebted to him and to Douglas Nelson, president of the foundation, for initiating the conference. Julia Lopez of the Rockefeller Foundation also provided valuable insights and ensured the full participation of state and local practitioners. Barbara Blum of the Foundation for Child Development and Mark Elliott of the Ford Foundation reviewed plans, agendas, and papers at all stages of the project. The contributions of these individuals cannot be overstated.

The discussions at the conference in April 1994 provided a vital forum for dialogue around the complex issues related to poverty, welfare and the labor market. We are grateful to all the formal speakers, moderators, and discussants listed in the front of this volume, for the time and energy they devoted to the conference. Special acknowledgment is due to Roger Weisberg and Dan Klein, co-producers of the Public Broadcasting System documentary, "Making Welfare Work," narrated by Walter Cronkite, which was previewed at the conference, and to Andrea Taylor of the Ford Foundation and William Rust of the Annie E. Casey Foundation for their ongoing support of that endeavor. Larry Haas devoted his full attention to every minute of the conference and prepared a written summary of the presentations and discussions.

We are particularly grateful for the advice and guidance provided by Peter Edelman and Wendell Primus of the U.S. Department of Health and Human Services, Thomas Glynn of the U.S. Department of Labor, and Ronald Haskins of the House Ways and Means Committee.

Urban Institute staff who worked tirelessly on conference planning deserve special recognition: Kristin Seefeldt, Mildred Woodhouse, Sharon Long, Janet Norwood, Rachel Pollack, Christina Card, Susan Brown, and Laura Wilcox. Without them, the conference would not have been such a success. Other Institute staff provided technical and logistical assistance at the conference: Rosalind Berkowitz, Deborah Chien, Mary Coombs, Sonja Drumgoole, Ernest Daniel, Grenda Hudson, Gregory Levine, Lori Schack, Minnie Tiller, and Andrea White.

The authors and editors are especially indebted to Felicity Skidmore, Scott Forrey, and CC Dietrich of the Urban Institute Press for their outstanding editorial and production effort under very tight time constraints. And finally, the book benefited greatly from the thoughtful review and comments of two anonymous reviewers.

CONTENTS

Tables

Figures

FOREWORD

A welfare policy built around the obligation to prepare for and seek work in exchange for benefits assumes both that the jobs are there and that they pay enough to be consistent with economic independence. In the current national debate on the welfare system, these assumptions have not been adequately examined.

Recognizing the crucial importance of such an examination, the Urban Institute welcomed the opportunity to host a conference in the spring of 1994, to direct the attention of the social policy and research communities to the challenges involved in achieving self-sufficiency among America's poor. We are equally pleased to publish *The Work Alternative*, the chapters of which are based on the papers presented at the conference and the insights derived from the conference discussion.

Achieving long-term economic self-sufficiency through work is a fundamental goal of our society. Reforming our public assistance system so that more Americans achieve that goal is a worthy policy endeavor. However, as they pursue the task of reform, policymakers need to face squarely some uncomfortable facts.

The job market may well have enough jobs for the majority, perhaps most, of the nation's current welfare recipients. But these jobs do not typically pay enough for a family to become self-sufficient. In addition, a considerable group, perhaps 20 percent or more, do not have the capacity to find and hold even a low-paying job in the regular labor market. Any viable reform will have to make provision for those who would need subsidized jobs, as well as those who would be unable to work. Moreover, no conceivable development in the labor market will solve the problem of poverty, even for those who work full-time all year round. It is our hope that the book will help highlight these important issues in the ongoing policy debate about the mutual responsibilities of society and its poorer members.

William Gorham
President

It is clear that the 1994–95 welfare reform debate will offer yet one more opportunity for a national referendum on welfare policy and, by extension, welfare recipients in the United States. Over the past twenty years or so, the Aid to Families with Dependent Children (AFDC) program has become one of the most universally unpopular government programs in American history, and has come to symbolize, to many American voters, the worst in bureaucratic ineptitude; waste, fraud, and abuse; and "social engineering". American welfare policy has been the target of at least a half dozen reform attempts over this period and has been an increasingly prominent issue in every presidential campaign since 1968. So much so that, as a candidate, President Clinton's pledge to "end welfare as we know it" was the top vote-getter in many parts of the country.

In some ways America's seeming perennial preoccupation with, and disdain for, the nation's principal anti-poverty program is puzzling. Federal AFDC payments to welfare recipients, estimated at approximately $12.8 billion for 1995, will consume less than one percent of the 1995 federal budget, and less than half the estimated $26 billion that will be expended for child exemptions for working families through the 1995 federal tax code. Both are intended to support America's children.

The most plausible explanation for America's angst over welfare may be a national intolerance for providing long-term support for unworking, and by implication, undeserving poor adults. The changing reality of the American family and the rising incidence of single working mothers has "raised the burden of proof" on the needs of poor. The consequent changes in public opinion have been mirrored in public policy. Beginning with the WIN demonstrations of the late 1970s and early 1980s, the paradigm for the nation's welfare program has steadily shifted toward the now widely accepted view that welfare recipients have an obligation to prepare for and seek work in exchange for their welfare benefits. By the mid-1980s, the nation had reached a strong consensus that welfare should be principally a transitional program. And with the passage of the Family Support Act of 1988, Congress went beyond the testing phase of the demonstrations and codified this transitional view by mandating participation in the JOBS Program. So there can be little wonder then why, in our current attempt at a 1990s version of reform, the government would move to further enforce that transition with a two-year time limit.

What has been missing from the transitional welfare debates, and particularly from the current proposal for time limits on cash assistance, is any consideration of the U.S. labor market and the extent to which it can actually provide the two to three million welfare recipients who might be subject to these new reform provisions with jobs that have wages and benefits adequate to support a family. In fact, it is the answer to this question that will largely determine whether welfare reform in the '90s will be a policy of hope or a policy of punishment for America's poor and needy.

Many observers believe that the current welfare reform debate will not be our last and that the nation will very likely revisit these issues yet again before the year 2000, perhaps with even less tolerance and public support than is evident today. While this kind of speculation is difficult to assess, it is reasonable to expect that the prospects of yet another, later round will increase markedly in proportion to the gap in public perception between the promise and the reality of next year's reform effort. The promise of "end(ing) welfare as we know it" may well set the stage for this later iteration. The question is whether the high expectations that have now been raised can be tempered or at least informed by an examination of the practical realities of employment for the poor.

Out of concern for this issue, The Annie E. Casey Foundation— joined by the Ford and Rockefeller Foundations and the Foundation for Child Development, in association with the Grantmakers Income Security Task Force—approached the Urban Institute to host a conference and create a national forum for raising these and other unanswered questions to the forefront of the current reform debate. The conference, held April 12–14, 1994, brought together 350 federal policymakers, state and local welfare officials, advocates, policy experts from government and academia, and journalists to critically examine the assumptions underlying current welfare policies and proposed new directions and to discuss the challenges involved in achieving a truly transitional welfare program. What follows is based on the papers and presentations shared with conference participants.

I believe I can speak for all who participated either as funders, presenters, discussants, or audience in expressing gratitude and congratulations to the Urban Institute for their tireless preparation and flawless execution of this forum.

James B. Hyman
Associate Director
The Annie E. Casey Foundation

Chapter One

WELFARE REFORM: HISTORICAL CONTEXT AND CURRENT ISSUES

Demetra Smith Nightingale

The United States welfare system comprises Aid to Families with Dependent Children (AFDC) and other programs such as Food Stamps and Medicaid. The system has evolved piecemeal in response to changes in the nature of the poverty problem and the performance of the labor market, and in social mores and public opinion about individual responsibilities and the role of government programs. AFDC, which was begun in 1935 ostensibly as a small program, covered about 15 million individuals by 1993, at an annual cost to federal and state governments of over $25 billion.

Although numerous incremental changes have been made over the years to the welfare system, there have also been many official attempts at major welfare reform. Cash and in-kind transfers have been the chief thrusts of antipoverty measures, but jobs and job training have also been central to the primary welfare reform efforts proposed or enacted. Since 1980, national policy has variously focused on (a) increasing financial incentives to encourage more welfare recipients to work; (b) providing more training and education to increase individuals' employability; (c) teaching job-finding skills; (d) having the government provide subsidized jobs as "employer of last resort"; and (e) stressing the obligation of public assistance recipients to prepare for and seek work in exchange for benefits.

As the nation nears the end of the 20th century, few are satisfied with the welfare system, despite many past attempts at reform. The American public endorses the idea of helping the poor, but they generally do not feel the current system is the appropriate way to help. Many resent that welfare recipients do not have to work to support their families. Recipients of welfare, in turn, often feel trapped by bureaucratic procedures that make it difficult for them to exit welfare for work, as well as by financial disincentives to becoming self-sufficient.

Reforming the welfare system was an important objective for President Bill Clinton even when he was still governor of Arkansas. His call to "end welfare as we know it" was positively received during the 1992 presidential campaign. Like previous federal attempts to reform welfare, President Clinton's approach is built around work, complemented by a strong focus on individual responsibility for one's self and children. His proposals are intended to make welfare a temporary, or transitional, state, "not a way of life." This would be accomplished by dramatically changing the incentives for and expectations of both welfare recipients and staff in welfare agencies. The most radical change would limit the length of time recipients may remain on welfare to two years. During the two years, the government would help improve skills and education; but after the two years, the recipient would be required to work, preferably in a regular job, but in a government-sponsored job if necessary.

President Clinton's plan is by no means the only call for welfare reform. In the past two years a flurry of welfare reform proposals has been introduced in Congress and in state legislatures. All the major ones emphasize work and jobs; and many, not just the president's, include the time-limit provision.

This book is not designed to critique the Clinton proposal or any other specific proposal. It has a wider purpose. Its intent is to examine the validity of the three main assumptions underlying most approaches to welfare reform: (1) that the labor market is the best route out of welfare and poverty; (2) that jobs are waiting for all at the end of the search and preparation process; and (3) that these jobs will pay enough to ensure economic independence for welfare recipients and their families.

The chapters in this volume address these assumptions in the context of today's labor market, and attempt to answer the following questions: Is today's labor market, in fact, able to generate earnings that will enable self-sufficiency for individuals now dependent on income support? Are enough jobs available to absorb welfare recipients who may be denied benefits under a time-limited system, and if not, can jobs be created? Will there not be a residual pool of adults who will be unable to secure and hold a job, no matter how effective the training and other services provided? If so, what policy alternatives should there be for these adults and their families? What does this imply for a new social contract between the government and recipients of public assistance?

These questions and concerns formed the basis of an Urban Institute conference in April 1994, funded by four major philanthropic foundations: the Annie E. Casey Foundation, the Ford Foundation, the Rockefeller Foundation, and the Foundation for Child Development, in association with the Grantmakers Income Security Task Force. Over 350 foundation officers; researchers; policy analysts; and federal, state, and local legislators, program administrators, and public officials participated in intense and far-reaching discussions sparked by the diverse policy and research papers prepared for the conference. Those papers are compiled here to provide an integrated examination of the role of the labor market in the achievement of economic self-sufficiency—defining and diagnosing the problem, identifying potentially promising solutions, suggesting strategies for stimulating employment and increasing opportunities, and reconsidering the social contract.

Before discussing the major conference themes as developed by the chapters in this volume, a brief historical overview provides the context for the welfare reform debate of the 1990s.

HISTORICAL CONTEXT: WELFARE REFORM AND THE LABOR MARKET

Over the years, federal programs have been enacted to address specific social welfare and employment security issues and problems. During the 1930s, federal social policy was built around Social Security, which aimed to provide income security for retired persons. Part of the social security package included income support for children whose fathers were deceased, a provision that soon was expanded to also cover their mothers (mainly widows). This eventually became AFDC, the most well-known welfare program today (see Holcomb 1993).

In time, the simple and straightforward objective of helping husbandless mothers with children became muddled as a result of changing economic and social factors: increasing numbers of women, including mothers, entered the work force; transportation technology made it easier for people to change job locations in response to economic and employment conditions; out-of-wedlock childbearing increased; and traditional two-parent families with children declined as more households were headed by divorced and never-married women. Simultaneously with these cultural changes, the structure of the labor market changed dramatically in the late 1970s and early 1980s, with a decrease in fairly well-paid manufacturing jobs and an increase in service sector jobs, many of which paid low wages. Although people with training and skills fared well in the labor market of the 1980s, those with few skills and little education fared badly.

The social implications of such changes are evident in the current nature of poverty, and in the role welfare plays in alleviating poverty. First, poverty has become particularly severe for persons in female-headed households and for children. Today about 40 percent of persons in female-headed households in the United States and over 20 percent of all children now live in poverty. This is compared to a poverty rate of about 14 percent for the population as a whole.

Second, many persons who work, even full-time, remain poor. Whereas full-time employment seemed to be an important route out of poverty in the 1960s and 1970s, by the 1980s, the economic reality had changed. Today, over 2 million persons have incomes below the poverty level, even though someone in their family works full-time or nearly full-time. Employment—even full-time—for those with few skills and little education is often insufficient to move families out of poverty.

Finally, more persistent, spatially concentrated poverty now exists in many inner cities. Concentrated poverty interacts with other elements of social and economic isolation to produce an alienated and economically, socially, and educationally disadvantaged population. Although the persistently poor comprise only about 6 percent of all persons in poverty, they are very visible. As such, they figure prominently in the general public's opinion about the poor. They are also most likely to have multiple problems and barriers to mainstream employment.

These changes in the character of poverty have exposed underlying ideological issues with which society and public officials have had to grapple. For example, it was easily accepted in the 1930s that women should not be expected to work in the paid labor market if they had small children; their job was to raise and care for their children. By the late 1960s, with over half of all mothers working, there was no longer such general agreement, but rather an increasing concern that society should not pay some mothers welfare and allow them to stay home while most nonwelfare mothers were employed outside the home. Perhaps the most important dilemma in the various rounds of welfare reform is the inherent conflict between providing an adequate level of income and support to the poor (especially children), and the maintenance of incentives to both work and keep families intact. This dilemma defines many of the issues surrounding today's debate over welfare reform.

Just as poverty has become more complicated with the changing, social, economic, and cultural character of the nation, the solutions are no longer as obvious or clear as they once were. Over the years, the nation's social policy has evolved from a focus on providing direct income support to programs designed to help the poor generate more income and thereby lift themselves out of poverty.

Although War on Poverty and Great Society rhetoric in the 1960s emphasized economic self-sufficiency and providing poor persons with access to various social, educational, political, and economic opportunities to help them improve their well-being, these programs in fact stressed income maintenance and cash transfers. By the 1970s, this emphasis resulted in a more complex system of delivering both cash and in-kind services. At the same time, it became clearer that the poor, including those on welfare, are not a homogeneous group, and that all would not benefit from the same package of services. A major issue became how to differentiate among (a) those who are not working but can work, (b) those who are working but are still poor, and (c) those who cannot reasonably be expected to work. Although no comprehensive welfare reform plan was passed during the 1970s, programs were developed for each of these three groups. However, even within the three groups, some persons have more serious difficulties than others. For example, for some portion of the poor expected to work, a number of different problems and barriers exist. Many need more than just a job: they may need a range of supportive services to compensate for a number of deficiencies or to overcome multiple barriers.

The employable poor have received considerable policy attention, as evidenced particularly by the increased focus on moving welfare recipients into the work force. In the 1970s, this was attempted through changes in the income and benefit incentive formulas in the AFDC program that allowed recipients to keep some of what they earn and still receive a welfare check. Later, the financial incentives were supplemented with employment, education, and training to help persons find better jobs. By the early 1980s, there was strong support for more mandatory work provisions, including requiring welfare recipients to work in exchange for their checks (i.e., workfare). Although research suggests that all of these approaches can, if well implemented, have some effect on employment and earnings, none have significantly increased earnings or reduced poverty rates or welfare dependency.

Although the emphasis on cash and in-kind transfers in the 1960s and 1970s relegated social services to a secondary position, by the late 1980s and early 1990s, policy tended to shift back toward the provision of social services, particularly coordinated services across related programs serving the same population. Expanded child care for welfare mothers in employment and training programs; integration of health care, substance abuse treatment, and housing assistance; and the creation of "one-stop" service centers are now the directions of choice for many policymakers and program operators.

Alongside today's service-oriented focus of programs is a new emphasis on individual obligations and behavior. Since the late 1980s, several states have proposed or enacted provisions requiring welfare recipients to behave in specific ways, including requiring children to attend school, having children immunized, participating in training, performing public service work, and limiting childbearing. There is, in addition, a new but strongly held belief that welfare receipt should be temporary, or transitional, and that public assistance recipients should be made aware of this. Despite numerous examples of fairly successful programmatic interventions that have evolved as part of the piecemeal changes in the welfare system, there is a growing consensus that the current system is not working well, and that it does not reflect the shift toward viewing welfare as a transitional program. Recipients, advocates, program managers, staff, and the general public agree that the system is broken, although there is much less agreement about how to fix it.

CHALLENGE OF WELFARE REFORM IN THE 1990s

The Clinton administration took office in 1993 with great expectations for substantially improving federal policies in a number of areas, including health care and welfare. President Clinton's promise to "end welfare as we know it" became a rallying cry for several welfare reform proposals by Democrats as well as by Republicans in Congress and in governors' mansions across the nation.

Among the central premises of President Clinton's proposals are:[1]

□ *Prevention and parental responsibility*—do not have a child until you are capable of and committed to supporting that child.

□ *Make work pay*, by linking welfare reform with expansions in the Earned Income Tax Credit and with health care reform that provides universal health insurance.

□ *Make welfare transitional*, by time-limiting benefits, and requiring work after the time limit is reached.

□ *Change the welfare "system,"* by changing operational priorities within local welfare offices from establishing eligibility and processing benefits to helping families become skilled, employed, and self-sufficient.

President Clinton's pledge to end welfare as we know it, in part by limiting a family's benefits to two years, raises a host of questions about whether welfare recipients can, on their own or even with government help, move into the economic mainstream. Some questions relate to the ability of the low-wage labor market to absorb all those who would be leaving welfare under such a scheme. Others address whether, even if enough jobs were available, those people leaving welfare would be able to find and keep jobs that pay enough to lift them and their families above the poverty line. Still others ask whether the labor market is the correct focus of reform efforts, or whether attitudinal or behavioral problems are not the most important factors underlying welfare dependency.

Diagnosing the Problem

Nathan Glazer, in chapter 2 of this volume, explores the reasons for the renewed urgency to again attempt welfare reform. This is a cogent issue, for as Glazer and subsequent authors point out, the nation has not had large-scale success with the employment-oriented policies or programs tried so far. In Glazer's view the public and politicians are supporting a new round of welfare reform as one means of addressing the nation's underlying social disorders. Welfare is equated in the public's mind with dependency, out-of-wedlock births by teenagers, inner city blight, homelessness, crime, and ghetto poverty.

Today, the conventional wisdom is that welfare and antipoverty programs should secure self-sufficiency through work. The labor market dimension of welfare and antipoverty policy, then, is largely premised on the assumption that the best route to self-sufficiency is through work. Glazer contends that the emphasis on requiring welfare recipients to work is appropriate, even if it does not lead to higher earnings or lower welfare receipt, because such policies reinforce an important societal norm that values work in and of itself. However, the nation should recognize, said Glazer, that work alone will not alleviate the underlying social problems that are manifested in welfare dependency.

In chapter 3, Rebecca M. Blank describes the labor market context within which work-based welfare reform must operate. Blank examines the structure of the labor market, trends in employment and wages for the low-skilled work force, and the nature of jobs at the low end of the labor market. She suggests that the labor market could absorb more low-skilled workers, especially women, so long as massive numbers were not expected to enter the work force all at once. But the jobs available to those with low skills have deteriorated over the past two decades, providing low wages and few opportunities for advancement. Of particular importance is that there are very limited earnings opportunities for low-skilled adult men in today's labor market. The situation for low-skilled women appears, on the surface at least, to be slightly better. Women's real earnings have remained stagnant over the past several years. But the lack of a decline in wages for women in large part reflects the fact that women have traditionally had very low wages.

Blank offers many reasons for this deterioration, one of which is that the demand for more-skilled workers is growing faster than the supply of skilled workers (thus pushing wages for this group up), while the demand for less-skilled workers is falling faster than the supply (thus keeping their wages down). She concludes that there is little reason to believe that these trends will reverse themselves, especially in the short run.

Gary Burtless, in chapter 4, focuses more directly on the labor market experiences of and job prospects for low-skilled women, especially those receiving AFDC. He notes that more than half of AFDC mothers in 1991 had not completed high school and had very limited basic skills, limitations that greatly restrict their job opportunities. Like Blank, he agrees that many welfare mothers could find jobs, but that most of these jobs would not pay earnings above the poverty level, and few of these would provide fringe benefits such as health insurance. He also warns that a major influx of unskilled workers could further depress the wages of all less-skilled workers.

Whereas Burtless agrees with Blank that in the 1970s the real wages of low-skilled women remained stagnant, he suggests that by the 1980s, low-skilled women, like low-skilled men, experienced significant wage deterioration. For high school dropouts, hourly wages declined by about 8 percent. Even women with a high school diploma saw their earnings erode by about 1 percent. This compares to about an 8 percent wage increase for women with a college degree.

Burtless also explains that the current problem does not result from a surplus of low-wage jobs, but, rather, from a surplus of low-skilled workers in a labor market increasingly requiring more skills. Thus, improving the skills of currently unskilled workers can reduce the number of low-wage jobs, but only if the skill-improvement occurs for a very large number of workers. Even then, the payoff in terms of an improved job situation would only occur in the very long run. Burtless concludes that, meanwhile, employment and training interventions alone, given their modest impacts in the past, will not move many families out of poverty.

Both Blank and Burtless offer convincing evidence that many low-skilled workers are active labor market participants and that some have very strong attachments to work. But whereas wages have continuously risen for high-skilled and educated workers, the real wages of low-skilled persons have declined substantially over the past two decades. Those families dependent on such workers have a low and declining chance of escaping poverty.

Searching for Solutions

Where, then, do policy solutions to poverty lie, not only for those who cannot find jobs in the regular labor market but for those who work but earn wages below poverty, and for young workers about to enter the labor force?

Rebecca A. Maynard, in chapter 5, suggests that even in a time-limited welfare system, not all recipients will in fact work in the regular labor market. Some will not want to work, some will have trouble finding or keeping a job, some will be geographically isolated, and some will have physical or mental handicaps or overwhelming family burdens. She estimates that, owing to serious barriers they face, about 20 percent of first-time welfare recipients, and a higher proportion of long-term recipients, will not obtain unsubsidized work even if faced with loss of welfare benefits. She contends that society has an obligation to maintain regular contact with and be ready to assist such families, and that the social and economic prosperity of the nation will be enhanced if all members of society are expected to engage in and are given opportunities for productive activity, even if they cannot work in the regular labor market. She proposes a combination of subsidized jobs; traditional education, training, and employment services; and non–labor market activities such as personal enrichment, parenting skills development, and community volunteering. Subsidized work, she states, is preferable to cash assistance alone, since individuals involved in any form of work generally feel good about what they are doing. The challenge is to create jobs that do not displace or compete with regular unsubsidized jobs.

For some portion of the welfare caseload, though, even low-pressure subsidized jobs are not realistic. For them, policy should encourage productive group activities—such as family literacy instruction, health education, and parenting skills—aimed at promoting greater responsibility for one's family and making greater contributions to the community.

In chapter 6, Laurie J. Bassi examines active labor market policies that have been adopted to assist low-wage workers, mainly adults, including welfare recipients. She provides an overview of policies that affect the supply of labor, those that affect the demand for labor, and those that affect matching the supply of workers with the demand for them.

Although no single approach has proven overwhelmingly successful, Bassi concludes that the nation needs all three types of policies. On the supply side, various policies such as tax credits and reemployment bonuses have been adopted to provide incentives to unemployed workers to return to work. And education, employment, and training policies aim to increase the quality of workers. There is some evidence that such policies can have a small effect, but Bassi explains that demand for labor is typically more of a constraint in the labor market than is supply.

National policy strategies to increase demand include tax credits to employers for hiring certain workers (e.g., the Targeted Jobs Tax Credit) or for increasing the number of new jobs added to the firm's payroll (e.g., the New Jobs Tax Credit in the late 1970s). Despite administrative difficulties in past tax credit efforts, Bassi suggests that well-designed employment credits could stimulate employment, although some windfall profit to employers is probably inevitable. Other policies provide training tax credits to employers, wage subsidies based on converting public benefits such as unemployment insurance or welfare payments into wage subsidies, and tax incentives and other financial advantages to firms locating in particular areas (e.g., enterprise and empowerment zones).

Bassi concludes that although each of these demand and supply strategies may have some effect, the evidence to date suggests that the impacts are small. She cautions that "policies that stimulate the supply of labor without affecting the demand for labor are likely to prove futile." She asserts that a combination of strategies that simultaneously address demand and supply will offer a greater chance to improve both the quantity and quality of jobs. Bassi proposes providing workers with better information about the labor market, and providing employers with incentives to increase both employment and firm-provided training.

Hillard Pouncy and Ronald B. Mincy, in chapter 7, address the special labor market situation facing youth—the nation's future work force. They explore both the potentials and weaknesses of universal policies designed to improve the work-force skills of the nation as a whole and policies specifically targeted on disadvantaged youth. Youth with economic and educational disadvantages, many of whom grow up in welfare families, become part of the growing low-wage labor force, as described earlier by Blank and Burtless.

Specifically, wage inequality in the United States has increased steadily in the past 20 years, with wages increasing slightly each year for the average American, but plummeting for the young and less educated. Young black men have suffered the most from the trend toward declining wages. Workers and job opportunities are often geographically mismatched: in economically depressed manufacturing centers, those needing jobs—a high proportion of whom are young black men—may lack information and access to openings in suburban industries. Of black men ages 25 to 34, 53 percent either do not work or do not earn enough to lift a family of four out of poverty; in inner-city neighborhoods, the employment rates are even lower. This figure was closer to 30 percent in 1969.

Pouncy and Mincy suggest that many of the most-disadvantaged young people may not have adequate access to programs available to the entire population, or even to those policies specifically targeted on youth, such as school-to-work transition programs and financial assistance programs for college. The limited opportunities for young black men as they approach working age means that they will have difficulty supporting their children, thus perpetuating another generation of poverty.

Instead of primarily emphasizing universal education and job training programs, Pouncy and Mincy propose that public policy intending to improve skills and opportunities for those youth at the lowest end of the labor market will do better to also invest seriously in programs targeted on disadvantaged youth. They particularly urge policymakers to work through community-based organizations to recreate a system of informal networking that has historically provided the best mechanisms for finding jobs, keeping jobs, and upward mobility.

CONCLUSION: EXPECTATIONS AND REALITIES

In the concluding chapter, Robert H. Haveman uses an overview of the conference discussion to underscore the tension between public expectations and economic reality. Although the public may demand welfare reform and expect that work will eliminate welfare, a responsible plan of action must take into account the harsh realities of the labor market. In addition, it is unlikely that the American public will support draconian policies that place poor children at more risk, as adamant as public opinion may be about imposing work obligations for their parents. Haveman outlines the main themes and areas of both consensus and disagreement that emerge from the preceding chapters and from the conference discussions.

Haveman contends that, for several reasons, welfare reform periodically surfaces on the policy agenda. The Clinton promise to end welfare as we know it made it politically infeasible not to put forth a welfare reform proposal. But more fundamental reasons for welfare reform are that current policy has failed to reduce poverty or to achieve other expected outcomes such as providing adequate income support while not discouraging productive activity including employment. Much of the public today believes, in fact, that welfare policy has done the opposite, contributing to dysfunctional social and economic behavior.

In part because the concerns about welfare policy date back several decades, it is not surprising to Haveman that the Clinton proposals include several constant themes including strengthening work requirements, making work more attractive than welfare, and having the government serve as employer of last resort. Some new themes, however, are also receiving top priority by the administration, including moving families toward self-sufficiency and off welfare. Mandates, rather than incentives, are the primary approach for achieving desired outcomes—what Haveman calls "public policy as moral suasion." And unlike past welfare reform efforts, there is little discussion about the adequacy of public assistance benefits or a concern about the stigma of welfare, nor is there concern about extending income support to the working poor. Welfare policy is clearly not antipoverty policy.

It is the labor market, though, that Haveman feels is the real "Achilles heel of the Clinton plan." Previous chapters revealed extreme skepticism about the ability of the labor market to absorb up to 2 million additional low-skilled workers at wages high enough to support their families. Haveman describes the intent to expect welfare reform through the low-wage labor market as "swimming against the tide." He contends that several strategies suggested in those chapters deserve closer examination, while recognizing the fiscal constraints imposed by the federal budget deficit. Among the most promising options are a new jobs tax credit to employers who increase the number of jobs they fill over some base employment level, a wage rate subsidy that would complement an expanded Earned Income Tax Credit (EITC). Other options worthy of more scrutiny include public service community jobs instead of welfare, mandatory participation in nonlabor market activities, case management, and mentoring.

The message from Haveman is that there is no cheap solution to the welfare problem. There seems to be consensus that work, or at least productive activity, is the desirable direction for policy, but the current trends in the labor market hold little promise that this direction will lead a family out of poverty. There is frustration about the complexity and severity of the problems facing poor families, especially in inner cities. And there is frustration that, despite several decades of experience, there are still areas about which policymakers and analysts know little. There is room for optimism, though, in that by continuing to gain knowledge and by integrating expertise and experience from different disciplines and sectors of society, more effective policy alternatives will emerge. Meanwhile, policymakers must continue to search for ways to balance the social obligation Americans feel to help poor children with the strong sense that able-bodied adults should work and that parents must assume full responsibility for their children.

Note

1. From comments by David Ellwood, assistant secretary for Planning and Evaluation, U.S. Department of Health and Human Services, at the Urban Institute conference on "Self-Sufficiency and the Low-Wage Labor Market: A Reality Check for Welfare Reform," Arlington, Va., April 12, 1994.

Reference

Holcomb, Pamela. 1993. "Welfare Reform: The Family Support Act in Historical Context." Washington, D.C.: Urban Institute.

Part One

DIAGNOSING THE PROBLEM

Chapter Two

MAKING WORK WORK: WELFARE REFORM IN THE 1990s

Nathan Glazer

Those of us who have followed welfare and welfare reform for the past few decades may well ask why a new welfare reform package is headed to Congress in 1994. Despite past developments that have alerted the public, politicians, and analysts to changes in welfare or in attitudes toward it that required attention and action, it is harder today to put one's finger on the new concerns that are triggering a new bout of welfare reform.

One answer, of course, is that Bill Clinton, campaigning for the presidency, pledged to end "welfare as we know it," and offered the exciting promise of limiting welfare receipt to two years. But what was happening in 1992 that made this campaign theme so popular when, after all, a substantial welfare reform package, the Family Support Act of 1988, had recently been passed, containing, in principle, virtually all the measures and objectives of the Clinton proposals? The central thrusts of the 1988 reform were that work was a norm that should be expected of all adults, even welfare mothers; that support for children should be expected from all parents; that implementation of measures to ensure work and child support should in large part be in the hands of the states; and that although we really did not know how to get more adult welfare recipients into the work force, we suspected the answer lay in the complexities of administration and in the provision of services to assist people to become employable. None of these themes, of course, is new in the past 30 years' discussion of welfare, but all got additional emphasis and support in the 1988 act.

The 1988 reforms no longer depended primarily on the power of economic incentives that operate through connections between monetary rewards from work and rewards from welfare to lure adult welfare recipients into the labor force. The Family Support Act of 1988 depended to a larger degree than previous legislation on compulsion, on the requirement to work if one could. In the language of the act, adult welfare recipients would be "encouraged, assisted, and required to fulfill their responsibilities to support their children by preparing for, accepting, and retaining such employment as they are capable of performing." One is struck by the word "required," and by the phrase "such employment as they are capable of performing." The issue is no longer "good jobs," or satisfying jobs, or jobs that are the first rung of a career ladder (the language of previous welfare reform), but employment, of any kind. Nor was there much concern over whether jobs provided more monetary return than welfare. Apparently it had long been accepted that there was no way of doing this when it came to persons of limited education, limited or no work experience, or poor skills. A generation of schemes to make work more rewarding than welfare had been abandoned. It couldn't be done. Welfare recipients would henceforth be led into work through compulsion, not monetary incentives. Work was a social norm, and an obligation, not something that was voluntary for adults without income.

HOW THE NEW CONSENSUS EMERGED

This was change enough from the welfare reform that was attempted, unsuccessfully, in the first Nixon administration with the Family Assistance Program, and then in the Carter administration with the Program for Better Jobs and Income and which was abandoned in 1981 with the Reagan administration's Omnibus Budget Reconciliation Act (OBRA), which eliminated longstanding economic incentives to work. At the time, the change was considered radical, part of the Reagan ideology. Liberal and independent welfare analysts thought it would work badly, leading those who could combine work and welfare to abandon work rather than welfare. This was only one of a number of predictions of the effects of the Reagan cuts that were not borne out by events.[1] It seemed that in the new ideology work behavior involved more than the monetary incentives that had been studied so intensely in the 1970s in the effort to implement inducements to work. By 1988, this concept of reform had become common wisdom accepted by many liberals as well as conservatives. "Only work works," pronounced Mickey Kaus in a 1986 article in the *New Republic* entitled "The Work-Ethic State," and whatever radicalism still accompanied this ringing statement in a leading liberal journal in 1986, there was nothing much surprising in it by 1988. The Family

Support Act had gone as far as legislators could figure in requiring work, and in assisting adult welfare recipients into the labor force. One could undoubtedly appropriate more money for work training, for child care, for various work-supporting social services, for government jobs of last resort, or for supplementing work in the private sector. But were those really the problems in "making work work"? What further changes could be implemented at the national level? This again brings us to the question, What can welfare reform do now?

True, the changes of 1988 came in the last days of the Reagan administration, which would strongly suggest to a Democratic administration that the reforms were in some ways wanting, but they were worked out by a Democratic Congress and bore the stamp of inveterate welfare reformer Senator Daniel P. Moynihan. So one might well have left welfare alone, allowing the inevitably complex and slow-moving reforms of 1988 to work themselves out at the state level, and awaiting further evaluations and analyses before again addressing welfare reform. However, to conceive of such a possibility is politically naive. Could we really expect a Democratic administration, coming to power after 12 years of Republican rule, to shrug its shoulders and say, "welfare has been fixed as much as it can be through national legislation?"

IS THERE A NEW WELFARE CRISIS?

There had however been surprising and substantial increases in the number of AFDC cases since 1989, after a long period during which the caseloads nationally had increased very little. But it was not clear what was driving these increases, aside from the worsening economy, and therefore what new policy interventions were suggested. The number of AFDC cases began to increase in the second half of 1989, and continued to increase through 1990 and 1991, but the rate of growth slowed down at the end of 1991. Overall, the number of cases nationally had risen by 1.2 million, or one-third, to 5.5 million in April 1993. The Congressional Budget Office, in an analysis of this increase, attributed more than one-half to the growth in the number of female-headed families, particularly the growth in the number of those who had never married, and one-quarter to the recession.[2] Other factors contributing to the increase, according to the CBO, were the fact that the recession hit particularly hard in the service sector and in California and the Northeast; the Immigration Reform and

Control Act of 1989; new Medicaid outreach efforts; and changes introduced in welfare by the Family Support Act of 1988. All these factors contributing to the increase in the caseload, except the increase in the number of female-headed families, could be expected to be short-range.

Why the growth in the number of female-headed families, which had after all already been increasing steadily through the seventies and eighties without much affecting the size of the caseload, should have had such surprising effects in 1989–93 is not fully clear to me from the CBO analysis. The argument of the CBO analysts is that while the growth in female-headed families should have increased the caseload by 100,000 a year in the 1980s (as against an average annual increase of only 17,000 cases 1983–89), "the expanding economy offset 55 percent of this upward pressure."[3] The fact remains that there were no marked signs that something significant had happened since 1988 that required another round of welfare reform. There was nothing like the explosion in the numbers on welfare in the late 1960s and early 1970s. The increase in costs was troubling at the state level but was dwarfed by Medicaid or the increase in costs for dealing with crime, building prisons, etc.

Nor did the analysis of this increase suggest what new measures might be taken in welfare. The increase was possibly well enough accounted for by the length and depth of the recession, and some of its special features, by the continuing increase in illegitimate births and by an unsettling uptick in the rate of this increase after 1988,[4] and by the continuing and perhaps accelerating relative decline in the wages that could be earned by workers with low skills.

WHAT IS DRIVING WELFARE REFORM TODAY?

I do not believe this increase in the numbers on welfare is driving welfare reform. Nor can the push be attributed to an excessive rise in expenditures: the federal AFDC expenditure of $13 billion in 1992 represented a smaller proportion of the federal budget than the $5 billion spent in 1975. Indeed, the costs of other programs aiding the poor had increased at much faster rates, with overall costs much larger than AFDC: Supplemental Security Income (Weaver 1994: A14), Food Stamps, housing subsidies, and the giant of them all, Medicaid. Moreover, the Earned Income Tax Credit was due to eclipse the costs of welfare at the federal level shortly (Scholz 1993–94: 1–11).

Whatever the numbers and costs of AFDC, these are not motivating welfare reform today. Rather, the issue has become what welfare symbolizes, not what it is. Welfare has come to stand for the rise of a permanent dependent population cut off from the mainstream of American life and expectations, for the decay of the inner cities, for the problem of homelessness, for the increase in crime and disorder, for the problems of the inner-city black poor. No one is worried much by high welfare levels in West Virginia, or by the fact that young teenagers there also have babies. Whatever the relationship between welfare and illegitimacy, or between being raised on welfare and doing poorly in school or becoming a juvenile delinquent, it is these latter presumed consequences that are the concerns of the public, rather than the fact that 5 percent of the population needs basic financial support.

Indeed, a substantial proportion of that 5 percent of the population will not be on welfare long, and is considered to have legitimate reasons for temporary welfare assistance. It is remarkable, then, that so much attention is paid to what narrows down to no more than 2 or 3 percent of the population—the long-term welfare recipients, disproportionately black, and confined to large central cities—for this is the image we think of in terms of welfare and welfare reform, and this is the image that drives the politics of welfare. (Note that a variety of studies, using measures such as concentration of persons in poverty, proportion on welfare, percentage of births out of wedlock, and so on, have yielded estimates of the size of the "underclass" that seem mystifying modest, in view of the prominence of "underclass" issues [in Ronald B. Mincy 1994: 125–31]. I have seen no discussion of this phenomenon.)

Ending "welfare as we know it" seems to promise some relief from these social disorders, and that is why policymakers and legislators are proposing welfare reforms at a time when there is not much to add to what was done in 1988. Further fueling reform, one suspects, are the scandals that erupt periodically, producing local outrage as they are aired in the media. In Boston, the recent scandal has been the use of Medicaid-paid drug treatments to induce fertility in women, more than half of whom were on welfare, and the majority of whom already had children ("Kennedy Hits Medicaid for Fertility Coverage", *Boston Globe*, 1994).[5] In New York it has been the discovery that a substantial number of New Jersey welfare recipients have been also collecting welfare payments in New York, a matter that emerged only when fare-beaters on PATH trains from New Jersey were arrested and found to have welfare identity cards from both New Jersey and New York, a story that made the front page of the *New York Times* (Levy 1994). One suspects it was the extra fillip that the two-state welfare collectors were also trying to ride free on the subway that made the story so notorious.

Finally, and perhaps most important, the 1988 consensus I have described as satisfying Democrats and Republicans, liberals and conservatives was not fully satisfactory. Although all agreed that adult welfare recipients should work, and that work was a norm for adults that was accepted by all Americans (as was the support of children by parents), there was less agreement on the conditions that would have to be satisfied before the norm of work was compelled. How much training? How much education? What kind of child support and how much? On these and other matters there was substantial dissent.

FROM POLICY TO ADMINISTRATION

Debate over what services are to be provided, when, for how long, just what is to be required of the welfare recipient, when, and with what penalties for noncooperation, might seem more the provinces of social work and social administration than of national policy and legislation. But nothing escapes politics and policy. In the years when we spoke of the end of ideology, some of us thought politics would be reduced to such issues as whether the National Health Service should pay for eyeglasses and false teeth. Much of politics has been reduced to such matters—and, one might add, a good thing, too. But major differences in social perspectives and philosophy do emerge when we consider these issues of eligibility, requirements, services. The daunting reality in the effort to replace welfare with work is that we will have to construct a variety of mechanisms, many quite obscure, to try to do for the employable poor what family, school, friends, individual motivation and adaptation, and the labor market currently do, albeit not without pain, and imperfectly, but with little assistance from government, for perhaps 95 percent of Americans.

The goal of "making work work" forces us to consider the fine grain of society and its institutions, and to ponder how we can recreate these for people who have been unable to become productive workers through the ordinary social and educational channels. Recent reforms, and the present one, require us to dissect the complex processes by which people prepare for and are prepared for work; by which they find the niches in which to work; and by which employers define jobs and select employees, and try to recast them administratively, in the shape of new requirements and new missions, for old bureaucracies.

What emerges most clearly in reviewing our recent experience with welfare and work and looking ahead to the next tasks is that we have moved first, from a period in which we tried to create *incentives* to work; to a subsequent period in which we imposed a *requirement* to work; to a period in which the main task will be to elaborate the *administrative structures* that put the requirement into effect. The first period saw economists happily doing what they do best, figuring out how these incentives would work, busily creating models for "a machine that would go of itself," to use a phrase that characterized the ambition of the Founding Fathers in framing the U.S. Constitution. The second period of work requirement expressed the outlook of moralists trying to impose norms of behavior. In the third period, the period of "making work work," it is not clear who will or can do the job. It will be harder work and less fun. As Lawrence Mead has written, "putting the employable poor to work is a problem in social administration, not social reform" (1992: 171). This strikes me as a key insight in considering welfare today. But what a complexity of tasks is wrapped up in the term "social administration," and in Mead's subsequent statement: "It requires mobilizing clients to participate in work programs and providing them with necessary support services, after which employment is usually possible" (1992: 171). "Mobilization" and "support services" have turned out to be enormously difficult to provide for a large portion of the adults on welfare, and the problem, I am convinced, is not only that the money for such efforts has been scanty. An examination of any report of the Manpower Demonstration Research Corporation (MDRC) on the variety of welfare-to-work programs implemented in the states, before and following passage of the Family Support Act of 1988, demonstrates the complexity of the task.

The argument over replacing work with welfare has, I believe, moved beyond some of the large questions of principle and policy—which makes things harder, not easier. For example, we have more or less settled the question of work for the mothers of children: for some time now most mothers have been working, even the mothers of quite young children, so the exemption for the welfare mother is settled by the question of equity. Under the old WIN (Work Incentive) program, mothers of children under age six were exempt from work requirements (primarily, under that program, the requirement to register). Under the stronger stipulations of the Family Support Act, only mothers of children under age three are exempt, and states may push that exemption down to one year of age. It is hard to believe that this rather draconian requirement will change. (Society may yet, in time, raise the question of whether it would not be better if more mothers *were* at home with their children, but I believe this minority view among conservatives will not soon change the terms of the debate.)

We have, furthermore, settled the question of what kind of work should replace welfare. The answer is, *any* work. As I pointed out earlier, we no longer worry much about whether the jobs into which we hope to direct adult welfare recipients are economically competitive with welfare. When one adds Food Stamps, housing subsidies, Medicaid, energy assistance, special food programs for the pregnant and for children, and the like, to the benefits available to many welfare recipients, it is hard to pull off this trick. However, if Medicaid is replaced by universal health insurance, and as the Earned Income Tax Credit expands, it will become easier to make work more attractive than welfare. Under the Family Support Act, there is no need for the job to pay more than welfare: "Participants may not be required to accept a job under the JOBS program unless the state agency assures that the participant's family will experience no net loss of cash income resulting from acceptance of the job" (U.S. Congress, House 1993: 610).

MODEST TARGETS OF FAMILY SUPPORT ACT

But despite the hard language of the Family Support Act, despite the apparently universal acceptance of the principle that work is the answer to welfare, and despite the widespread popularity of the idea of "ending welfare as we know it," the Family Support Act, designed on the basis of work and welfare demonstrations in various states, sets remarkably limited numerical goals. That is undoubtedly because the act's authors were sobered by the administrative complexities of moving any large number of adult AFDC recipients off welfare and into jobs. I think the same administrative constraints will prevail in any welfare reform, despite increased funds. So the experience of FSA and state demonstrations leading up to it are still relevant.

Thus, there must be reasonable exemptions of adults from the requirement to participate in the work program. In the FSA JOBS— Job Opportunities and Basic Skills Training—program, those "ill, incapacitated or of advanced age; needed in the home because of the illness or incapacity of another member of the family; parents caring for a young child under age 3 . . . ; employed 30 hours or more a week; . . . under age 16 or attending, full time, an elementary, secondary or vocational school; a woman who is at least in the second trimester of pregnancy . . . ." (U.S. Congress, House 1993: 608) are exempt.

These exemptions—and they could not be very different under any reform—mean that more than half of the adults in AFDC will ordinarily be exempt from the JOBS program. For those not exempt, the Family Support Act called for a minimum participation rate for eligible individuals of 7 percent in fiscal year 1991, 11 percent in 1992–93, 15 percent in 1994, and 20 percent in 1995. In two-parent families, the targets are higher: 40 percent in 1994, rising to 75 percent in 1997 and 1998. These targets apply to one of the two parents. In 1992 16 percent of nonexempt AFDC recipients were participating in JOBS programs, or 7 percent of all adult AFDC recipients. The best states reached about 15 percent of adults (U.S. Congress, House 1993: 608; Kane and Bane 1994: 24–25). Most of those participating in the JOBS program were at the first and most modest rung of the ladder of services and opportunities: they were in job search, which means participating in "jobs clubs," learning how to apply for a job, or spending required hours on the telephone finding out about and applying for jobs (U.S. Congress, House 1993: 636–37).[6] These participation targets and rates, it should be stressed, do not refer to percentages of people actually employed but simply to the proportion of individuals engaged in activities potentially leading to work, including education, job training and readiness activities, job search, and the like. When one reviews the state programs that have pioneered in this approach, one sees that the range of activities short of and separate from jobs can be imaginatively broad. A number of questions therefore arise: Why are our objectives in this brave new approach so limited and so far from ending "welfare as we know it"? Can't we do better? What areas, specifically, need improvement? Most significantly, are adult recipients on AFDC deficient, and our capacities to assist them to become employable so slight, that we must accept that in this population nonwork will remain the norm?

LEARNING FROM STATE PROGRAMS

The answer to the first question, Why are our objectives so limited, and so far from ending "welfare as we know it"? is that these objectives are the best we can expect on the basis of experience with a range of welfare-to-work programs in various states. The Manpower Demonstration Research Corporation's reports on these programs include flow charts of what happens to 100 eligible JOBS program participants over the course of the program. I have already indicated that the eligibles will be at best half the numbers on welfare. Generally the number participating in the program drops off rapidly.

Consider, for example, a recent report on Florida's Project Independence, a program initiated before passage of the Family Support Act, and which became Florida's JOBS program (Kemple and Haimson 1994). The MDRC's typical research pattern is to contrast a group of persons on welfare not receiving the services whose impact is being analyzed with an experimental group who are. Of course, there are many complexities in managing an evaluation of a public program where services may be received as a right or may be mandated, but the high quality of MDRC evaluations is well known.

Of 100 Floridians referred to Project Independence orientation from the Public Assistance Unit, 77 attended an orientation, 43 "participated in at least one activity" (job search or job club, education or training; 25 were only in job search or job club), 23 were still "registered" at the end of the 12-month follow-up period (which I assume means they were still on welfare and without enough work earnings to exit welfare), and 11 of these 23 were still participating in some activity. Throughout this process, persons not pursuing further activities in the project dropped out, at times because they found employment (which might or might not have paid enough to get them off welfare). Thus, of the 23 persons who were referred to but did not attend orientation, 16 were employed at some point in the research period: although it would be hard to attribute their employment to the orientation they did not attend, perhaps the activities subsequent to it contributed to their finding employment.

There were penalties for nonparticipation in the Project Independence program. About half of those who did not appear for orientation did not have a good reason and were referred for an AFDC grant reduction—a "sanction"; 10 percent of these referrals resulted in actual grant reductions. The evaluations suggest that some kind of employment at some time is available for most of those eligible, and that in terms of finding some employment, there is not much difference between those who get some services and those who don't.

The Florida results are in no way atypical. The main point emerging from this and similar MDRC flow charts is that it is difficult to provide a flow of services for a troubled population such as this that will lead to steady work off welfare. As Lawrence Mead wrote of an earlier program in Chicago: "Some of this dropoff [from stage to stage] reflects administrative confusion and normal turnover, with many clients leaving welfare before they can participate in workfare. Much of it, though, is due to clients disappearing or declining to show up for required activities" (1992: 173). The Project Independence story suggests that adding sanctions does not change much. It is also clear that sanctions are hard to administer.

Much of the effort in evaluations such as these is devoted to determining the "bottom line": how many participants went off welfare? To what extent were the earnings of program participants greater than the earnings of the controls? How much was saved in welfare costs? What was the cost-benefit ratio? On all these measures, these programs tend to show positive effects, but the effects are remarkably small. Consider these results of the Florida program:

> At the end of the first year of follow-up, just over 64 percent of those who were referred to the program were receiving AFDC compared to just under 69 percent that did not have access to the program. . . . [This 5 percent difference between controls and experimentals in staying on welfare seems typical.] The program produced first-year earnings gains (again, compared to the control group) of $157 per person referred to the program. (This average includes individuals who did not work, worked part-time, or worked for only part of the year.) (Kemple and Haimson 1994)

Project Independence included parents of children between ages three and six, which reduced its impact on earnings compared to other state programs, but otherwise the project's results were comparable.

ARE MORE EXPENSIVE PROGRAMS BETTER?

Some programs have done better, but not much better. Thomas J. Kane and Mary Jo Bane characterize the Baltimore Options Program as one of the early successes. The program included job search, on-the-job training, and thirteen weeks of work experience. . . . In this program, 28 percent of the participants were off welfare in the fifth quarter after they came on the rolls, compared with 26 percent of the control group—a positive, though hardly earth-shattering, finding. The Options Program appears to be cost-effective under reasonable assumptions about costs and about the permanence of earnings gains. But the total net benefits amount to only about $600 per participant—modest gains, to say the least. (Kane and Bane 1994: 23)

The Baltimore Options program seems to have been more intensive than Florida's Project Independence, and it would seem reasonable that more and lengthier services would produce somewhat better results. However, the results of even the best programs are only modestly better than those of no program. Without getting into the charged field of welfare dynamics, it is the case that 35 percent of all recipients have been on welfare for two years or less, and that half of all spells will last less than two years (Kane and Bane 1994: 29). Thus, for a large proportion of the welfare population, if the aim is to get people off welfare, it hardly matters what we do. Perhaps that is why the programs show such modest overall results in this respect.

One of the most successful programs described by Kane and Bane is the Massachusetts ET Choices, which was voluntary. "It provided both work opportunities and supporting services, such as child care and transportation. . . . Clients were assigned to a case manager who assisted them in developing a Family Independence Plan" (Kane and Bane 1994: 22). The approach of the welfare offices, which as described by Kane and Bane commonly concentrates almost exclusively on eligibility—that is, getting the paperwork to justify or legitimate a grant right—changed, as well as the behavior of welfare clients: "Many more of them were going out to education or training, or working or looking for work, than in the typical welfare system" (ibid.: 22).

Whereas "proponents of Massachusetts' ET program claimed large employment gains and welfare savings," the caseload decreased only 5 percent—

a drop comparable to that in other states without work-welfare programs—though also without the substantial welfare benefit increases that occurred simultaneously with ET. Especially given the great strength of the Massachusetts economy during the period . . . , the 5 percent drop in caseloads suggests that even an enthusiastically implemented and well-managed work-welfare program on this model is likely to have only a modest impact on who goes off welfare and how fast. (Kane and Bane 1994: 22)

One must keep in mind in evaluating this program's results that participation in ET was voluntary.

The programs described here are relatively cheap. The most expensive programs, however, do not offer much to be enthusiastic about, including, for instance, the well-known Supported Work program for welfare mothers. The cost per person in the Supported Work experimental group was $17,981, of which $8,534 was for wage subsidies. In the first year, the difference in earnings between experimentals and controls was large, and the savings in welfare were substantial. By the third year the difference in earnings was $1,076—large in comparison to other, cheaper, programs—and the savings in welfare per experimental participant were $401 (Friedlander and Gueron 1992: 157). However, results such as these do not get people out of poverty: "Even Supported Work, with its large earnings impact, produced only a small and not statistically significant reduction in the number of families below the poverty line" (ibid.: 187).

I do not doubt that a well-administered program can get a large number of welfare recipients to find and accept work. What is unlikely is that the work they will find, taking into account the level of education, skills, and motivation characteristic of most of the AFDC population, will make it possible for them to leave welfare. This is the conclusion of those who have analyzed what kind of jobs are available to the poorly skilled, such as Rebecca M. Blank and Gary Burtless.[7] It suggests the answer is not two years and out, but insistence on some work, even if it is insufficient to provide an income that matches welfare. Thus the concentration on the question, will there be enough jobs available after two years of training, is misguided: Some kind of job is in most places available. If one restates that question to ask, will there be jobs that pay better than welfare for most welfare recipients who have had the typical kind of training that work training programs provide, the answer is no.

WHAT IS TO BE DONE?

I return to my initial query: Why welfare reform now? Do we know that much more than we knew in 1988 to warrant new legislation? I don't think so. Do we feel confident enough about the programs we prescribed for states in 1988 to put substantially larger sums into them? It seems doubtful to me. Can we get a substantial proportion of long-term welfare clients off the welfare rolls by increasing their earned income through investments in learning how to work, basic education, training programs, and the like? We cannot. In the search for remedies to the welfare dilemma, we find an "infinite regress" in prescriptions from one expert to the next. The welfare expert, for example, finding no answer in changes in the welfare system, refers his problem to the education expert, who will probably tell us the problem really lies with the family. Meanwhile, no one program or course of action has been demonstrated as clearly better than another. To those who are confident, for example, that investments in work training and education are the answer, James Heckman's study demonstrates the phenomenal amount of investments necessary to overcome the problem of low wages for the poorly qualified.[8]

There are good ideas in the welfare field. (I call them good because they seem sound to me, not because research demonstrates they are better than other things.) I think that to concentrating on the welfare mother with one child is a good idea, as well as ensuring that she first completes her high school education. The Family Support Act calls for such targeting. (On the other hand, we are told these young people are harder to work with than older welfare mothers.) In addition, I think concentrating on jobs first, rather than education and work-training, is a good idea—it is too easy for the latter to simply become a career (see Etzioni 1994). Putting more effort into collecting support payments from fathers, and determining who the fathers are, are also good ideas—though we have had legal requirements on child support for decades, and we may be reaching the limit of our resources in this area. I think it is a bad idea to count too much on jobs provided by government as a last resort, because I doubt that government supervisors will impose the work discipline required. I think we ought to allow states, counties, and cities more freedom to pursue strategies for welfare reform—two worthwhile approaches that come to mind are "Learnfare" in Wisconsin and, in New Jersey, capping welfare benefits regardless of more births.

Until we know more, a major new effort to reform welfare is not, in my opinion, justified, and I suspect the effort to "end welfare as we know it" will lead, for the most part, to welfare by some other means, under other names. The insistence on work for welfare recipients is right, regardless of whether it increases earnings, or gets people off welfare, or raises them out of poverty, because it expresses a national norm and a national consensus. In this regard, one should be careful not to undermine this central thrust by adding too many conditions (such as child care that is acceptable to the child-care professionals, when most mothers seem satisfied with and prefer something different, and cheaper [Offer 1994: 18–19]). The underlying social problems that drive the concern for welfare reform remain. Welfare is only one manifestation of these problems, and so long as that is so, we will worry about welfare reform.

Notes

1. See Glazer (1988: 198, n. 18) and Blank (1994). Concerning the elimination in the 1981 OBRA of the provision that working welfare recipients could retain $30 a month and 30 percent of earnings without reduction in their benefits (from an economist's point of view, this is a 100 percent tax on earnings), Blank writes: "A number of researchers studied the effects of this change by comparing the work behavior of AFDC recipients before and after the legislative change. . . . Surprisingly, these studies showed almost no decrease in work effort among continuing AFDC recipients after the new rules were implemented. (p. 182)"

2. CBO Staff Memorandum, "Forecasting AFDC Caseloads, With an Emphasis on Economic Factors," Congressional Budget Office, pp. 1, 3.

3. Ibid., p. 3.

4. See Daniel P. Moynihan (1994: 24, charts accompanying letter to William F. Buckley).

5. The Kennedy referred to is Senator Ted Kennedy, which shows how far we have come in welfare reform.

6. Of JOBS participants, 11.9 percent were in job search, .4 percent were in on-the-job training, .2 percent were in work supplementation, 2.8 percent were in Community Work Education programs, and 3.5 percent were in other programs.

7. See their chapters in this volume (chapters 3 and 4).

8. Assuming a 10 percent return on investment in education and work training, he calculates, for example, that to restore average male high school dropout earnings in 1989 to average real earnings of male high school dropouts in 1979 would cost $214 billion.

References

Bane, Mary Jo, and David T. Ellwood. 1994. *Welfare Realities: From Rhetoric to Reform.* Cambridge, Mass.: Harvard University Press.

Blank, Rebecca M. 1994. "The Employment Strategy: Public Policies to Increase Work and Earnings." In *Confronting Poverty*, edited by Sheldon H. Danziger, Gary D. Sandifur, and Daniel H. Weinberg. Cambridge, Mass.: Harvard University Press, pp. 168–204.

Boston Globe. 1994. "Kennedy Hits Medicaid for Fertility Coverage." March 16.

DeParle, Jason. 1994. "Sharp Increase Along the Borders of Poverty." *New York Times*, March 31.

Etzioni, Amitai. 1994. "Starting Over on Welfare." *Wall Street Journal*, March 31.

"For the Record." 1994. *National Review*, February 7: 12.

Friedlander, Daniel, and Judith M. Gueron. 1992. "Are High-Cost Services More Effective than Low-Cost Services?" In *Evaluating Welfare and Training Programs*, edited by Charles F. Manski and Irwin Garfinkel. Cambridge, Mass.: Harvard University Press.

Glazer, Nathan. 1988. *The Limits of Social Policy*. Cambridge, Mass.: Harvard University Press.

Heckman, James J. 1994. "Is Job Training Oversold?" *Public Interest* (Spring): 91–115.

Kane, Thomas J., and Mary Jo Bane. 1994. "The Context for Welfare Reform." In *Welfare Realities: From Rhetoric to Reform*, edited by Mary Jo Bane and David T. Ellwood. Cambridge, Mass.: Harvard University Press.

Kaus, Mickey. 1986. "The Work-Ethic State." *New Republic*, July 7: 22–33.

Kemple, James J., and Joshua Haimson. *Executive Summary. Florida's Project Independence: Program Implementation, Participation Patterns, and First-Year Impacts*. New York: Manpower Demonstration Research Corporation, January.

Levy, Clifford J. 1994. "Two States to Join in System to Stop Welfare Fraud." *New York Times*, March 30.

Mead, Lawrence M. 1992. *The New Politics of Poverty*. New York: Basic Books.

Mincy, Ronald B. 1994. "The Underclass: Concepts, Controversy, and Evidence." In *Confronting Poverty*, edited by Sheldon H. Danziger, Gary D. Sandifur, and Daniel H. Weinberg. Cambridge, Mass.: Harvard University Press.

Moynihan, Daniel P. 1994. Letter, *National Review*, April 4: 24.

Offer, Paul. 1994. "Day Careless," *New Republic*, April 18: 18–19.

Scholz, John Karl. 1993–94. "Tax Policy and the Working Poor: The Earned Income Tax Credit." *Focus* 15 (3, Winter): 1–11.

U.S. Congress. House. Committee on Ways and Means. 1993. *Green Book*. Washington, D.C.: U.S. Government Printing Office.

Weaver, Carolyn. 1994. "Welfare Reform Is Likely to Leave This Monster Intact." *Wall Street Journal*, April 6: A14.

Chapter Three

OUTLOOK FOR THE U.S. LABOR MARKET AND PROSPECTS FOR LOW-WAGE ENTRY JOBS

Rebecca M. Blank

If welfare-to-work programs are to be successful, jobs must be available for welfare recipients that help them move toward economic self-sufficiency. Thus, those concerned with welfare reform must pay close attention to the availability of jobs and to the nature of those jobs in the labor market. The last several decades have seen substantial changes in the U.S. labor market. On the supply side of the market, there have been notable changes in family composition and work behavior. On the demand side, there have been substantial shifts in occupation and industry demands, changes in the geographic location of jobs, and changes in the returns of education and experience in the labor market. Increasing evidence indicates that entry-level job opportunities for less-skilled workers have deteriorated over the last 15 years. This chapter reviews that evidence, with particular attention to job prospects for less-skilled women.

There are two primary ways by which labor market opportunities can worsen. First, the availability of jobs for less-skilled workers may fall, with a growing number of unskilled workers unable to find work. Second, jobs may remain available, but may be less attractive along a number of dimensions, including wages, other compensation, and long-term earnings potential. The first two sections of this chapter evaluate the evidence for each of these propositions. I argue that there is little evidence that jobs, per se, have become less available, particularly for less-skilled female workers. In fact, women's unemployment rates have fallen relative to men's over the past decade. But there is substantial evidence that the job attributes of available jobs have deteriorated, although this problem has been much less acute for women workers than for men. In many ways, the story for less-skilled women is one of stagnation. Despite substantial growth in the earnings opportunities of their better-educated sisters, these women continue to face a labor market with low earnings and few advancement opportunities.

After discussing these problems, this chapter reviews other aspects of job quality, including the availability of nonwage benefits, access to promotion and job mobility, and the availability of full-time (versus part-time) work. There is no evidence that these other job attributes are improving among less-skilled workers, and some aspects seem to be deteriorating along with wage opportunities.

The labor market facing an individual worker is not the only determinant of economic well-being, however. It is possible that expanded hours of work could offset declining wages, that many low-wage workers may be in households also containing higher-wage workers, or that nonearned income sources (such as government transfers) may offset earnings patterns. The third section of the chapter investigates the total family income available to workers in low-wage jobs, to see whether these labor market changes for individual workers have translated into changes in the income available to families. The last section of the chapter provides a summary of findings and relates changes in the labor market to specific issues in the welfare reform debate.

TRENDS IN AVAILABILITY OF JOBS

The availability of jobs to workers who seek employment is a major concern to political and economic analysts. One of the most frequently cited measures of economic prosperity is the unemployment rate. Substantial increases in unemployment among Western European countries since the mid-1970s have caused social and political unrest, have produced major changes in economic policy, and have spawned a seemingly endless stream of economic reports analyzing the causes of and potential cures for this problem (Blank and Freeman 1994). By contrast, the United States has been a model of job growth and (relatively) lower unemployment.

The United States has experienced sustained and long-term growth in employment over several decades. Table 3.1 contrasts aggregate population growth over the past three decades with aggregate employment growth. In every decade, employment growth has outstripped population growth, meaning that the labor market has been able to absorb a growing share of workers in the population. These new jobs have been necessary to meet a growing demand for employment due to demographic and social changes. The rise in female labor force participation, driven by a combination of labor supply

Table 3.1 CHANGES IN U.S. POPULATION AND EMPLOYMENT, 1960–90

	Percentage Change in Population	Percentage Change in Employment	Change in Number of Employed Workers (000)
1960–70	16.9	19.6	12,900
1970–80	22.4	26.2	20,625
1980–90	12.1	18.7	18,611

Source: *Economic Report of the President* (1994: table B-33).

and demand factors, has increased the share of adult women in the labor force from 42 percent in 1970, to 51 percent in 1980, and to 58 percent in 1990 (*Economic Report of the President* 1994: table B-37). At the same time that women's labor force participation grew, the large post–World War II population bulge known as the baby boom reached adulthood and entered the labor force between the late 1960s and early 1980s. The fact that the U.S. labor market absorbed these two large increases in the supply of workers with only moderate increases in the underlying unemployment rate suggests that aggregate job creation has not been an economic problem for the U.S. economy.

Figure 3.1 plots U.S. unemployment rates over the past three decades for men and women. Although there was a steady rise in the underlying unemployment rate from 1970 through 1982 (due to both reduced economic growth and growing labor force participation), after 1982 unemployment rates fell back to their mid-1970 levels. Surprisingly, despite the large growth in employment demand by women, unemployment rates among women have actually fallen relative to male unemployment rates over this time period. The recent period of slow growth (1990–92) resulted in rising unemployment, but unemployment rates in this period stayed well below their very high levels of a decade earlier, and appear to be falling rapidly now that economic growth has resumed. Thus, aggregate unemployment does not appear to be a more difficult problem in 1993 than it was 15 years ago; there is little evidence of any recent deterioration in job availability and unemployment.

Clearly, different groups face different labor market experiences, and some particular groups have long faced higher unemployment rates. Table 3.2 shows recent unemployment rates by race, age, and sex. Among black workers, unemployment rates are more than twice those of whites, while youth unemployment rates are typically three times the level of adult workers. Data similar to table 3.2, tabulated for years in the 1970s and 1980s, show different underlying unemployment rates but the ratio of unemployment rates between groups

Figure 3.1 U.S. UNEMPLOYMENT RATES BY SEX: CIVILIANS, AGES 16 AND OVER

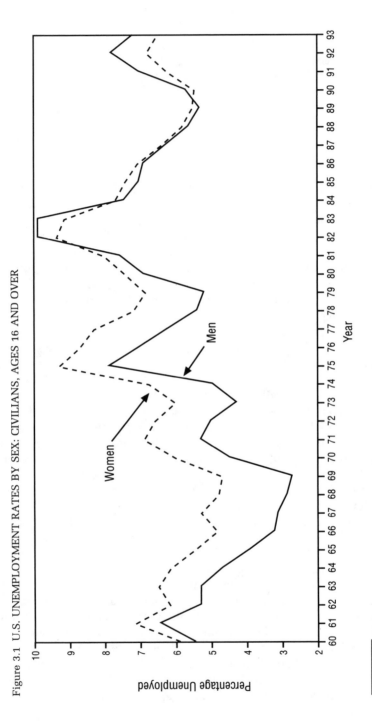

Source: *Economic Report of the President* (1994: table B-34).

Table 3.2 U.S. UNEMPLOYMENT RATES BY RACE, AGE, AND GENDER, 1993

	All Races (%)	White (%)	Black (%)
All ages	6.8	6.0	12.9
Adult men	6.4	5.6	12.1
Adult women	5.9	5.1	10.6
Youth (ages 16–19)	19.0	16.2	38.9

Source: *Economic Report of the President* (1994: tables B-40, B-41).

is quite similar. The only noticeable change is among adult women, whose unemployment rates were consistently about one point higher than those of adult males in the 1970s and are now consistently lower. The fact that the distribution of unemployment across race and age groups has not changed underscores the reality that employment opportunities have been and still are more limited for younger workers and for workers from minority racial backgrounds. But there is little evidence that these experiences have worsened in recent years.

Figure 3.1 and table 3.2 both indicate that women's relative job availability seems to have improved. Lower unemployment rates for women over the last decade are reflective of the fact that manufacturing jobs (disproportionately filled by less-skilled men) have experienced an increase in turnover and layoff rates relative to service and clerical jobs, which are more likely to be filled by less-skilled women.

Of course, looking at aggregate unemployment rates does not differentiate between the unemployment experiences of those in better-paid versus lower-paid jobs. In general, unemployment is heavily concentrated at the bottom of the income distribution. Figure 3.2 graphs the share of total weeks of unemployment in each year from 1967 to 1991 experienced by workers living in families in the bottom quintile of the family income distribution.[1] In 1991, workers in families in the bottom 20 percent of the income distribution experienced 27 percent of the weeks of reported unemployment over the year, as indicated by the solid line. Among all individuals who were the head of their household in 1991, 40 percent of the reported weeks of unemployment occurred among heads in the bottom quintile of the family income distribution, as indicated by the dashed line. Furthermore, the share of total weeks of unemployment experienced by those in the bottom quintile of the family income distribution increased somewhat over the past two decades, although most of this increase occurred from 1970 to 1983, and there has been little change in the unemployment burden of poorer families over the last decade.

Figure 3.2 U.S. UNEMPLOYMENT SHARES IN BOTTOM QUINTILE
(BASED ON ANNUAL WEEKS OF UNEMPLOYMENT)

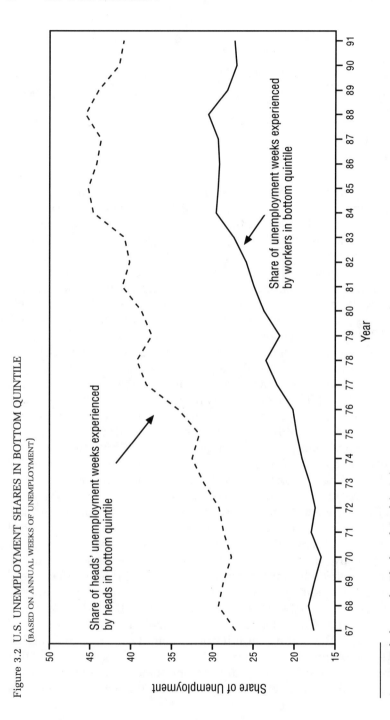

Source: Tabulations by Blank and Card (1993).

Table 3.3 DISTRIBUTION OF U.S. UNEMPLOYMENT ACROSS SKILL LEVELS, MARCH 1992

Education Level	Unemployment Rate (%)	Ratio of Unemployment Rates in Each Skill Group to Unemployment Rates among College-Educated Workers (%)		
		Total	Male	Female
Less than high school	16.3	4.9	4.8	4.8
High school degree	8.8	2.7	2.7	2.6
Some post–high school training	6.4	1.9	1.9	2.1
College degree or higher	3.3	1.0	1.0	1.0

Source: Tabulations from U.S. Bureau of the Census, Current Population Survey, March 1992.

Table 3.3 shows the distribution of unemployment rates across skill levels and the ratio of unemployment rates among less-skilled workers to those of college-educated workers by sex in March 1992. Less-skilled men and women experienced almost five times as much unemployment as college-educated men and women. Calculations based on 1979 data show very similar patterns between the unemployment rates of more- and less-skilled workers by sex. Both less-skilled men and less-skilled women experienced a disproportionate share of the burden of unemployment, an imbalance that, over the 1980s, does not seem to have shifted much.[2]

The results in this section indicate that job availability, at least as measured by unemployment rates, deteriorated in the 1970s. Less-skilled workers may have been particularly hard hit by this change, as shown by an increase in the share of unemployment experienced by workers at the bottom of the income distribution. Over the 1980s, however, unemployment fell substantially; as mentioned earlier, even the recent growth slowdown has not brought unemployment near the levels of a decade ago. Unemployment rates among women workers have fallen even faster than rates among men, lowering women's relative unemployment situation. Unemployment rates among white workers are lower than black unemployment rates, indicating more limited job availability for black workers, but this differential does not seem to have changed much over the 1980s. Thus, any discussion of deteriorating labor market options for less-skilled workers must focus on changing attributes of available jobs;

the actual availability of jobs to those that seek them does not seem to have substantially worsened in recent years.

A few caveats to this conclusion should be kept in mind, however. First, the much higher rates of unemployment among less-skilled and minority workers make it necessary to emphasize that although unemployment has not increased over the past decade, it remains a serious problem for many workers. Second, the fact that aggregate unemployment has improved over the past 15 years says little about the specific unemployment situation in particular cities or regions. There have always been spatial mismatches between the location of jobs and workers. Even in the absence of any aggregate problem with unemployment, there will surely be some areas where jobs are less available and where workers consequently suffer more serious unemployment problems. Third, the fact that long-run U.S. employment growth remains strong does not imply that the labor market could immediately absorb a sharp increase in the number of working adults. Phased-in increases in employment among limited numbers of welfare recipients and low-skilled workers can occur in most regions without problems. But any short-term massive increase in the number of those seeking work in an area will drive up unemployment rates. The economic experience of this country indicates that, over time, jobs would become available for many of these workers, but this employment growth would not happen overnight.

NATURE OF AVAILABLE JOBS

Growing Wage Inequality

A growing body of evidence indicates that earning opportunities for less-skilled workers have deteriorated since 1980. Most of this research, however, focuses on the experiences of less-skilled men. The primary conclusions of these studies are three-fold:[3] First, the wage distribution among men is widening, with real wages among less-skilled workers falling and real wages among more skilled workers rising. Both high school dropouts and high school graduates have seen a steady drop-off in the wages they can command in the labor market since about 1979. This change appears to be occurring within all sectors of the economy. Less-skilled men in both manufacturing and nonmanufacturing industries have experienced similar real wage declines. Thus, the long-term sectoral shift away from manufacturing and into services is not the primary cause of these changes; they would have occurred even in the absence of that shift.

Second, although younger male workers have experienced these changes to a greater extent than older workers, even less-skilled workers with many years of experience have seen their absolute and relative wage positions worsen. This rules out the hypothesis suggested by some that these wage declines are primarily due to a deterioration in worker quality among younger, less-skilled workers.

Third, although at least half of the rising inequality in the labor market is due to growing gaps between workers in different skill and experience categories, half of the inequality is occurring *within* those categories. In other words, within all age and experience groups inequality is rising, so that the earnings experience of similar groups of workers is becoming more diverse (see, especially, Murphy and Welch 1993). This means that rising inequality in wages is not just the result of the increasing divergence between more- and less-skilled workers; causal explanations must explain more than growing skill differences in earnings.

A somewhat different picture is emerging with regard to earnings opportunities for less-skilled women. Whereas women have experienced rising wage inequality between different skill categories, this is almost entirely due to the growth in wages among more-skilled women. Less-skilled women have faced essentially stagnant wage levels since 1979, not experiencing the real declines of less-skilled men, but also not experiencing any of the real growth that their more-skilled sisters have witnessed.

Table 3.4 presents evidence of these trends among men and women by education level. Over the 1980s average weekly earnings among men with less than 12 years of education have fallen by 13 percent, while they have risen 11 percent among men with more than 12 years of education. In contrast, women without a high school degree have faced virtually stagnant weekly earnings since 1969, while women with more than 12 years of education have seen their earnings grow by 25 percent.[4]

It is also worth noting that even though less-skilled men have experienced a large earnings loss, they still earn far more than women at all education levels (table 3.4). Aggregate earnings data from the last decade indicate that women's earnings relative to men's are improving; median weekly earnings among women working full-time were 75 percent of those of full-time male workers in 1992, up from 62 percent in 1979 (U.S. Department of Labor, *Employment and Earnings*, January 1980 and January 1993). But among less-skilled

Table 3.4 AVERAGE WEEKLY EARNINGS BY YEARS OF SCHOOL AND SEX AMONG EMPLOYED NONELDERLY ADULTS IN UNITED STATES
(IN 1992 DOLLARS)

	Men ($)			Women ($)		
	1969	1979	1989	1969	1979	1989
All workers	593	580	613	282	299	364
Percentage change		−2.2	+5.7		+6.0	+21.7
Less than 12 years of education	470	440	384	221	224	223
Percentage change		−6.4	−12.7		1.4	−0.4
Twelve years of education	580	548	526	278	280	308
Percentage change		−5.5	−4.0		+0.7	+10.0
More than 12 years of education	763	693	768	366	362	453
Percentage change		−9.2	+10.8		−1.1	+25.1

Sources: Tabulations from U.S. Bureau of the Census, Current Population Surveys, March 1970, 1980, and 1990, based on civilian population, ages 18–65. Inflation adjustments based on gross domestic product deflator.

workers, this closing of the male/female wage gap is occurring because men are losing wages, rather than because women's wages are growing.

If the data in table 3.4 are separated by race and sex, black and white women in 1989 have quite similar weekly earnings in all educational categories. This means that black women have experienced real wage growth since 1969, with particularly large increases among more-skilled black women. In contrast, differences between white and black men's earnings at different skill levels continue to exist.[5] Given this chapter's emphasis on the labor market opportunities facing less-skilled women workers, racial differences in earnings are less important to analyze.

Another look at these distributional changes is provided in table 3.5, which presents the matrix of the working population, distributed by skill categories and wage categories in 1979 and 1992. In 1979, only 4 percent of the population reported earning less than $5 per hour (in 1992 dollars). This reflects the fact that the 1979 equivalent of $5 per hour was just below the minimum wage in that year. By 1992, 10 percent of the entire population and almost one-quarter of non–high school graduates earned less than $5 per hour.[6] Among high school graduates, by 1992 11 percent were in this bottom category, and even 10 percent of those with some post–high school training were also at this earnings level. At the other end of the spectrum, among those with a college degree or better, only 22 percent earned more than $20 per hour in 1979, but almost 30 percent were in this category by 1992.

Table 3.5 indicates that skill levels are strongly correlated with earnings, but that there is a substantial minority of less-educated workers in high-earnings categories, as well as a substantial minority of more-educated workers in low-earnings categories. The correlation between earnings and skills has become tighter over time, however. In 1979, 34 percent of high school dropouts earned more than $10 per hour; by 1992, only 23 percent had earnings at this level. Similarly, among college graduates in 1979, 26 percent earned less than $10 per hour; by 1992, only 21 percent were at this level of earnings. One way to interpret the data in table 3.5 is that it was harder to escape a poor education in 1992 than it was in 1979.

Causal Analysis of Growing Wage Inequality

The reasons behind these changes in wage opportunities have been much debated among researchers. Most of the evidence indicates

Table 3.5 DISTRIBUTION OF WAGES BY EDUCATION CATEGORY IN UNITED STATES, 1979 AND 1992

| | | | Wage Categories (in 1992 dollars) | | | | | |
| Education | Less than $5/Hour (%) | | $5 up to $10/Hour (%) | | $10 Up to $20/hour (%) | | $20/Hour or Higher (%) | |
Category	1979	1992	1979	1992	1979	1992	1979	1992
Less than high school	6.8	24.1	59.1	53.1	31.6	21.3	2.4	1.5
High school degree	3.9	11.0	52.0	47.6	38.8	36.8	5.3	4.6
Some post–high school training	3.2	10.0	45.7	41.0	42.5	41.3	8.6	7.7
College degree or more	2.2	2.7	24.2	18.5	51.7	49.0	21.9	29.8
All skill levels	4.0	10.1	47.1	38.9	40.4	39.4	8.4	11.6

Source: Tabulations of workers in outgoing rotation groups of Current Population Survey data, May 1979 and March 1992.
Note: Entries for each year sum across to 100 percent within each education category, and represent distribution of working population at that education level across wage categories.

that changes in demand are the primary driving force behind these numbers: demand for more-skilled workers is growing faster than the supply, while the demand for less-skilled workers is falling faster than the supply. Note that this is true even though the share of less-skilled workers in the U.S. economy has steadily declined over time, while the share of more-skilled workers has steadily increased. But labor supply changes occur slowly as younger workers make education and training decisions and as older (on average, less-skilled) workers leave the labor market.

One aspect of changing demand is the growing importance of international competition to U.S. firms. Skilled workers in the United States have a comparative advantage in the global labor market, while less-skilled labor is at a comparative disadvantage (see, e.g., Blackburn et al. 1990, Katz and Murphy 1992, Murphy and Welch 1993, and Revenga 1992). One can hire unskilled workers much more cheaply in developing countries, but only the United States has so large a concentration of college-educated workers. The growth in international economic competition is not adequate by itself to fully explain the wage changes, since even in nontraded sectors (such as public administration) there has been a sharp increase in wage differentials, but there is evidence that international economic shifts are at least one of the factors behind wage shifts. In addition, the fact that a number of other industrialized countries (but not all) are facing similar wage shifts indicates that the phenomenon is not due to changes in the U.S. economy alone.[7]

A second aspect of changing demand is the possibility of technological shifts that have been demand-increasing for more-skilled workers and demand-decreasing for less-skilled workers (see Bound and Johnson 1992; Davis and Haltiwanger 1991; and Berman, Bound, and Griliches 1993). The rapid spread of computer-based technology in all industries and occupations is often mentioned as an example of this. But despite evidence that technology shifts of this sort might have occurred, it is difficult to directly measure technological change. Following a long tradition in economics, many articles interpret unexplained residual effects as technological change. While these results provide evidence consistent with a technological change story, more direct measurement of the effect of technological innovations would be more convincing.

Institutional changes in the U.S. economy may also be affecting wage inequality. The decline of unionization has been associated with about 20 percent of the change in relative wage rates (Blackburn et al. 1990; Card 1992). (Clearly, changes in unionization are simulta-

neously determined with other demand changes.) Much less significant was the decline in the real minimum wage over the 1980s; this
was responsible for only a small amount of the relative decline in
earnings among less-educated workers (Blackburn et al. 1990; Horrigan and Mincy 1993).

Changes on the supply side of the labor market have also been
substantial, although their impact on wages is rather uniformly
agreed to have been relatively small. There is evidence that the demographic bulge of the baby boom reduced wages among this group
about 1 to 2 percent. There is little evidence that this contributed
much to the distributional changes, however. In fact, as noted earlier,
the large increase in women's work effort, which should have
increased competition among women in largely "feminized" occupations, has not had notable effects. Employment rates and wages
among women have risen, relative to men. A more likely labor supply
effect may be the increased competition in the low-skill labor market
from new immigrants in the United States, which has kept the pool
of less-skilled workers higher than it would have been otherwise
(Borjas et al. 1992). There is substantial evidence, however, that
immigration has not greatly depressed wages among native-born less-
skilled workers in the recent past (see, e.g., Altonji and Card 1991).
Instead, at least some evidence indicates that immigration increases
employment, by creating new jobs both within the immigrant community and among employers who hire immigrants for jobs that
native workers may find less attractive. In general, those who have
investigated supply-side explanations of deteriorating wage opportunities among less-skilled workers have not been able to explain a
substantial amount of the change in wage distributions and wage
levels over the past decade.

A key question for those interested in entry-level jobs among
women workers is why wage patterns among women have not
changed in the same way as among men. Strikingly, no current
research has addressed this question. At least two possible explanations are consistent with what we know about labor market changes
over the 1980s. First, it is possible that the jobs that women have
traditionally filled have not been as affected by demand shifts. For
instance, hardest hit over the last decade are unionized jobs in manufacturing, an area of the economy where women have never had
much representation. In addition, it is possible that men, due to
greater political and economic participation, were better able to capture the extra rents available to U.S. businesses when the U.S. economy dominated world markets. Women, who were often explicitly

excluded from these jobs, have not been as badly affected by the loss of these rents. Indeed, to the extent that less-skilled women have historically been crowded into a limited number of feminized occupations, their wages may always have been subject to greater competition.

Second, some have suggested that one hallmark of the changing U.S. economy is the rising importance of "soft" skills, such as effective interpersonal communication with customers or the ability to work in teams. Women have long been in service jobs requiring some of these skills, and may have a comparative advantage in them due to gender-specific socialization processes. If this is true, then unskilled women may be better prepared to move effectively into the new low-wage jobs available in the 1990s than are unskilled men.

Both of these explanations of gender differences in recent wage trends are speculative and would benefit from supporting evidence. Consistent with these theories are data on wage changes by men and women within manufacturing and service sectors of the economy. Unskilled women have experienced only small earnings losses in manufacturing jobs, and have experienced no earnings losses at all in service sector jobs. They have also seen less of a shift between these sectors, largely because they were less present in the manufacturing sector to begin with. Unskilled men, on the other hand, have experienced large earnings losses in both sectors and a large shift from manufacturing to services.[8]

Although we have yet to fully understand what is behind these labor market changes, there is broad agreement that the changes are unlikely to be reversed in the near future. The linkages between the U.S. economy and the world economy are expected to remain and to grow. Moreover, there is little reason to believe that recent technological innovations have come to an end. While the U.S. labor force will continue to increase its skill levels, the demand for more skilled workers will also continue to rise. There is no likelihood that workers who have experienced serious declines in their earnings ability will see a reversal of this situation. In fact, wages for unskilled work are likely to persist in their downward course.

The U.S. Bureau of Labor Statistics regularly projects growth by occupational category. Table 3.6 shows the distribution of the labor force across occupations in 1992, the growth in these occupations between 1979 and 1992, and the projected growth by occupation from 1992 to 2005. Two broad groups of occupations are projected to grow most rapidly in the future (and have grown most rapidly in the past): occupations that disproportionately require higher-than-

Table 3.6 CURRENT OCCUPATIONAL DISTRIBUTION AND PAST AND
PROJECTED OCCUPATION CHANGE IN UNITED STATES

| Occupational Category | Percentage of Labor Force, 1992 | Percentage Change | |
		Actual, 1979–92	Projected, 1992–2005
Executives: administrative and managerial	10.0	50.4	25.9
Professional specialty	13.7	43.0	37.4
Technicians and related support	3.5	57.6	32.2
Marketing and sales	10.7	30.7	20.6
Administrative support, including clerical	18.5	15.0	13.7
Service	16.0	24.6	33.4
Agriculture, forestry, fishing, etc.	2.9	−5.2	3.4
Precision production, craft, and repair	11.2	4.3	13.3
Operators, fabricators, and laborers	13.5	−10.3	9.5
All occupations	100.0	19.0	21.8

Source: Silvestri (1993: table 1).

average education levels, such as managerial, administrative, and professional jobs; and occupations that disproportionately require lower-than-average education levels, primarily service jobs. Jobs that have historically provided less-skilled men with higher earnings are projected to continue to shrink as a share of employment.

Changes in Distribution of Nonwage Compensation

Wages are only one piece of compensation. Slightly over 15 percent of total compensation is represented by nonwage benefits (Woodbury 1990; table 2). Changes in the distribution of nonwage compensation may have exacerbated or offset changes in wages over the past decade.

In general, we know that nonwage compensation is not equally spread across the wage distribution. Woodbury and Bettinger (1991) indicated that workers at lower education levels, lower earnings levels, and with less experience are substantially less likely to be covered by pension or health plans. On the other hand, when workers do receive these benefits, they are typically not fully prorated. This means that, relative to earnings, low-wage workers with benefits often receive a higher share of nonwage compensation than do high-wage workers with benefits. For instance, even though the incidence of health insurance receipt is lower among workers with low earnings, Acs and Steuerle (1993) have reported that health benefits had a small net equalizing effect on the distribution of total compensation in the 1980s because lower-wage employees who receive health benefits get proportionately more relative to their salary than do high-wage workers.

Although a large number of studies have investigated changes in the distribution of wages over the 1980s, there has been much less analysis of changes in the distribution of nonwage compensation, in part because measurement of nonwage benefits is more difficult and this information is less frequently collected. A notable exception to this is Acs and Steuerle (1993), who compared the distribution of health benefits in 1979 and 1989. They found that the availability of health benefits to low-wage workers fell over that decade, and that this decline was more marked among men than among women, largely because low-wage women had always been unlikely to receive health insurance on their jobs. The value of health benefits among those who continued to receive them, however, grew over the decade. Thus, the distribution of health insurance dollars remained largely unchanged, even though the incidence of health insurance became more unequal. Acs and Steuerle concluded that inequality in total compensation tracked inequality in wage compensation over the 1980s.

The decline in unionization, which has contributed to the decline in wages among less-skilled workers, has also contributed to a decline in nonwage compensation (Woodbury and Bettinger 1991). Unionized workers typically receive not only higher wages but more nonwage benefits. As the availability of union jobs has declined for unskilled workers, nonwage benefits have also declined.

Finally, there has been a rapid increase in the use of contingent employees in the U.S. labor market. Contingent employees are workers who are not permanently attached to a firm, but are hired only to complete a particular job. Some of these employees operate as private, self-employed contractors, while others may be attached to temporary service firms. There is no widely accepted definition of contingent work and no regular data on this phenomenon. Evidence from special studies by the Bureau of Labor Statistics indicates that there has been a substantial increase in the number of temporary workers, self-employed workers, and business-service providers over the 1980s (Belous 1989). These jobs may range from highly paid consultants who provide special types of financial analysis, to workers hired from a temporary agency to do maintenance and cleaning.

Contingent work is typically believed to have fewer nonwage benefits associated with it than is permanent employment with a firm, although direct evidence on this is sparse. For instance, there is not much evidence, either, on the extent to which the growing number of temporary agencies do or do not cover their employees for health or pension benefits. Since equivalent noncontingent workers in unskilled jobs often have few nonwage benefits, it is not clear that unskilled workers who are attached to temporary agencies are worse off. There is also not much evidence about the availability of nonwage benefits for the growing number of self-employed workers in the economy.[9] Further evidence on the compensation structure of these jobs is important, particularly if they continue to expand as part of the U.S. labor market.

Virtually all of the recent research documenting deteriorating labor market prospects for less-skilled workers has focused on wages. In general, however, there is little reason to believe that these trends have been offset by growth in nonwage compensation. If anything, the evidence seems to indicate that nonwage compensation has also deteriorated among low-wage workers. This suggests that less-skilled workers have lost even more ground than simple wage comparisons would indicate.

Changes in Job Mobility and Long-term Promotional Opportunities

This discussion has so far focused on point-in-time comparisons of job opportunities in the labor market. Traditionally, however, many workers have viewed the labor market as a ladder to be climbed as they gain experience. Historically, many low-wage entry-level jobs have provided workers with the opportunity for promotion and advancement into more economically secure positions. The current changes in the labor market for less-skilled workers suggests, however, that these workers will not only earn less when they enter the labor market but that as they acquire experience they will be less able to increase their wages. There is little direct research evidence on whether mobility opportunities over time for less-skilled workers have declined, but there is much indirect evidence supporting this claim.

In part, it appears that job ladders within firms may have become more attenuated. There is evidence of this particularly for unskilled manufacturing workers. In the century past, the classic view of promotion within American manufacturing firms was "when the president retires, the firm hires a new stock boy." In the post–World War II era, the link between production line and management jobs almost disappeared, as college degrees and (more recently) master's degrees in business administration were required for entry into management-level positions. Some have argued that recent technological changes have attenuated job ladders for less-skilled workers even more sharply over the past decade.

Certainly the research cited previously here on earnings changes within education and experience groups indicates that unskilled but experienced male workers are earning less now than their equivalent counterparts 10 and 20 years ago. This implies that wages are growing more slowly with experience, suggesting that promotional opportunities for these workers are more limited. Direct proof of this phenomenon, following cohorts of workers over time or studying changes in the job structure and promotional opportunities for workers within specific firms in either the manufacturing or service sector, is notably absent, however.

In contrast, there is some reason to believe that job ladders for less-skilled women have not deteriorated and may even have improved slightly over the past two decades. With the advent of antidiscrimination laws and the increase in the availability of female workers, large numbers of companies in the 1970s tried to provide opportunities for women in traditionally low-wage feminized jobs (particularly clerical workers) to be promoted into lower-level administrative and managerial positions. Again, there is little evidence on the extent of this shift, and we do not know exactly which group of women workers it has most benefited. But it suggests that women's job ladders within firms may not have suffered as much deterioration in recent decades as have men's, another potential reason why wages among less-skilled women may not have eroded as much.

If jobs available to experienced but less-skilled workers become more limited, this not only blocks the promotional opportunities within a firm, but it also makes it less possible to increase earnings through a job change. There is substantial evidence that job changes are typically associated with real salary increases for workers. Thus, many workers have moved up the earnings scale by moving to new jobs after they establish a good work history in a less-skilled entry-level position. If, however, there are no better-paying jobs available to workers whose main skills are good work habits, then low-paying entry-level jobs become permanent positions.

We have little research on patterns of job progression and promotion among less-skilled workers across firms, either historically or currently. As table 3.5 demonstrated, educational credentials appear to have become increasingly important in the labor market, making it more difficult to improve one's earnings by experience alone. Declining internal promotional opportunities for experienced but unskilled workers almost surely means that firms are also not hiring such workers from outside for these positions. Discussions with those who run job placement programs for women on public assistance indicate that their clients perceive that they have few advancement opportunities beyond entry-level jobs; this is a major reason why some of them have not actively sought work. If less-skilled workers perceive few opportunities for promotion and increased future earnings, this may limit their willingness to accept a low-wage entry-level job. This indicates the importance of looking at the entire set of future employment options available to potential workers.

Changes in Availability of Full-time Jobs

Finally, a number of persons have suggested that there is an overlap between job availability and job quality through the growth of part-time work. For instance, if the only available jobs are part-time, this will seriously constrain a worker's earning ability and is evidence of deterioration in both job availability and job quality.

Figure 3.3 depicts the share of male and female workers who work part-time. A relatively constant share of women have worked part-time over the past 25 years, around 26 percent to 28 percent. If anything, this number has declined slightly since the late 1970s. Thus, there is little evidence that women have become more constrained by part-time work. In contrast, there has been a steady increase in part-time work among men over the past 25 years, from about 8 percent to almost 13 percent of male workers. Part-time work among men is also more cyclical than among women. Thus, as with wage trends, the part-time work trends indicate a deterioration among men's employment situations but little change among women's.[10]

The key issue in part-time work, however, is probably not "How much part-time work is there?" but "How much part-time work is involuntarily chosen?" For instance, in 1992 close to 75 percent of female part-time workers indicated that they were working part-time because they wanted to or because they only sought part-time work. Among men in 1992, 60 percent of all part-time workers indicated that they were voluntarily working part-time. Trends in voluntary part-time work are also graphed in figure 3.3. For both men and women, the share of involuntary part-time work has grown by about

Figure 3.3 SHARE OF PART-TIME WORK BY WOMEN AND MEN IN UNITED STATES

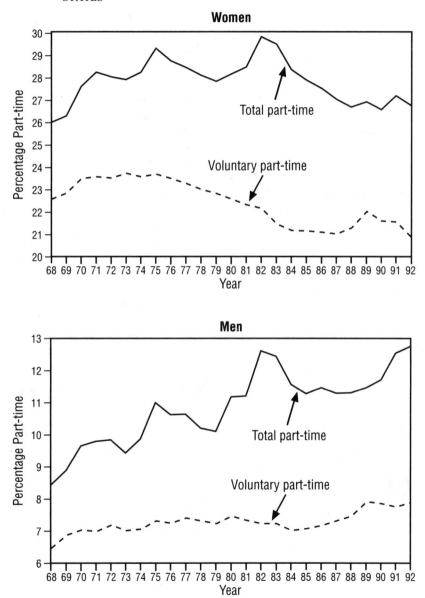

Sources: Years 1967–88 from U.S. Department of Labor (1989: table 23); years 1989–92 from U.S. Department of Labor, *Employment and Earnings*, January, various issues, and table 7 in Household Data Annual Averages.
Note: Both plots based on all civilian workers, ages 16 and over, at work in nonagricultural industries.

five percentage points over the past decade, indicating there may be increasing constraints on hours in the labor market.

If less-skilled men are experiencing increasing involuntary part-time employment, this would also be correlated with declines in their wage and nonwage compensation, since part-time jobs are typically worse along both dimensions (Blank 1990). At best, however, the small changes in part-time work in the U.S. labor market over the past few decades indicate that this is probably a secondary issue with regard to the deterioration of job prospects for unskilled workers.

In summary, there is evidence of more limited earnings opportunities for adult men in today's labor market, and stagnant earnings opportunities among women. There is little reason to believe that these trends are going to reverse themselves, although their causes are not fully comprehended. To the extent that they are related to the internationalization of the U.S. economy, to ongoing technological changes, and to other only partially understood changes in the labor market, job opportunities may continue to deteriorate for less-skilled workers in the years ahead. While we have less evidence on changes in nonwage compensation for less-skilled workers or in their long-term earnings mobility, if these other aspects of the labor market have also become worse for less-skilled workers, then the labor market problems facing less-skilled workers may be even greater than wage changes alone indicate.

DO LOW WAGES CORRELATE WITH ECONOMIC DISTRESS?

The previous section's evidence about deteriorating job opportunities for less-skilled workers does not necessarily mean that economic distress among individuals has increased. In particular, declining earnings opportunities must be discussed along with other variables that affect total income. First, individual earnings are the result of both wages and work effort. If individuals increase their work effort in the face of earnings declines, then economic need may not increase (although, by most economic models, the well-being of the person will have decreased, since the same income level is being achieved with a greater input of labor market time). Second, changes in household composition and in the earning behavior of households could offset declines in earning power among some individuals. For example, if all low-wage workers are adolescents who live with their parents, their low wages may have little impact on their economic

Table 3.7 U.S. LABOR FORCE PARTICIPATION RATES BY SKILL LEVEL, 1979–92

Education Category	Men		Women	
	1979	1992	1979	1992
Less than high school	75.9	70.0	42.7	42.9
High school degree	90.2	86.6	60.2	66.6
Some post–high school training	85.4	82.9	62.6	71.9
College degree or more	93.3	91.5	70.9	80.1
All education levels	86.2	83.7	57.5	66.7

Source: Tabulations from U.S. Bureau of the Census, Current Population Survey, May 1979 and March 1992.

well-being. Third, earnings are only one source of income for families. Changes in earnings may be offset by changes in public or private transfers that help families maintain income levels even in the face of earnings losses. The sections following examine each of these issues in turn.

Labor Effort and Earnings

The substantial changes noted here in the labor force participation of Americans have been particularly interesting because they are so different by gender. Among women, labor force participation has steadily expanded, whereas it has declined among men. These aggregate trends hide significant differences among workers of different skill levels, however.

Table 3.7 shows trends in labor force participation over the past decade among adult women and men by skill level. Whereas labor market participation among women with more education has increased measurably, among less-skilled women labor market participation has been essentially stagnant. Coleman and Pencavel (1993b), in a comprehensive review of women's labor market behavior since 1940, indicated that this trend has been evident throughout the post-World War II period. In fact, they concluded that skill differences were more important to understanding women's pay in 1990 than were gender differences, as more-educated women's work effort moves closer to that of more-educated men.

Table 3.7 also shows recent labor market participation trends among adult men by skill level. In contrast to women, adult men's labor market participation has declined markedly, with most of the decline concentrated among men at lower education levels.[11] Coleman and Pencavel (1993a), in a comprehensive review of long-term male labor force behavior, suggested that work hours among highly skilled men have actually increased in the United States, whereas there has been a slight decline in hours and a substantial decline in participation among less-skilled men.

Analysis of the causes behind these trends in male labor force participation point to changing factors over the past 25 years. Juhn (1992) indicated that the decline in men's labor force participation from 1967 to the mid-1970s appeared to be due to behavioral changes, exclusive of the labor market. Since the mid-1970s, however, falling wages for less-skilled workers can explain most of the decline in work effort, assuming reasonable elasticity responses among men to earnings opportunities.

Trends in female labor force participation reflect very different changes. Increases in real wages for many (particularly more-skilled) women are important, as are smaller families, higher education levels, and changes in household work. But some amount of the rise in female labor force participation is unaccounted for by standard economic and demographic factors, and appears to reflect long-term changes in women's (and men's) expectations about their economic role.

It is worth noting, however, the extent to which labor participation trends among both men and women track wage trends. As wages for less-skilled men have fallen, so has their willingness to work. Stagnant wages for less-skilled women are associated with an unchanging labor supply. More-educated women, whose earnings opportunities have greatly expanded, have responded by expanding their work effort. At a minimum, this indicates how important earnings and job opportunities are in inducing work effort. Attempts to increase employment among less-skilled women in the face of stagnant or declining earnings opportunities will be difficult, at best.

In conclusion, among less-skilled workers, individual work effort has tracked earnings opportunities over the past 15 years. There is no evidence that labor supply changes have in any way offset the changes in hourly wages among individual workers. Instead, they have been a reinforcing factor. It is true, however, that changes in work behavior within households, as well as changes in family composition, have been important. It is to this issue that I turn next.

Household Composition and Economic Well-being

Individual earnings are only one component of economic well-being. For persons who live in families, multiple earners can offset or reinforce earnings changes. Over the last 15 years, family income inequality has risen slowly, but more slowly than wage inequality. There is also not much evidence of substantial income declines among workers at the bottom of the distribution; much of the rise in family income inequality is due to increases in income at the top.[12]

Two issues are crucial in understanding how family income changes are related to changes in individual earnings. First, one must examine changes in family formation and composition to see how many households are dependent on single adults for economic well-being. Second, one must look at changes in earnings within multiple-adult households to see whether increases in wives' earnings are offsetting declines in husbands' earnings.

Family composition changes have substantially increased the vulnerability of many families to the labor market. Over the past three decades, the splintering of households has meant that more persons are reliant upon only their own earnings as the primary source of economic well-being. Two trends should be mentioned here. First, there has been a growing propensity for single individuals to live alone rather than in shared housing arrangements. Blank and Card (1993) have indicated that single persons without children have increased from 16 percent of all households in 1967 to 29 percent in 1991. Second, the rising number of single-parent families has meant that both children and their custodial parents are more vulnerable to poverty. In fact, the rise in children's poverty rates over the 1980s can be almost entirely attributed to the continuing growth in the number of children who live in single-parent families. Blank and Card (1993) reported that the share of single parents with children has almost doubled among all households. Among low-income families with children, well over 50 percent are single-parent families, a striking change from several decades ago.

With the growth in single-adult households, the labor market opportunities of that one adult are increasingly important in determining economic well-being. Note that the problem here is *not* single-earner households, but single-adult households. Many households in the past relied only on a single earner, but had multiple adults. This meant they had the potential to increase work effort by adding another earner, and also allowed them to substitute time in home production for labor market earnings. There are fewer ways to cushion the effects of stagnant or falling earnings among less-skilled workers when they are the sole adult in their family. Cancian, Danziger, and Gottschalk (1993) and Karoly and Burtless (1993) have documented that the breaking apart of families is a primary cause of widening family income inequality. The correlation between changes in family composition and changes in wage inequality together explains much of the rising inequality in family income.

In addition to the growth in single-adult families, it is important to look at joint earnings trends among husbands and wives in multiple-adult families. Wives' earnings have long acted to equalize the family income distribution, largely because women in lower-income households were more likely to work. Cancian et al. (1993) have indicated that wives' earnings continue to have an equalizing effect on the income distribution, and have somewhat offset the effect of falling real wages among less-skilled men. In fact, the primary reason that low-income married couples have not experienced greater income declines is because wives have increased their work effort. Burtless and Karoly (1993), however, contended that rising inequality in men's wages has been directly responsible for about one-third of the rise in family income inequality. In conclusion, deteriorating wages among less-skilled workers have not always translated into a dollar-for-dollar decline in family income, but they have had some effect on family income levels and income inequality.

Table 3.8 looks at the cross between individual earnings and family income. Across the top of the table are the quintiles of the family income distribution in 1991. On the lefthand side are the quintiles of the individual earning distribution in March 1992. The table tabulates the cross-distribution of an individual's current placement in the wage distribution with his or her placement in the family earnings distribution in the previous year.

There are several things to note about table 3.8. First, higher-income families tend to have fewer individuals in them. Thus, although 20 percent of all families are in the bottom quintile of the family income distribution, 28 percent of all individuals are in families in this bottom quintile. Second, the table demonstrates that individuals who are not working or whose wages place them in the bottom of the earnings distribution are more likely to be in the bottom of the family income distribution as well. For instance, 31 percent of persons in the first quintile of the wage distribution are also in the first quintile of the earnings distribution. Only 26 percent of persons in the top quintile of the wage distribution are in the bottom quintile of the earnings distribution.

Third, table 3.8 shows that a large number of persons with high wages are in families with low incomes. These are typically either persons who work little over the year, but who earn a good wage when they do work, or persons who are moving from a low earnings

Table 3.8 DISTRIBUTION OF INDIVIDUALS IN WAGE QUINTILES BY FAMILY INCOME QUINTILES IN UNITED STATES: 1991 AND 1992

Hourly Wage Quintiles (in March 1992)	Family Income Quintiles (in 1991)				
	Bottom Quintile	Second Quintile	Third Quintile	Fourth Quintile	Top Quintile
Not working	28.8	22.0	18.8	17.4	12.9
Bottom quintile	31.2	21.2	19.6	16.0	12.0
Second quintile	29.6	20.9	17.6	18.6	13.4
Third quintile	27.6	19.6	19.3	18.9	14.6
Fourth quintile	27.4	19.2	18.5	18.8	16.1
Top quintile	26.1	18.4	19.0	17.4	19.1
All persons	28.5	20.6	18.8	17.8	14.4

Sources: Tabulations from U.S. Bureau of the Census, Current Population Survey, March 1992. Family income quintiles based on reported income in 1991; hourly wage quintiles based on wages per hour last week, reported in March 1992.

Note: Entries sum across to 100 percent within each wage quintile. Each row represents distribution of persons within each wage category across family income quintiles.

situation in the previous year (they may have been in school or at home with a young child) to more extensive earnings on their current job. At the same time, a large number of persons with low wages are in high family income situations. Twenty-eight percent of persons in the bottom of the wage distribution are in the top 40 percent of the family income distribution. Interestingly, whereas women are somewhat more likely to be among this group, a substantial number of men are also in this situation. These are predominantly persons in households with other earners whose income compensates for their own low wages.

The message from table 3.8 is that there are a substantial number of persons at the bottom of the wage distribution who are also at the bottom of the family income distribution. But not all low-wage workers are in poor or even near-poor families. To characterize all low-wage work as a problem for economic well-being would be inappropriate. Presumably, concern about changes in the low-wage labor market should focus primarily on those workers whose low earnings are directly related to low family income.

Other Income Sources beyond Earnings

Even among workers who are the sole adult in their family, declining earnings opportunities could be offset by expansions in other income sources, particularly public and private transfers. The public income sources available to workers in low-income families include Aid to Families with Dependent Children (AFDC, the cash assistance program that is available primarily to single mothers and their children) or in-kind assistance such as Food Stamps or rent supplements. Wage supplementation is available through the Earned Income Tax Credit (EITC). Private income sources might include gifts and transfers from other family members, or child support payments to custodial parents.

In general, with the exception of expansions in the EITC (discussed later here), other income sources have not expanded for low-wage workers. AFDC cash benefits have declined in real terms throughout the 1980s. Food Stamp benefits have remained relatively constant in real terms over the last decade, after a slight cut in the early 1980s.[13] Gramlich et al. (1993) have investigated the net effect of transfer changes over the 1980s, and concluded that these changes not only did not offset the rising inequality in income and earnings but actually reinforced it.

Private transfers to low-income families are harder to track, since we have less data on them. For instance, we have no reliable time series on inter-family gifts, so we do not know if they have been increasing or decreasing in size over time. There is evidence that low-income adults receive about the same amount of financial assistance from their parents as their higher-income siblings, indicating that inter-family transfers in general do not do much to offset income differences. Child support payments have risen, but so have the number of single mothers and children. The share of single parents collecting child support does not seem to have increased a great deal over the last decade, despite real efforts at providing a more extensive child support system. Average child support payments per eligible child have also not grown much (U.S. Congress, House 1993).

The only transfer that has expanded in direct response to the declining wages among less-skilled workers is the Earned Income Tax Credit (EITC). The EITC is an earnings supplement available to low-wage workers in low-income families. It is paid through the federal income tax system, typically as a lump-sum refund at the end of the tax year. The exact structure of the EITC has been well-described elsewhere (see Hoffman and Seidman 1990) and is not reviewed here.[14] Essentially, the EITC supplements earnings up to a given point, and then slowly tapers off as earnings go above this level. For instance, in 1980, the EITC provided an additional $.10 per $1 of earnings on the first $5,000 of earnings. By 1994, this had increased to a supplement of an additional $.30 per $1 of earnings on the first $8,400 of earnings for a family with two children. Under the Clinton administration, the EITC is undergoing a further major expansion. By 1996, most low-wage workers with children will receive a supplement large enough to ensure that full-time work, together with Food Stamps, will raise them out of poverty.

Because the recent large expansions in the EITC are just now occurring, and because we lack good data on who uses the EITC and when they receive it, we know little about the effect of the EITC on the economic well-being of families. On the one hand, a substantial number of eligible families (around 80 percent) seem to be receiving the supplement.[15] There is no doubt that this increases their family income and offsets any earnings declines that they may have experienced. On the other hand, few recipients appear to have any clear understanding of how the EITC operates; thus it is uncertain that it provides them with any additional work incentives.

Moreover, most recipients continue to receive the EITC as a lump-sum payment at the end of the year, which means that it does little to supplement regular monthly income. It is treated as "forced savings" by many recipients, who use it to make special once-a-year purchases that require larger sums of cash. The net effect of these expenditure patterns on economic well-being is hard to judge. A better understanding of the extent to which the EITC offsets some of the economic problems caused by declining wages among less-skilled workers will become increasingly important as the EITC expands for low-wage earners.

CONCLUSIONS

Extensive changes have occurred in the labor market for low-wage workers over the past several decades. Less-skilled men have experienced a deterioration in earnings opportunities both at the entry level and at higher levels of experience. At least some evidence indicates that nonwage compensation for these men may also have declined. These changes are directly related to the declining labor market participation among this group over the past 15 years.

Among women, the picture is not quite so bleak. For reasons still not clearly understood, less-skilled women seem to have been somewhat protected from the labor market changes impacting men. Wages for unskilled women have been essentially unchanged over the past two decades, as has their labor market participation. Women with moderate to high skill levels have seen major wage increases, correlated with substantial increases in their labor market involvement. There is also reason to believe that promotional opportunities for women have not become as attenuated as for men.

It is worth noting, however, that entry-level wages for less-skilled women remain well below those of men, and the jobs women take are still substantially less likely to provide nonwage compensation such as health and pension benefits. Essentially, unskilled women have always had access to bad jobs at bad wages, and little has changed for them over the past few decades. Their earnings opportunities are no worse, but also no better than they were one or two decades ago.

Labor market opportunities and earnings are not the sole determinants of individual economic well-being, although they are correlated. A substantial number of low-wage workers, both male and female, live in higher-income families and are presumably less affected by these changes. Married couple, two-earner families have also protected themselves somewhat from declining male earnings. In addition, the Earned Income Tax Credit provides low-wage workers a subsidy to their earnings, and recent expansions to the EITC will increasingly offset earnings declines. On the other hand, as more and more individuals find themselves in single-adult families, the adults and children in these families will be highly vulnerable to deterioration in earnings opportunities for less-skilled workers.

It is only somewhat encouraging that these labor market changes have not produced substantial increases in unemployment among less-skilled workers (although this has probably been helped by the decline in labor market participation among less-skilled men). Evidence seems to indicate that job availability, per se, remains strong. While less-skilled workers experience higher unemployment than more-skilled workers, their relative position in the labor market in terms of job availability has not declined. This suggests that the changes in the U.S. labor market are not leading to the elimination of jobs for less-skilled workers, but to the reconfiguration of those jobs into lower-paid positions that provide fewer opportunities for advancement into higher-wage positions. The good news is that less-skilled persons can still find work. The bad news is that their long-term earnings opportunities have eroded, and there is little reason to believe that these changes will be reversed in the near future.

With respect to efforts to increase employment among welfare recipients, this description of the current U.S. labor market is not promising. It suggests that there is little prospect that women with low skill levels will be able to work their way into middle-income employment opportunities. At best, they face a labor market much like that faced by their mothers or grandmothers, with low-paid jobs, relatively high unemployment and high turnover, and few fringe benefits.

Serious efforts to move these women into employment will have to grapple with problems of long-term low-wage prospects. In particular, even after one or two years of steady employment, a woman still may be unable either to find a job providing health insurance or to fully cover her child care expenses. It would be foolish for work/welfare programs to assume that women who find jobs will make steady economic progress toward substantially higher wages. Some welfare recipients will be able to follow this model (particularly those with more education), but this is unlikely to be the typical experience among women who lack high school diplomas or even among those who have a high school degree.

There is some good news in this chapter for welfare-to-work efforts, however. First, employment efforts focused on less-skilled women are going to be easier to implement than those focused on less-skilled men. Women's earnings opportunities are at least no worse than they have been in the recent past, and their relative unemployment rates have improved. Second, these women will, in general, be able to find jobs. The problem will not be employment, but the nature of that employment. So long as the government is willing to provide wage subsidies and assistance for child care and other family needs, greater employment is very possible.

Third, it is even possible that less-skilled women are benefiting relative to less-skilled men from the structural shifts in the U.S. economy. To the extent that these women have better interpersonal skills, and have long relied upon skills other than their physical strength to find a job, they may be in a better position than their male counterparts to take advantage of the strong job growth for less-skilled workers that is projected to occur in retail, service, and health care industries. In fact, the decline in male labor market participation may well open up new job opportunities to women in the years ahead.

Finally, it is worth noting that widespread acceptance of the idea that welfare reform efforts should be focused on increasing employment among single mothers is itself the result of the fundamental labor market changes that have occurred over the past several decades. As women's education, employment, and earnings opportunities have expanded, we have increasingly come to view single mothers as *earners*, and to demand work from them in the same way we have long demanded that adult men support themselves. It is perhaps an inevitable result of women's increasingly important role in the labor force that women would no longer be viewed by the social assistance system as dependent, but would come to be seen as workers. The irony, of course, is that these expanded labor market opportunities are not occurring among women at the bottom of the wage distribution. By demanding that welfare recipients should be working more in today's economy, we are perhaps guilty of making false inferences from the experience of the average woman, whose earnings and employment opportunities have expanded, and applying these inferences to a population whose labor market opportunities have been much more stagnant.

Just as the growth of single-mother families has created a new set of family-related demands on less-skilled women, the social redefinition of women as earners rather than as dependents is now adding a new set of employment-related demands. In a world of expanding employment and growing real wages, efforts to move welfare recipients from welfare to work could piggyback on the incentives provided by expanded economic opportunities. Unfortunately, labor market opportunities for unskilled women show little promise of improving. As a result, we cannot expect rapid success from efforts to increase employment among welfare recipients. This does not imply that such policies should not be pursued, but that they must be viewed as long-term efforts.

This chapter also underscores the extent to which successful efforts to promote work among welfare recipients must involve more than job placement assistance. The growing importance of skills in the labor market emphasizes the importance of efforts to help women acquire more training or to persuade young people to stay in school. The likelihood that low-wage entry-level jobs will not lead to high-wage jobs indicates the need to plan on potentially long-term earnings supplements to these women, through cash or in-kind benefits such as child care assistance. In short, welfare-to-work programs cannot be cheaply or quickly formulated if they are to be effective in helping women escape poverty permanently. Attempts to simply cut women off welfare without making other services available will merely cast them and their children into an increasingly hostile labor market where many less-skilled persons in single-adult families cannot earn enough to survive on their own.

Notes

I thank Rebecca London for excellent research assistance.

1. Data in figure 3.2 are based on calculations from the data set described in Blank and Card (1993).

2. It is worth noting that racial differences in unemployment are significant even after controlling for skill and gender, with blacks at each skill level experiencing about 1.5 times higher unemployment rates than whites. In addition, the ratio of unemployment rates between high- and low-skilled workers is somewhat smaller in the black population.

3. Evidence summarized in this section can be found in Blackburn, Bloom, and Freeman (1990), Juhn, Murphy, and Pierce (1993), Karoly (1993), and Levy and Murnane (1992).

4. If table 3.4 were extended through the early 1990s, declines in women's earnings would be visible due to the recession. The 1979 to 1989 comparison is more useful, however, since it depicts two relatively similar years in the business cycle.

5. For a discussion of differential changes in the distribution of black and white men's earnings, see Juhn, Murphy, and Pierce (1991).

6. The minimum wage in 1992 was $4.25.

7. For a summary of the cross-national evidence on widening wage inequality, see Freeman and Katz (1994).

8. Information in this paragraph is based on work in progress by Frank Levy and Vandy Howell.

9. There is some evidence that self-employed workers in the 1980s had somewhat lower earnings than wage and salary workers, which reflects a deterioration in the position of the self-employed (Aronson 1991).

10. A comparison between the U.S. experience and that of many Western European countries is also instructive. In a number of countries, almost all of the employment growth over the last decade has been in part-time jobs. In comparison, the increase in part-time work in the United States is almost unnoticeable.

11. Blackburn et al. (1990) also documented that declines in labor force participation among men have all occurred among the less skilled.

12. In 1979, mean income in the bottom quintile of the family distribution was $6,379; in 1989 it was $6,368. In the top quintile, mean family income rose from $72,038 to $83,195 over these years (calculated from data set described in Blank and Card 1993).

13. For a discussion of trends in benefit programs and their overlap with the labor market, see Blank (1994).

14. For a discussion of recent expansions and changes in the EITC, see Scholz (1994b).

15. In fact, recent evidence indicates that a number of noneligible persons are trying to claim the EITC (Scholz 1994a).

References

Acs, Gregory, and C. Eugene Steuerle. 1993. "Trends in the Distribution of Non-Wage Benefits and Total Compensation." Urban Institute Working Paper. Washington, D.C.: Urban Institute.

Altonji, Joseph G., and David Card. 1991. "The Effects of Immigration on the Labor Market Outcomes of Less-skilled Natives." In *Immigration, Trade, and the Labor Market*, edited by John M. Abowd and Richard B. Freeman. Chicago: University of Chicago Press.

Aronson, Robert L. 1991. *Self-Employment: A Labor Market Perspective.* Ithaca, N.Y.: ILR Press.

Belous, Richard S. 1989. "How Human Resource Systems Adjust to the Shift toward Contingent Work." *Monthly Labor Review* 112 (3, March):7–12.

Berman, Eli, John Bound, and Zvi Griliches. 1993. "Changes in the Demand for Skilled Labor within U.S. Manufacturing Industries: Evidence from the Annual Survey of Manufacturing." National Bureau of Economic Research Working Paper 4255. Cambridge, Mass.: National Bureau of Economic Research, January.

Blackburn, McKinley L., David E. Bloom, and Richard B. Freeman. 1990. "The Declining Position of Less Skilled American Men." In *A Future of Lousy Jobs?*, edited by Gary Burtless. Washington, D.C.: Brookings Institution.

Blank, Rebecca M. 1990. "Are Part-time Jobs Bad Jobs?" In *A Future of Lousy Jobs?*, edited by Gary Burtless. Washington, D.C.: Brookings Institution.

―――――. 1994. "The Employment Strategy: Public Policies to Increase Work and Earnings." In *Combatting Poverty: Prescriptions for Change*, edited by Sheldon Danziger, Gary Sandefur, and Daniel Weinberg. Boston: Harvard University Press.

Blank, Rebecca M., and David Card. 1993. "Poverty, Income Distribution, and Growth: Are They Still Connected?" *Brookings Papers on Economic Activity*, no. 2. Washington, D.C.: Brookings Institution.

Blank, Rebecca M., and Richard B. Freeman. 1994. "Evaluating the Connection between Social Protection and Economic Flexibility." In *Social Protection versus Economic Flexibility: Is There a Tradeoff?*, edited by Rebecca M. Blank. Chicago: University of Chicago Press.

Borjas, George J., Richard B. Freeman, and Lawrence Katz. 1992. "On the Labor Market Effects of Immigration and Trade." In *Immigration and the Work Force*, edited by George J. Borjas and Richard B. Freeman. Chicago: University of Chicago Press.

Bound, John, and George Johnson. 1992. "Changes in the Structure of Wages in the 1980s: An Evaluation of Alternative Explanations." *American Economic Review* 82(3, June):371–92.

Cancian, Maria, Sheldon Danziger, and Peter Gottschalk. 1993. "Working Wives and Family Income Inequality among Married Couples." In *Uneven Tides: Rising Inequality in America*, edited by Sheldon Danziger and Peter Gottschalk. New York: Russell Sage Foundation.

Card, David. 1992. "The Effect of Unions on the Distribution of Wages: Redistribution of Relabelling?" National Bureau of Economic Research Working Paper 4195. Cambridge, Mass.: National Bureau of Economic Research, October.

Coleman, Mary T., and John Pencavel. 1993a. "Changes in Work Hours of Male Employees, 1940–1987." *Industrial and Labor Relations Review* 46(2, January):262–83.

―――――. 1993b. "Trends in Market Work Behavior of Women since 1940." *Industrial and Labor Relations Review* 46(4, July):653–76.

Davis, Steven J., and John Haltiwanger. 1991. "Wage Dispersion between and within U.S. Manufacturing Plants: 1963–86." *Brookings Papers on Economic Activity: Microeconomics*, no. 1 (pp. 115–80). Washington, D.C.: Brookings Institution.

Economic Report of the President. 1994. Washington, D.C.: U.S. Government Printing Office, February.

Freeman, Richard B. 1993. "How Much Has De-Unionization Contributed to the Rise in Male Earnings Inequality?" In *Uneven Tides: Rising*

Inequality in America, edited by Sheldon Danziger and Peter Gott-schalk. New York: Russell Sage Foundation.

Freeman, Richard B., and Lawrence F. Katz. 1994. "Rising Wage Inequality: The United States versus Other Advanced Countries." In *Working Under Different Rules*, edited by Richard B. Freeman. New York: Russell Sage Foundation.

Gramlich, Edward M., Richard Kasten, and Frank Sammartino. 1993. "Growing Inequality in the 1980s: The Role of Federal Taxes and Cash Transfers." In *Uneven Tides: Rising Inequality in America*, edited by Sheldon Danziger and Peter Gottschalk. New York: Russell Sage Foundation.

Hoffman, Saul D., and Laurence S. Seidman. 1990. *The Earned Income Tax Credit*. Kalamazoo, Mich: W. E. Upjohn Institute.

Horrigan, Michael W., and Ronald B. Mincy. 1993. "The Minimum Wage and Earnings and Income Inequality." In *Uneven Tides: Rising Inequality in America*, edited by Sheldon Danziger and Peter Gottschalk. New York: Russell Sage Foundation.

Juhn, Chinhui. 1992. "Decline of Male Labor Market Participation: The Role of Declining Market Opportunities." *Quarterly Journal of Economics* 107(1, February):79–122.

Juhn, Chinhui, Kevin M. Murphy, and Brooks Pierce. 1991. "Accounting for the Slowdown in Black-White Wage Convergence." In *Workers and Their Wages*, edited by Marvin H. Kosters. Washington, D.C.: AEI Press.

————. 1993. "Wage Inequality and the Rise in Returns to Skill." *Journal of Political Economy* 101(3, June):410–42.

Karoly, Lynn A. 1993. "The Trend in Inequality among Families, Individuals, and Workers in the United States: A Twenty-Five Year Perspective." In *Uneven Tides: Rising Inequality in America*, edited by Sheldon Danziger and Peter Gottschalk. New York: Russell Sage Foundation.

Karoly, Lynn A., and Gary Burtless. 1993. "The Effects of Rising Earnings Inequality on the Distribution of U.S. Income." Working Paper, Brookings Institution. December.

Katz, Lawrence F., and Kevin M. Murphy. 1992. "Changes in Relative Wages, 1963–87: Supply and Demand Factors." *Quarterly Journal of Economics* 107(1, February):35–78.

Levy, Frank, and Richard J. Murnane. 1992. "U.S. Earnings Levels and Earnings Inequality: A Review of Recent Trends and Proposed Explanations." *Journal of Economic Literature* 30(3, September):1333–81.

Murphy, Kevin M., and Finis Welch. 1993. "Industrial Change and the Rising Importance of Skill." In *Uneven Tides: Rising Inequality in America*, edited by Sheldon Danziger and Peter Gottschalk. New York: Russell Sage Foundation.

Revenga, Ana. 1992. "Exporting Jobs? The Impact of Import Competition of Employment and Wages in U.S. Manufacturing." *Quarterly Journal of Economics* 107(1, February):255–84.

Scholz, John Karl. 1994b. "Tax Policy and the Working Poor: The Earned Income Tax Credit." *Focus.* Madison, Wis.: Institute for Research on Poverty, Winter.

———. 1994a. "The Earned Income Tax Credit: Participation, Compliance, and Antipoverty Effectiveness." *National Tax Journal* 47 (1, March): 59–81.

Silvestri, George T. 1993. "Occupational Employment: Wide Variations in Growth." *Monthly Labor Review* 116(11, November):58–86.

U.S. Congress. 1993. House Committee on Ways and Means. *1993 Green Book.* Washington, D.C.: U.S. Government Printing Office.

U.S. Department of Labor, Bureau of Labor Statistics. 1989. *Handbook of Labor Statistics.* Bulletin 2340. Washington, D.C.: U.S. Government Printing Office.

Woodbury, Stephen A. 1990. "Current Developments in Employee Benefits." In *Research in Labor Economics, Volume 11*, edited by Laurie J. Bassi and David L. Crawford. Greenwich, Conn.: JAI Press.

Woodbury, Stephen A., and Douglas R. Bettinger. 1991. "The Decline of Fringe-Benefit Coverage in the 1980s." In *Structural Changes in U.S. Labor Markets: Causes and Consequences*, edited by Randall W. Eberts and Erica L. Groshen. Armonk, N.Y.: M. E. Sharpe.

Chapter Four

EMPLOYMENT PROSPECTS OF WELFARE RECIPIENTS

Gary Burtless

Public assistance recipients in the United States suffer from extreme disadvantage in the labor market. Adults who receive the most important form of cash assistance, Aid to Families with Dependent Children (AFDC), are often young women with limited schooling and very low scores on standardized tests of ability and achievement. Even if these women were not responsible for the care of young children, they would face severe problems finding and holding well-paid jobs. Child care responsibilities make their employment problems even more formidable.

This chapter examines the job prospects of welfare recipients by concentrating on recent labor market developments among young women with characteristics similar to those of women receiving AFDC. Most calculations are performed using data over the last 10 to 15 years from the National Longitudinal Survey of Youth (NLSY) and from the Current Population Survey (CPS) of the U.S. Bureau of the Census. Data in both surveys suggest that adult AFDC recipients face grim employment prospects.

The weak labor market preparation of most public assistance recipients, especially of those who rely most heavily on AFDC payments, is obvious from simple tabulations of their work experience, educational attainment, and standardized test scores. Among women in their mid-twenties who are most dependent on AFDC, roughly half have not completed high school. Less than one out of eight has received any schooling beyond high school. More than 70 percent of the most dependent 25-year-olds obtained a score on the Armed Forces Qualification Test (AFQT) that places them in the bottom *quarter* of all test takers in their age group.

The employment prospects of women with poor educational credentials have never been particularly favorable. In 1979 a woman aged 20–34 who had not completed high school could expect to earn less than $16,000 per year (in 1993 dollars) if she worked year-round on a full-time schedule. Few AFDC recipients can expect to earn wages this high, of course, because their child care responsibilities prevent them from working full time. Since the late 1970s, the job prospects facing young women with limited education have worsened. Between 1979 and 1989, for example, average full-time earnings received by young female dropouts fell 10 percent. Among female dropouts between the ages of 20 and 24, full-time earnings fell nearly 20 percent. Real earnings received by young, poorly educated women have continued to fall since 1989.

Not only have real earnings fallen on average among young women with limited schooling, but individual career prospects have worsened as well. Wage data on both the CPS and NLSY show that women who have not completed high school can expect to receive very meager earnings gains over the early years of their careers. Women who have not completed high school can ordinarily expect slower annual wage improvement than women with greater school attainment. High school dropouts interviewed in the NLSY saw their hourly wages climb just $0.07 (1.2 percent) per year between the ages of 21 and 29. In contrast, women completing one to three years of college by age 24 saw their average wage climb $0.45 (5.7 percent) per year from age 21 to age 29. The steeper wage profile of better-educated workers means that women who may be low-wage earners in their early twenties can usually look forward to moderately well-paying jobs when they reach their early or mid-thirties. Steady advancement in a career is much more unusual among women who have done poorly in high school or failed to complete it.

This chapter is divided into six sections. The first section sketches the trend in public policy and popular attitudes toward paid work among poor single mothers. The second and longest section describes employment and earnings trends among a group of young AFDC recipients, showing their experiences from age 18 through their early thirties, as contrasted with those of similar groups of women who did not collect welfare. This analysis documents the bleak job prospects of single mothers who collected AFDC in an era when comparatively few women were forced to accept employment or training as a condition for receiving welfare. The third section of the chapter considers how job prospects of AFDC mothers would change if many or most of them were forced to find jobs as a condition for retaining AFDC eligibility.

The analysis in the first three sections focuses on the actual employment experiences of poor single mothers over the past 10 or 15 years. The fourth section examines the future job prospects of poor mothers in light of recent job market trends that continue to erode average real wages earned by less-skilled workers. The fifth section considers whether increased spending on education or job training can significantly improve the earnings capacity of welfare recipients. It seeks to answer two questions: First, can education and training programs boost unskilled workers' earnings by enough to erase their recent setbacks in the labor market? Second, if welfare benefits were limited to two years, could training programs help offset the loss of AFDC benefits and lift welfare recipients out of poverty? The chapter concludes with a brief survey of the policy implications of the analysis.

TRENDS IN PUBLIC POLICY AND ATTITUDES TOWARD WELFARE

When Aid to Dependent Children was established in 1935, one of its principal goals was to enable widows and other single mothers to care for their children without being forced to hold a job. In the 1930s, mothers were expected to act as caregivers and homemakers, not as breadwinners, even when they were unsupported by a working spouse. The 1960s and 1970s witnessed a major shift in social attitudes toward work among mothers. Because job holding was increasingly common among married mothers, including mothers with very young children, many voters saw little reason to excuse single women from the obligation to work solely because they are responsible for rearing children.

Moreover, the nature of the population receiving AFDC changed. When Aid to Dependent Children was established in the Depression, the target population consisted mainly of widows and their children, easy objects of sympathy for most voters. Over the 1960s a growing percentage of the welfare caseload consisted of families where the mother had been separated, divorced, or deserted by her husband or had never been married. By 1971 more than three-quarters of families receiving AFDC were headed by women in these categories. Many taxpayers find it hard to be sympathetic with these kinds of families.

As popular views on public assistance recipients have evolved, lawmakers have been forced to modify the basic rules under which able-bodied adults can receive aid. The first notable public program to encourage work among mothers on public assistance was the Work Incentive (WIN) program, established in 1967. The WIN amendments changed the formula for calculating AFDC benefits, permitting recipients to keep a higher percentage of their earnings if they found a job. The amendments also instituted a counseling and training program to help recipients with older children find private jobs. Although the federal government attempted to require that local welfare agencies refer eligible mothers to the program, in practice only a small percentage of the caseload received much help. The level of resources available to help mandatory participants in the WIN program was very modest. In many parts of the country, participation in WIN activities, such as counseling, training, work experience, or job search, was effectively voluntary for most women who were required to register in the program.

In 1981 President Ronald Reagan and the U.S. Congress authorized states to experiment with tougher work and training obligations than the ones that had been permitted under WIN. For example, states were given the authority to institute mandatory work experience (or workfare) programs in which able-bodied AFDC recipients could be required to perform short-term, unpaid community service in exchange for their welfare grants. Such programs had been tried before, although infrequently (and seldom with much success).

In 1988 the president and Congress strengthened assistance recipients' obligation to search or train for work with passage of the Family Support Act. Viewed by some as a landmark in the history of public assistance, the new law obligated state governments to transform AFDC from an income maintenance program into a jobs program. A central provision of the law requires single parents on welfare whose children are at least four years old to find regular employment. If a job cannot be found right away, recipients are required to enroll in education or job training programs and, eventually, in a state-organized employment program. To make job finding feasible, the law authorized $3.3 billion in new federal spending over a five-year period for training, transportation, and child care assistance. Much of this money has gone unspent, however, because state governments have been slow to implement large-scale employment and training programs. So far, the Family Support Act has had little measurable effect in moving public aid recipients from welfare rolls onto payrolls. Between 1988 and 1992, the number of families collecting AFDC climbed from 3.7 million to 4.8 million.

The 1992 presidential campaign brought renewed interest in the problem of finding jobs for public assistance recipients. During the campaign, candidate Bill Clinton proposed limiting regular AFDC payments to a restricted period, perhaps just two years. Recipients who remained dependent on aid at the end of the two-year period would be referred to public or private jobs or would face termination or sharp reduction of their monthly AFDC check. For this strategy to be affordable and successful, most AFDC recipients would need to find private-sector jobs. The cost of offering public jobs to all able-bodied AFDC recipients is prohibitively high in an era of tight public spending constraints. A crucial question, then, is whether enough jobs exist in the private sector to provide reasonable incomes for parents who will be forced to leave the welfare rolls.

EARNINGS CAPACITY OF WELFARE RECIPIENTS

One way to assess the employment prospects of welfare recipients is to examine the work experiences of people who are similar to those now receiving AFDC. The U.S. Department of Health and Human Services (DHHS) periodically publishes information about character-istics of AFDC recipients based on data obtained from its quality control survey. This information suggests that many recipients would face serious obstacles in finding and holding well-paid jobs.

Table 4.1 presents data from the department's quality control sur-veys over the period from 1979 to 1991. The first four rows in the table show the age distribution of children collecting AFDC. The caseload has recently grown younger, as the percentage of children younger than age six, and especially under age three, has climbed. Women, whether married or unmarried, who rear very young chil-dren ordinarily find it much harder to work full-time than do women who are childless or whose children are six years old or older.

The educational attainment of AFDC mothers, though improving, remains painfully limited. The DHHS quality control survey shows that fewer than 55 percent of AFDC mothers had completed high school in 1991. In comparison, more than 85 percent of all 25–34-year-old American women had completed high school in that year. About 1 percent of AFDC mothers have graduated from college, whereas 23 percent of all 25–34-year-old women have a college degree. Part of the discrepancy in educational attainment can be explained by the extreme youth of many AFDC mothers. About 8 percent are under age 20 and nearly a quarter are between 20 and 24. Even so, the percentage of AFDC mothers with some college education is remarkably low. Only 13 percent report one or more years of college, whereas slightly more than half of all 25–34-year-old women have attended at least a year of college.

Table 4.1 CHARACTERISTICS OF AFDC CASELOAD, 1979–91
    (PERCENT)

Characteristic	March 1979 (%)	1986 (%)	1991 (%)
Ages of children			
Under 3	18.9	21.0	24.8
3 to 5	17.5	21.1	21.4
6 to 11	33.0	32.4	32.6
12 and over	29.8	24.3	21.4
Education of mother			
8th grade or less[a]	18.2	11.9	11.2
1–3 years high school[a]	39.8	35.5	35.1
4 years high school[a]	36.0	42.9	40.7
Some college[a]	5.2	8.4	12.2
College graduate[a]	0.8	1.2	0.8
Unknown	47.8	59.7	49.9
Mother's employment status			
Full-time job	8.7	1.6	2.2
Part-time job	5.4	4.2	4.2
Cases with reported earnings	12.8	7.5	7.9

a. Percentage distribution among mothers whose educational attainment is known.
Source: U.S. Congress, House, Committee on Ways and Means, 1993, *1993 Green Book* (696–97). Washington, D.C.: U.S. Government Printing Office.

National Longitudinal Survey of Youth

The job qualifications of AFDC recipients can be examined in greater detail using data from the National Longitudinal Survey of Youth. The NLSY is a nationally representative survey of young men and women who were first interviewed in 1979. Nearly all the analysis in this chapter focuses on young women rather than young men, since women are far more likely to collect AFDC, especially for long periods of time. Approximately 13,000 young people were interviewed in the 1979 survey, when respondents were between 14 and 22 years old. The education and labor market data analyzed here were collected in 13 annual surveys spanning the period 1979 to 1991.

About a year after they entered the survey sample, most respondents completed a cognitive test known as the Armed Services Vocational Aptitude Test Battery, an examination ordinarily given to select and classify recruits into the U.S. military services. One part of the test, the Armed Forces Qualification Test (AFQT), is used to determine which applicants are eligible to enlist in the military. The AFQT composite score reflects the test taker's weighted scores in arithmetic reasoning, numerical operations, word knowledge, and

Table 4.2 EMPLOYMENT QUALIFICATIONS AND EMPLOYMENT STATUS OF
25-YEAR-OLD U.S. WOMEN
(PERCENT)

	Number of months received AFDC (%)			All Women (%)
	12	1–11	None	
Educational attainment by age 24				
Less than 4 years high school	52	44	14	17
4 years high school	35	48	40	39
1–3 years college	12	8	24	23
4 or more years college	0	0	22	21
Total	100	100	100	100
Composite score on AFQT				
Bottom quartile	72	52	22	26
Second quartile	17	33	26	25
Third quartile	9	14	26	25
Top quartile	3	2	25	24
Total	100	100	100	100
Employment or labor earnings				
Employed at interview date	11	37	77	72
Earnings during last 12 months	30	58	86	83

Source: Author's tabulations of National Longitudinal Survey of Youth (NLSY),
1979–91.

paragraph comprehension. The composite score is considered a reliable indicator of a person's general problem-solving ability.[1]

Women interviewed in the NLSY can be followed for up to 12 years, starting in 1979 and continuing through 1991. Since respondents were aged 14 to 22 when first interviewed, we can observe the educational attainment and employment experience of a nationally representative group of women from age 14 up to as late as age 34. Table 4.2 contains information about respondents when they were 25 years old. (Tabulations for ages 21 through 29 would show similar patterns.) Women have been divided into three classes, depending on their receipt of AFDC benefits during the 12 months before their interview at age 25. The most dependent group of women consists of those who received AFDC during all 12 months. The least dependent group received no AFDC at all, though, of course, some members of this group received AFDC in earlier or later years. In all, about 8 percent of 25-year-old women received AFDC. Three percent received benefits during at least 1 month but less than 12 months of the previous year; 5 percent received benefits during all 12 months.

Like the DHHS quality control survey, the NLSY shows that women collecting AFDC face serious deficiencies in educational attainment.[2] Whereas only 17 percent of all 25-year-old women have failed to complete high school, among 25-year-olds who are most dependent on AFDC the comparable figure is 52 percent (see table 4.2). Among 25-year-olds who receive AFDC in 1 to 11 months out of the previous year, 44 percent have not completed high school. The educational shortcomings of AFDC recipients are reflected in their very poor performance on standardized tests of ability and achievement. Among 25-year-old women in the most dependent category, 72 percent obtained a test score on the AFQT that places them in the bottom quarter of all test takers. Only 12 percent received a score that places them in the top half of test takers. Women who are moderately dependent on AFDC achieved better test scores, but their performance on the test was well below the national norm. Only 16 percent obtained a score placing them in the top half of test takers.

Earnings Trends among AFDC Recipients

The low educational attainment and poor test scores of welfare-dependent mothers severely restrict the kinds of jobs most of them can obtain. The contrast between the job prospects of dependent and nondependent young women is illustrated in figure 4.1, which shows the trend in real hourly wages among two groups of women, both between 18 and 22 years of age in 1979. The lower line traces the wage gains of women who collected AFDC during part or all of at least one year between 1979 and 1981; the upper line shows average wage gains among women who collected *no* AFDC benefits in those three years.[3] From 1979 to 1990 the average real wage of AFDC-dependent women rose from $6.18 to $6.85 an hour—an annual wage gain equivalent to just $0.06 per hour, or a bit less than 1 percent a year. Among women who received no AFDC benefits between 1979 and 1981, the average wage climbed from $6.07 to over $10.00 an hour—a wage gain of 4.8 percent or $0.37 per year.[4]

These hourly wage figures may be more understandable if they are converted into flows of annual earnings. In 1979 women in both groups earned a wage that would yield slightly more than $12,000 a year for a person working on a full-time, year-round schedule (2,000 hours per year). By 1990 women who were dependent on AFDC sometime between 1979 and 1981 earned a wage that would provide $13,700 a year to a person working on a full-time, year-round schedule. Women who received no AFDC between 1979 and 1981 earned a 1990 wage that would yield an annual income of $20,400—about

Figure 4.1 AVERAGE HOURLY WAGE OF YOUNG WOMEN IN NLSY, 1979–90

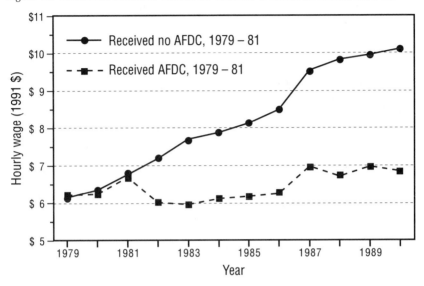

Source: Author's tabulations of NLSY.

50 percent more than the comparable figure for AFDC-dependent women. What is more, women in the nondependent group were clearly receiving faster wage increases, boosting their chances of earning even higher wages in the future.

The problem of slow wage growth for AFDC-dependent mothers is similar to that faced by other women who have limited job qualifications. Figure 4.2 shows real wage trends among all women with recorded wages during the 1979–90 period. Once again, the tabulations are based on the experience of women in the NLSY sample who were between 18 and 22 years old in 1979. The light lines in the figure show wage trends at selected points in the overall wage distribution. The top line, for example, shows wage gains received by women in the 90th percentile of all women who had recorded hourly wages. A lower line accented by a solid box shows the trend in the median wage. The lowest line traces wage movements among women in the 10th percentile of the overall distribution. The heavy line near the bottom of the figure shows the trend in the median wage of women who received AFDC during at least one month between 1979 and 1981. Note that this line corresponds almost exactly to the trend in wages among women at the 25th percentile of the *overall* female wage distribution. In other words, women who

Figure 4.2 HOURLY WAGES AT SELECTED POINTS IN THE WAGE
DISTRIBUTION OF YOUNG NLSY WOMEN, 1979–90

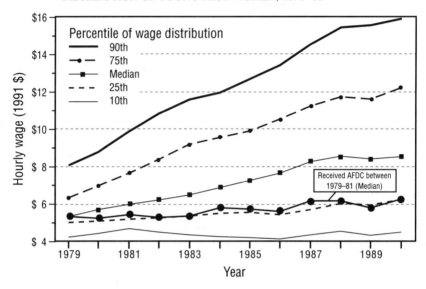

Source: Author's tabulations of NLSY.

received AFDC, even if only briefly, between 1979 and 1981 received
wage gains equivalent to those obtained by women at the 25th percentile of the wage distribution.[5]

Women near the bottom of the wage distribution obtained comparatively slow wage gains for a couple of reasons. First, as a result of
economy-wide factors described in the paragraphs following, nearly
all U.S. workers with wages near the bottom of the distribution have
suffered slow wage growth or declining real wages over the past
decade and a half. Second, workers with advanced levels of education
and skill typically receive very rapid wage gains during their twenties
and early thirties. The wage gains of less-educated workers at the
start of their careers are typically much slower than those enjoyed
by workers with college and professional degrees.

The point is illustrated in figure 4.3, which shows real wage trends
in four different groups of women who did *not* collect AFDC and
for whom there is enough information to calculate hourly wages on
the NLSY. Instead of showing average real wages in selected calendar
years, the figure displays wages at five different ages—21, 23, 25,
27, and 29. Women are classified according to two criteria, their
educational attainment by age 24 and their composite AFQT score.

Figure 4.3 TRENDS IN REAL WAGES BY EDUCATIONAL ATTAINMENT AND
AFQT SCORE

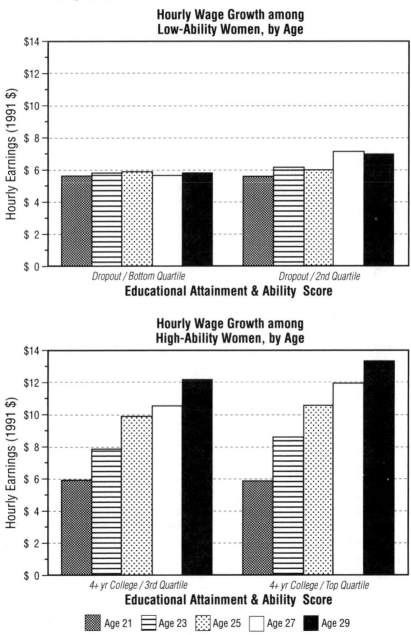

Source: Author's tabulations of NLSY.

The top panel shows real wage trends among two groups of school dropouts with below-average AFQT scores; the bottom panel shows wage trends among two groups of women who graduated from college by age 24 and achieved above-average composite scores on the AFQT exam. At age 21 the average hourly wage in all four groups falls within a very narrow range, just below $6 per hour. By age 29 the gap in wages is wide and growing steadily. Dropouts in the bottom AFQT quartile continue to earn about $6 an hour, but college graduates in the top AFQT quartile earn more than $13 an hour. The experience reflected in the top panel is obviously the one most relevant to women who collect AFDC benefits. Almost half of 25-year-old women who collect AFDC steadily for 12 months are high school dropouts with AFQT scores in the bottom half of the score distribution. Approximately 42 percent of 25-year-old women who collect AFDC for at least 1 month but fewer than 12 months fall into the same category. The wage gains enjoyed by college graduates are less relevant to AFDC recipients. As noted previously, only a minuscule fraction of the AFDC caseload has completed college.

The job prospects of AFDC recipients are probably even less favorable than implied by figures 4.2 and 4.3. Recall that the median and average wages of young women are calculated using the wages of workers who actually have a recorded wage. This introduces a bias in the calculation of average wages, especially of wages of women who collect AFDC. In 1987, for example, only about 50 percent of the women who had collected AFDC between 1979 and 1981 reported an hourly wage. Nonworking women probably had fewer qualifications than those who worked, so it is likely that their potential wages were even lower. By contrast, about 70 percent of all women provided enough information to calculate an hourly wage. The bias in measuring wage trends among all women is thus smaller than it is for the women who received AFDC between 1979 and 1981.

Women who were dependent on AFDC between 1979 and 1981 enjoyed one advantage over other women, however. Since many fewer of them worked during the late 1970s and early 1980s, they had a much better chance of improving their earnings as a result of entry into the job market and increases in annual hours of work. Figure 4.4 shows the percentage of women who reported labor earnings during the previous 12 months on each of the NLSY interviews conducted between 1979 and 1990.[6] As before, women are divided into those who received AFDC sometime between 1979 and 1981 and those who received no AFDC benefits. The gap in employment in 1979 was wide—90 percent of nonrecipients had labor earnings

Figure 4.4 FRACTION OF NLSY WOMEN WITH WAGE EARNINGS IN PREVIOUS
YEAR, 1979–90

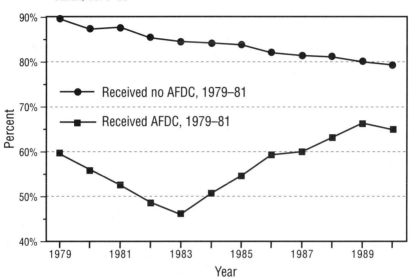

Source: Author's tabulations of NLSY.

versus just 60 percent of AFDC recipients. The proportion of AFDC-
dependent women who have earnings continued to fall until 1983,
when it dipped as low as 45 percent. After that year, the percentage
with earnings climbed fairly rapidly, though even by 1990 it remained
below 65 percent. The employment pattern of nondependent women
is very different. Whereas slightly more than 90 percent had earnings
in 1979, the percentage with earnings edged down over the next
decade as women married, bore children, and temporarily withdrew
from the labor force to care for their young children.

The implications of these trends for annual earnings of women
who received AFDC between 1979 and 1981 are displayed in figure
4.5. The top line in the figure is the *predicted* annual earnings of
women who work 2,000 hours a year and earn the average wage
received by AFDC-dependent women for whom an hourly wage rate
is observed. This line may be thought of as a typical AFDC recipient's
"potential" annual earnings path. The year-to-year movements in
this line reflect changes in the average hourly wage received by these
women (see figure 4.1). The middle line in figure 4.5 shows the trend
in *actual* annual earnings of AFDC-dependent women who reported
some earnings during the year. In 1979 the actual annual earnings

Figure 4.5 ACTUAL AND PREDICTED EARNINGS AMONG WOMEN WHO
RECEIVED AFDC IN 1979–81

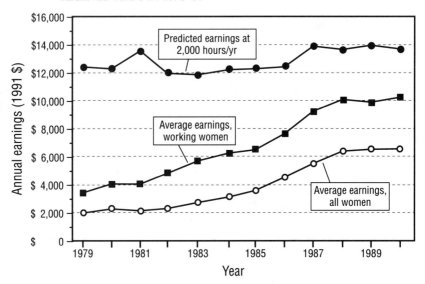

Source: Author's tabulations of NLSY.

of these working women was only about a quarter of the "potential" earnings they could have received if they had worked year-round on a full-time schedule. After 1981, the actual earnings of women who had earnings rose faster than "potential" earnings, but nonetheless remained well below potential earnings. Women who had earnings increased the amount of time they worked each year, but they continued to work less than 2,000 hours. By 1990 actual earnings were about 75 percent of "potential" earnings ($10,200 versus $13,700, respectively).

The lowest line in figure 4.5 shows the trend in annual earnings among *all* women who received AFDC between 1979 and 1981, including the women who did not work. After 1983 this measure of average earnings began to climb, both because working women spent more time at work during an average year and because the fraction of women at work began to rise. By 1990, the average earnings of all women who received AFDC between 1979 and 1981 were nearly one-half of "potential" earnings ($6,700 versus $13,700, respectively). This represents a sharp increase from the corresponding figure in 1979–81, when AFDC-dependent women earned only about 15 percent of their "potential" annual earnings.

Implications for Reform

The trends displayed in figure 4.5 offer two important lessons for welfare reform. First, conservative critics of the welfare system are correct in arguing that single mothers on welfare can substantially increase the amount of self-support they derive from their own earnings. Among young women who received AFDC benefits between 1979 and 1981, real earnings nearly tripled between 1980 and 1990, rising from $2,300 to $6,700. Among women who actually had wages, annual earnings rose 155 percent during this period, climbing from $4,000 to $10,200. But there is still much room for improvement. If all of the young women who collected AFDC in 1979–81 had worked on a year-round, full-time job in 1990, their average earnings would have been $13,700—about twice their actual level of earnings and about one-third higher than the average earnings of women who actually worked.

The second lesson from these statistics is much more disturbing. In the unlikely event that single mothers could all find and retain full-time, year-round jobs, their annual incomes would remain distressingly low. In 1991 the poverty threshold for a family consisting of one adult and three children was nearly $13,900, slightly higher than the *average* "potential" full-time earnings of women who collected AFDC between 1979 and 1981. Average "potential" earnings are of course higher than the earnings most women could hope to achieve. First, the median observed wage is lower than the average observed wage. Whereas average "potential" earnings is $13,700 per year, the median "potential" earnings of women with an observed wage is just $12,500—10 percent below the poverty line for a family of four. This means that half of all women who collected AFDC between 1979 and 1981 can expect to earn less than 90 percent of a poverty-level income, even if they work full-time and year-round.[7] Second, as already noted, the average wage among women for whom a wage is observed overstates the wage that nonworking women could expect to earn if they found jobs. Finally, it is unrealistic to expect that all single women with young children will be able to work full-time on a year-round basis. Many will choose to work part-time in order to make childrearing more feasible. Others will spend part of the year without jobs as a result of involuntary unemployment, illness, or difficulty in arranging child care. Unemployment is a particular hazard for these women, because many of them only qualify for jobs where turnover rates are high (and hourly wages are low).

Another point deserves mention. The AFDC-dependent women whose earnings are tabulated in figure 4.5 include many young women who received AFDC only briefly and then never received welfare again. Of the 15–23-year-old women who received AFDC in 1980, for example, less than half received AFDC benefits 5 years later in 1985; only one-third received benefits 10 years later in 1990. In fact, only 27 percent of 25–33-year-old AFDC recipients in 1990 had received welfare benefits in 1980; less than one-third had received benefits some time between 1979 and 1981.

At any point in time, the welfare caseload contains many women who will remain on the rolls briefly and many others who will receive benefits off and on for an extended period. Most welfare reform proposals aim to provide services or to change the behavior of women in the latter category. Women who are on the welfare rolls for lengthy consecutive or interrupted periods are typically much more disadvantaged than women who collect benefits only briefly. The potential earnings of long-term recipients are substantially overstated by the numbers shown in figure 4.5, which reflect the experiences of many women who remained on welfare briefly and then left the rolls. If the numbers had been calculated based solely on the experiences of women who received benefits for lengthy periods, the earnings trends would have appeared even worse.

The earnings estimates shown in figures 4.1 to 4.3 and figure 4.5 have important implications for welfare reform. The labor market does not provide outstanding earnings opportunities for young mothers who have poor educational qualifications and low scores on scholastic aptitude tests. The idea that AFDC recipients can easily obtain employment that will remove them from dependency is clearly contradicted by the data. Even full-time employment would not remove an important minority of AFDC recipients from poverty. Among the 18–22-year-old women who received AFDC benefits in 1979–81, 25 percent of those who managed to find jobs by 1990 earned an hourly wage of $4.69 or less; 10 percent earned a wage of $3.97 or less (see appendix figure 4A). A woman who earned $4.69 per hour in 1990 would need to work nearly 3,000 hours a year to obtain enough income to escape poverty. At a wage of $3.97 an hour, she would need to work 3,500 hours a year—or about 70 hours a week—to escape poverty. These illustrations do not show that job finding is impossible for women who receive AFDC. They do show that many women who eventually find jobs will earn too little to support themselves and their children with any degree of comfort.

JOB AVAILABILITY

Many critics of work programs for welfare recipients argue that it is unrealistic to believe the market can produce enough jobs to absorb the able-bodied recipients who would be forced to seek jobs under a system of time-limited welfare. With roughly 7 million jobless workers, even at full employment, is it plausible to expect that employers could offer an additional 2–3 million jobs for AFDC recipients forced to leave the welfare rolls? Surprisingly, most labor economists probably believe the answer to this question is yes.

An individual welfare recipient, if she is able-bodied and moderately resourceful, can almost certainly find an employer willing to offer her a job if she is willing to accept a low enough wage and a meager package of fringe benefits. In many urban labor markets, for example, jobless workers with few qualifications apply to temporary employment agencies for short-term work. Although the employment is uncertain and irregular, workers who are diligent and persistent can usually obtain temporary work assignments, at least occasionally, and can often find permanent employment if their job performance impresses a manager who has provided a short-term assignment. Other job opportunities for less-qualified workers are found in low-wage retailing, business protection and cleaning services, and informal child care.

None of these job opportunities is particularly appealing, in the sense of offering high wages, good fringe benefits, comfortable working conditions, or decent prospects of future promotion. The point is, however, that job opportunities exist for applicants who are willing to accept them, a fact confirmed by the job-finding success of unskilled immigrants. Many immigrants enter this country suffering even worse disadvantages than those possessed by long-term welfare recipients. Immigrants who illegally reside in the United States are not eligible to collect income transfers, except emergency medical aid, so they must rely on their own earnings or transfers from relatives in order to survive. The great majority of undocumented adult immigrants almost certainly relies on labor earnings.

Even if *individual* welfare recipients could be expected to find jobs in the current labor market, it is questionable whether *millions* could find jobs if forced to find them on short notice. For example, if welfare rules were changed, denying regular benefits to able-bodied adults who collected AFDC for 24 months or longer, up to 2 million additional recipients might be forced to seek employment within a couple of years. Could the job market absorb this influx of new workers? In the short run, many new job applicants would certainly face problems. During the second half of the 1980s the American labor force grew by approximately 2.1 million potential workers a year. Many of the new entrants were well educated and reasonably highly skilled. Less than half the new entrants brought skills to the labor market as limited as those possessed by welfare recipients. If the labor force grew by *an additional* 2 million less-skilled workers within a one- or two-year period, employers would need to double or even triple their net rate of hiring new unskilled workers if all AFDC recipients were to find jobs. Since this seems unlikely, many aid recipients would undoubtedly suffer long spells of involuntary unemployment. In addition, some AFDC recipients who succeeded in finding work would displace other single mothers from jobs, pushing up applications for AFDC as jobless mothers turned to public assistance to replace their lost earnings.

Over the long term, however, the U.S. labor market seems capable of absorbing the great majority of extra workers without a significant rise in joblessness. From 1964 through 1989 the labor force grew by 50.4 million persons, or slightly more than 2 million a year. Over the same period, the number of Americans holding jobs climbed by 47.7 million, or slightly more than 1.9 million workers a year. About 95 percent of new job seekers were able to find jobs, even though the number of people available for work swelled by 67 percent. The unemployment rate rose only slightly, from 5 percent to 5.2 percent. To be sure, unemployment climbed steeply in the 1970s and early 1980s when the labor market was unable to absorb the enormous number of new entrants. But most of the rise in joblessness during those decades was due to business cycle developments, not to the rapid pace of increase in the available work force.

Many people find it implausible that so many extra job seekers could be absorbed by the labor market. They fail to consider the fact that in the long run employers are free to change their production methods to exploit the availability of abundant, low-wage labor. Moreover, they ignore the possibility that wages may change in response to the entry or exit of large numbers of potential workers. In the 1970s, for example, the relative wages received by younger workers fell in comparison with those earned by older workers, in part because younger workers became so much more abundant. Wages received by new college graduates fell in comparison with wages received by young workers with less education, in part because of the rapid rise in college attendance and college completion. Faced with a huge increase in the availability of workers who had limited job experience, employers adopted production methods that took full advantage of less-experienced workers. Restaurant meals were prepared and served by 11th-grade students and high school dropouts rather than by experienced cooks or waiters. Gardening and domestic cleaning were performed by unskilled and semiskilled employees rather than by experienced nursery people or homeowners themselves. In the end, 95 percent of new job seekers were successful in finding jobs, albeit many of these jobs were not well paid.

Thus, even though most AFDC recipients would eventually find jobs if forced to do so, the influx of unskilled workers could depress the wages received by less-skilled workers. If 2 million AFDC recipients were forced to accept jobs, the wage trends shown in figures 4.1, 4.2, and 4.5 could represent a significant overstatement of the wage gains new workers could expect to receive. Employers might modify some existing jobs and develop new ones to take advantage of the abundance of less-skilled single mothers, but, again, a likely long-term effect of an influx of less-skilled workers is a reduction in hourly wages. With fierce competition for unskilled and semiskilled jobs, wage rates would be driven down, at least modestly, and AFDC recipients would face worse job prospects than those faced by women who left the rolls during the 1980s.

FUTURE EARNINGS PROSPECTS

The labor market problems faced by young mothers with limited schooling are similar to those faced by less-educated young men. Since the late 1970s, wage earners of both sexes and all ages have seen a sizable jump in wage inequality. For men, the rise in inequality has been accompanied by a substantial drop in earnings among young workers with the least skills. Until recently, rising inequality among women involved wage stagnation or slow wage growth among the least skilled, but no sizable loss in real hourly or annual earnings. In the past few years, however, less-skilled women have also experienced significant losses in hourly earnings. Figure 4.6 shows trends in hourly wages at selected points in the wage distribution for male and female workers over the period from 1979 to 1992.[8] The dark bars represent changes in male wages; the light bars, changes in women's wages. Although on average women have enjoyed faster wage gains than men, women in the bottom quarter of the wage

Figure 4.6 GROWTH IN REAL HOURLY WAGES, 1979–92

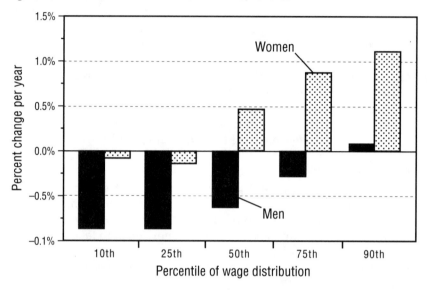

Source: Lynn Karoly, unpublished tabulations of Current Population Survey (see Karoly 1993: 48–56).

distribution have seen their hourly wages fall since 1979. By contrast, men and women at the top of the distribution have enjoyed increases in hourly wages.

The recent jump in earnings inequality has been the topic of a large and rapidly growing literature. Many labor economists have tried to determine why earnings have grown less equal.[9] Census statistics show that part of the growth in earnings inequality has been due to increased returns to education, skill, and work experience, especially among younger workers. Absolute declines in earnings have been particularly severe among the young and those with limited education. Figure 4.7 shows changes in real annual earnings among young women who work year-round on a full-time schedule. The figure shows changes in earnings between 1979 and 1989 for two different age groups, women aged 20–24 (on the left) and those aged 25–34 (on the right). Within each age group, earnings changes have been separately tabulated for women in four different groups classified by educational attainment.

Women with the least schooling have experienced the largest earnings losses. For example, 20–24-year-old dropouts saw their real earnings fall by 19 percent between 1979 and 1989; 25–34-year-old

Figure 4.7 CHANGE IN U.S. WOMEN'S ANNUAL EARNINGS BY AGE AND
EDUCATIONAL ATTAINMENT, 1979–89

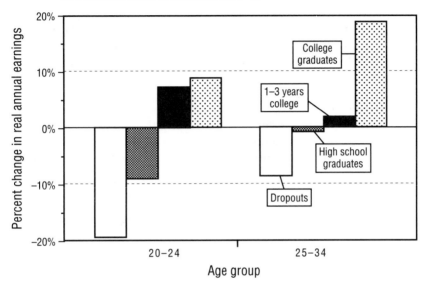

Source: Author's tabulations of Current Population Survey.
Note: Data apply to full-time year-round workers.

dropouts suffered earnings losses of 8 percent. Even women who
completed high school experienced some loss in earnings. By contrast, 25–34-year-old college graduates enjoyed substantial earnings
gains. Real earnings climbed 8 percent among 20–24-year-old college
graduates and 19 percent among 25–34-year-old graduates.

Explanations for Recent Trends

Two developments are responsible for most of the surge in earnings
inequality. As just noted, inflation-adjusted earnings of less-skilled
workers have dropped significantly relative to those received by more
skilled workers, who of course earned better wages to begin with.
Although this trend is apparent among many groups of American
workers, younger less-skilled men have lost the most ground. A less-
well-known but more important source of extra inequality is the
steadily widening disparity over the past two decades in wages paid
to workers who have nearly identical characteristics. The earnings
of the best-compensated workers have not only risen much faster

than the earnings of workers at the bottom of the wage distribution, but they have far outpaced earnings gains of middle-income workers.

Most economists who study earnings trends emphasize movements in the supply and demand of labor when explaining relative wage changes. Average wage growth has slowed or stopped altogether because of the adverse trend in labor productivity. Relative wages of different groups have changed, in part, because the supply of some groups has climbed faster than demand for the labor services of those groups. As noted earlier, young workers saw their earnings decline in comparison with older workers during the 1970s because of the influx of the huge baby boom generation into the labor market. Young college graduates saw their earnings fall relative to young high school graduates because a sharply increased percentage of young people completed college in the 1970s.

Changes in relative supply cannot satisfactorily explain all movements in relative wages, however. The percentage of young adults with college diplomas continued to rise in the 1980s, but the relative wages of young college graduates soared (see figure 4.7). Most economists interpret this rise to mean that the demand for better-educated and better-skilled job market entrants has grown or, more plausibly, the demand for less-skilled and less-well-educated workers has plunged.

The fall in demand for less-skilled workers (or, equivalently, the relative growth in demand for better-skilled workers) is linked partly to a change in the kinds of industries that are demanding extra workers and in the types of industries that are shrinking. Shrinking industries, like manufacturing, offered well-paying jobs to unskilled and semiskilled workers, especially men. Growing industries offer well-paying jobs mainly to people with better educational credentials and better occupational training. The change in the relative size of different U.S. industries has thus contributed to the shrinking demand for less-skilled workers.

The change in the relative size of U.S. industries explains only a small part of the shifting pattern of demand for workers in different skill categories, however. Most economists who have closely examined employment patterns conclude that within individual industries there has been a widespread and fairly steady decline in demand for less-skilled and less-educated workers. Thus, the increase in overall wage inequality has been driven primarily by growing wage disparities within individual industries, not by the sinking fortunes of industries that offer the best job opportunities to less-skilled workers. Good job opportunities for less-skilled workers are becoming more scarce in nearly all U.S. industries, not just in those that formerly offered good jobs to the unskilled.

One explanation for this pattern is that changes in technology have favored workers with the greatest skill and have reduced the demand for workers with average or below-average skill. Another partial explanation might be that free international trade has disproportion-ately affected workers with skills similar to those of overseas workers who are paid much lower wages. Because very poorly paid unskilled workers are abundant overseas, unskilled U.S. workers have been hurt most by this trend.

The reasons for the growth in within-group inequality are hotly debated among economists. People who work within the same indus-try and have the same educational credentials and job experience receive wages that have grown increasingly unequal over time. Some economists believe this form of inequality can be explained by the same factors that have driven up disparities between workers with different educational or skill credentials. According to this theory, poorly paid high school graduates have seen their relative earnings fall over time because of the drop in demand for less-skilled workers in general. The high school graduates whose earnings have increased in recent years have benefited from the continued strong demand for highly skilled workers. Other theories can explain the pattern of growing within-group inequality, however, so the debate about the root causes of this development has not been resolved.

One factor contributing to greater inequality has special signifi-cance for welfare recipients. Since the early 1970s the labor force has experienced large changes in the flow and composition of immigrant workers. The annual rate of immigration has nearly doubled in recent decades. The skills and educational attainment of recent immigrants are much more limited than they were among immigrants in the 1950s and 1960s. Immigrants to the United States were once drawn mainly from Europe or from well-educated groups in less developed countries, but are now drawn increasingly from less-skilled popula-tions in the Third World. Today immigrants comprise one-quarter of U.S. workers with less than a high school education. Perhaps one-fifth of the recent deterioration in the relative wages of high school dropouts may be due to increased immigration of less-skilled workers (Borjas, Freeman, and Katz 1991).

The labor market facing unskilled workers is dismal, and it contin-ues to deteriorate. Most of the trends in wages and employment can be explained if there has been a growing demand for skilled workers and a declining demand for the less skilled. This has occurred not so much because there has been a shift in the level or distribution of demand across different kinds of industries, but because companies and industries have attempted to change their production methods in a way that requires a more able and skilled work force. Because unskilled workers have become relatively much more abundant, their wages have shrunk, increasing the income gap between them and workers with better educational qualifications.

Less-skilled young women have suffered along with unskilled men as a result of this shift. Their earnings have fallen compared with the wages received by better-educated and more-skilled women. The problem they face is not a surplus of bad jobs, as widely assumed, but a surplus of less-skilled workers in a market requiring more skill than ever. In some respects, the labor market position of less-skilled workers might be improved if the economy produced *more*, not fewer, jobs requiring limited skill. Their wages might then be bid up and the wage gap with more skilled workers closed.

EDUCATION, JOB TRAINING, AND OTHER REMEDIES

If skill deficiencies are the source of welfare recipients' job market problems, education and job training might offer a remedy. A variety of work and training programs for welfare recipients has been attempted over the past quarter century. Analysts have now accumulated considerable evidence about programs that succeed in improving recipients' earnings and about the reasons for their success. Much of this evidence suggests that education and training programs are worthwhile. None of it suggests that education and training alone can eliminate the job market problems faced by long-term welfare recipients.

How the Programs Work

Most policymakers and analysts who favor work and training programs assume their main goal is to prepare unskilled adults for the labor market. Welfare recipients are taught how to search for jobs, are required to file job applications with a variety of employers, or are enrolled in basic education and training programs. If a program succeeds, policymakers probably believe that welfare recipients will find decent jobs and leave the welfare rolls. If the program fails, recipients will remain on the rolls.

The programs may encourage or deter entry onto the AFDC rolls in another respect, however. If welfare recipients come to believe the work and training program is successful, some single mothers might be tempted to apply for AFDC in order to obtain work and training benefits that are available solely to welfare recipients. On the other hand, if the work and training program is found to be burdensome or ineffective, some potentially eligible adults will be deterred from applying for AFDC. When recipients are required to participate in an ineffective program as a condition for obtaining cash benefits, a small percentage of potential applicants will decline to enroll in AFDC.

Experimental Programs

After President Reagan and Congress authorized states to experiment with tougher employment and training requirements in 1981, a number of states established demonstration programs to test the effectiveness of different approaches to job training, voluntary or mandatory job search assistance, and mandatory work experience. The response of states to the 1981 federal legislation has been described in a number of reports (e.g., U.S. General Accounting Office 1987; Nightingale and Burbridge 1987; Congressional Budget Office 1987; Burtless 1989; and Greenberg and Wiseman 1991). By far the most interesting results from the state demonstrations emerged from the experiments designed and evaluated by the Manpower Demonstration Research Corporation (MDRC) (see Gueron and Pauly 1991). The MDRC, in cooperation with about a dozen states, conducted thorough evaluations of a variety of work-welfare initiatives. In eight states, officials were persuaded to measure the effectiveness of their programs using controlled randomized trials. That is, administrators assigned welfare recipients to a particular work program or to control status using the flip of a coin. This analytical method yields unusually reliable estimates of behavioral response to social programs.

Although the MDRC experiments usually required participants to engage in some kind of work-related activity, the demonstrations used a variety of approaches in accomplishing this goal. In one state, unpaid work experience, or workfare, was the main method used to push AFDC recipients into work. In another site, administrators relied primarily on encouraging recipients to participate in job training and job search assistance programs. Other states placed greater emphasis on forcing aid recipients to participate in job search training and individual or group-oriented job search programs.

A number of experimental programs instituted community work experience (or workfare) programs, but the rate of participation in these programs was low.[10] Some people enrolled in the experiments undoubtedly had good excuses for nonparticipation. Others left the welfare rolls before a workfare position could be found. Still others participated in some alternative activity, such as education, job training, or a part-time job, that precluded their participation in workfare. But many probably failed to report for a workfare job without any good reason.

The demonstration programs proved that administrators can dramatically raise the percentage of welfare recipients who participate in some kind of work or training program. Many programs accomplished this without spending much money. Most of the tested education and training programs cost less than $500 per client served. The training offered in the majority of the programs was modest. Participants were taught how to fill out a résumé, prepare for an employment interview, and hunt for job leads. In some cases, they were provided with a limited amount of general education or occupational training. After they received training, welfare recipients were expected to search systematically for work, and penalties were occasionally imposed if clients could not provide evidence that they had searched hard enough.

The most expensive experimental state programs were conducted in Baltimore and San Diego. The Maryland program, which cost a little over $1,000 per enrollee, offered genuine skills training—but only to 17 percent of enrolled welfare recipients. Because training consumes real resources, the Maryland approach can be costly; however, the cost was held down by limiting the number of participants who actually received training. The San Diego program, in addition to investing real resources in education and training, devoted considerable effort to implementing an effective job search program for enrolled clients. Moreover, the program invested substantial administrative time in tracking program enrollees to ensure that few of them escaped their obligation to participate. The direct cost of the San Diego program was approximately $850 per enrollee (Gueron and Pauly 1991: 256).

The virtue of these types of experimental programs is that they are simple to administer and comparatively cheap. They are inexpensive enough so that states can offer some type of service to all able-bodied welfare recipients who do not already hold a job. If one aim of reform is to expose a large fraction of welfare recipients to the world of work, evidence from the past decade suggests that this goal is within our reach.

Many of the programs also succeeded in improving the earnings or reducing the dependency of welfare recipients. The MDRC found evidence that the experimental treatments raised enrollees' earnings in most (though not all) of the sites (Gueron and Pauly 1991). There was little detectable influence on enrollee earnings in states that relied almost exclusively on community work experience programs or that invested little in establishing an effective job search assistance program. The largest short-term impacts were found in the San Diego experiments. Over the second through the sixth calendar quarters after participants enrolled, the MDRC found that the San Diego programs raised average treatment-group earnings by about 25 percent ($450–$550 per year). Moderately large earnings gains were also registered in the Maryland program, especially in the period starting 12 or 18 months after enrollment. For example, annual earnings rose $400 in the second year after enrollment and about $500 in the third year after enrollment. These gains represent 17 percent of average earnings in the Maryland control group (Gueron and Pauly 1991: 265). Other states attained less impressive earnings improvements, but spent substantially less to achieve them. It should be noted, however, that much of the earnings gains in all of the sites was temporary. Within four years after entering the experimental program, welfare recipients enrolled in the work or training program usually received quarterly wages that were only slightly higher than those received by recipients enrolled in the control group (Friedlander and Burtless 1994).

The states involved in the MDRC experiments realized smaller improvements in welfare caseloads and spending than they did in participant employment and earnings. The largest reductions in AFDC caseload and spending occurred in the San Diego experiments, where AFDC benefits in the treatment group fell $250 to $550 per year, or about 8 percent to 14 percent of average benefits paid to members of the control group. Welfare reductions were smaller and less reliably estimated in the other states, although it is notable that reductions occurred in some states that offered low-cost programs where no measurable effect on employment or earnings had been detected. Surprisingly, very little welfare savings were achieved in Maryland, the state that offered the most expensive and ambitious program (see Gueron and Pauly 1991: 140–45). Nor were major welfare savings obtained in some of the low-cost programs. Even in some states where the programs managed to raise participants' earnings, they failed to reduce measurably the size or cost of the welfare caseload.

Other experimental programs have tested more ambitious—and much more costly—treatments. The Supported Work Demonstration, conducted by the MDRC during the late 1970s, tested the effectiveness of a carefully structured program of work experience. Measured in 1990 dollars, the services offered in the demonstration cost nearly $22,000 per enrolled welfare recipient (Gueron and Pauly 1991: 256–57). The treatment offered up to 12 months of intensive work experience to welfare recipients drawn from an especially disadvantaged population—single mothers who had been dependent on welfare for an average of more than eight years.

In spite of the extreme labor market disadvantage of the population enrolled, the Supported Work program succeeded in substantially raising unsubsidized employment and earnings. Employment during the first full post-treatment year rose by 8½ percentage points (21 percent), while annual earnings rose about $1,800 (46 percent of the control-group mean). The program achieved significant savings in AFDC and Food Stamp benefits as well. During the first full post-program year, combined AFDC and Food Stamp transfers fell over $1,500—about 23 percent of the average transfer benefits received by members of the control group (Board of Directors, Manpower Demonstration Research Corporation 1980). Although these reductions in transfer outlays resulted in clear gains to taxpayers, they represent losses in the well-being of disadvantaged single mothers (explained in the next subsection). In fact, the loss in transfer benefits is nearly as large as the gain in gross wage earnings. Participants in the Supported Work program enjoyed far smaller gains in post-program net income than are suggested by the large percentage gains in their wage earnings.

The AFDC Homemaker–Home Health Aide Demonstrations were nearly as ambitious—and about half as costly—as the Supported Work Demonstration. The Homemaker–Home Health Aide Demonstrations were authorized by Congress in the early 1980s to give training and subsidized employment to AFDC recipients, who in turn were expected to provide home health care services to functionally impaired clients. Abt Associates, a social science research firm, collaborated in designing the demonstrations and evaluated their impacts (Enns, Flanagan, and Bell 1986, and Orr 1986). The results from the demonstrations suggest that expensive work programs for welfare recipients can be a cost-effective way of raising recipients' employment and earnings. Not surprisingly, participants' total earnings, including the subsidized earnings they received as home health aides, were substantially higher than the wages earned by members of the control group. But several of the demonstrations also produced significant gains in participants' *unsubsidized* earnings after the subsidized work experience was completed. During the second post-program year, average earnings gains across the seven demonstration sites amounted to a little over $1,300 per year (Enns et al. 1986: 48). In several of the sites, the gain in earnings was matched by a decline in AFDC caseloads and spending on public transfers.

Implications of Experiments

Although more-expensive training programs offer the greatest promise for large payoffs, even inexpensive programs achieved modest improvements in employment and welfare caseloads. Employment and earnings probably rose in the more-expensive programs because participants' skills were tangibly affected by training. Employers recognized the improvement in client's skills, and they rewarded it by offering a job.

Inexpensive work programs achieved their impact through a different route. Welfare recipients' skills were left almost untouched by an annual investment that may amount to as little as $300 or $400. Employment gains occurred because clients found jobs they would not previously have sought out. If a welfare recipient is obliged to file 20 job applications every month, there is a reasonable chance she can obtain a job offer she would otherwise have missed. If the offer is good enough, she may even accept the job and leave the welfare rolls. The training or job search program has not achieved this effect because of the fact that it has improved the skills of participants; it has simply made life on the rolls more vexing than before the work or training requirement was imposed. A few recipients might decide that the extra effort involved in receiving benefits is not worth the modest monthly check. Instead of accepting welfare and its attendant burdens, they decide to leave the rolls. Several experimental programs almost certainly raised participant earnings and reduced assistance outlays by imposing extra costs on welfare recipients.

The evidence from these evaluation studies shows that good employment and training programs can significantly raise the earnings of welfare recipients and can do so in a cost-effective way. That is, they can raise participants' earnings by enough to offset the direct and indirect cost of administering the programs. But the evidence offers a more depressing lesson, as well. Even the most successful programs fail to raise earnings enough to make a large difference in the poverty status of poor mothers and their children. Some programs caused participants' earnings to rise by one-third or more. Unfortunately, this large percentage gain does not translate into a substantial improvement in most recipients' standard of living. The reason is simple: People on welfare earn very little money. Even if their wages doubled or tripled, few would earn enough to bring their families up to the poverty line. A number of programs have been found to work, but none has been found to work miracles.

This point can be illustrated using the statistics on welfare recipients' earnings shown in figure 4.5. Recall that the 1991 poverty line for a family consisting of one adult and three children was $13,900. The Supported Work and Homemaker–Home Health Aide Demonstrations produced large and statistically significant gains in participant earnings, gains that are far larger than those produced by less-costly training programs for welfare recipients. The two demonstrations raised participants' annual wages by as much as $1,300 to $1,800 in the period immediately after services ended. Note in figure 4.5 that 1990 earnings among former welfare recipients averaged about $6,700 per woman enrolled in AFDC between 1979 and 1981. The earnings gains achieved in the Supported Work and Home-maker–Home Health Aide Demonstrations represent only about one-eighth of a poverty-line income and one-quarter of the average poverty *gap* faced by former welfare recipients and their children. The most successful work programs will not close much of the deficit between single mothers' earnings and the poverty line, even if working mothers were permitted to keep all of their earnings gains.

Unfortunately for welfare recipients, the earnings gains achieved in work programs must be divided between recipients and taxpayers. Welfare recipients do not keep all of the extra income they earn as a result of finding new jobs. The loss of AFDC and Food Stamp benefits offsets part of the earnings gain that is achieved in a successful education and training program. Additional child care expenses soak up some of the rest. In several of the programs mentioned previously, benefit losses and added spending on child care wiped out the income gain from higher earnings. As a result, the standard of living of participating families was raised by substantially less than the improvement in pretax earnings.

This discussion highlights the shortcomings of focusing extra education and training solely on welfare recipients. Even though training can improve the earnings prospects of women who are dependent on AFDC, it will not cause enough of an improvement to remove many low-wage single mothers from poverty. A more broadly targeted training strategy, though obviously more costly, offers some hope of reducing the percentage of breadwinners who earn extremely low wages. By improving the skills and earnings capacity of a large number of low-wage workers, this strategy would reduce the competition for the narrow range of jobs requiring limited skills. Poor single mothers would benefit from this strategy in two ways. Their own skills would be improved, increasing the range and quality of jobs they could hold. Perhaps more important, the number of workers with limited skills would be reduced, possibly reversing the trend toward lower wages in unskilled jobs.

CONCLUSION

The earnings capacity of most women who collect welfare is extremely low, and it rises only slowly with age. Recent labor market developments have depressed the potential earnings of recipients below the modest levels attainable in the 1970s and 1980s. Most assistance recipients, if forced to rely on their own wage earnings, would almost certainly remain poor even if they worked full-time on a year-round basis. Nonetheless, the actual earnings of welfare recipients can be substantially increased, even if demand for unskilled workers remains weak. Most recipients work less than could be expected if they devoted their best efforts to finding and keeping a job. A program that forces aid recipients to seek private-sector jobs could substantially raise the employment rate of poor single mothers, thus boosting their earnings. However, unless the program supplements private-sector earnings with a generous wage subsidy, most new workers would remain poor.

A primary shortcoming of the strategy to force aid recipients to find jobs is the large surplus of low-productivity workers now available in the labor market. Modest improvements in welfare recipients' job skills can certainly improve their chances of finding and keeping a job. But forcing AFDC recipients off the rolls will swell the number of poor single parents who are seeking work, adding to the downward pressure on wages paid to less-skilled workers.

Can a training strategy reduce the number of poor parents who are dependent on public aid? One perspective on the job market may be helpful in answering this question. The U.S. market currently offers a large number of low-productivity, low-wage *jobs*. While the nation can plausibly hope to raise the skills of some of its least-skilled workers, it is much harder to engineer the elimination of all of the poorly paid jobs. So long as those jobs exist, some people will hold them. If the job holders happen to be single parents with dependent children, their families are likely to be poor. Unless the poor bread-winners receive public aid in one form or another, they will remain poor.

Improving the job skills of unskilled workers can eventually reduce the number of very poorly paid jobs, but only in the very long run after employers have modified a large percentage of jobs to reflect the higher average level of worker skills. Over the next decade, how-ever, it is hard to be confident that an employment and training strategy by itself will significantly raise the percentage of single par-ents who can support themselves with their own earnings. Work programs and training obligations can yield small but meaningful benefits to the dependent poor, but such programs are not likely to yield large enough benefits to reduce child poverty significantly. In view of this harsh reality, an employment and training strategy, by itself, can be expected to leave many single-parent families stuck in poverty.

Notes

Josh Teitelbaum of the Brookings Institution, Washington, D.C., provided excellent research assistance for this chapter.

1. A cursory analysis of the composite scores shows, however, that their distribution is far from smooth within the NLSY sample. Moreover, the scores differ significantly among younger and older test takers. To remove the correlation between the composite score and each test taker's age, I calculated percentile scores separately within each age category of female test takers. Respondents were then classified into four equal-sized ability groups (AFQT quartiles) within each single-year-of-age group. Twenty-five percent of the entire sample (and 25 percent of each age group) are therefore classified as part of the lowest ability group; 25 percent are classified as part of the next lowest ability class; and so on.

2. Women are defined as completing high school if they report obtaining 12 years of schooling by the time they were interviewed at age 24. Note that some women who have completed 12 years of schooling may have failed to obtain a high school diploma.

3. More precisely, I have defined "dependent" women as those who received AFDC at least once in any of the 12-month periods before the 1979, 1980, or 1981 NLSY interviews. Note that figure 4.1 shows average hourly wages only among women for whom a wage rate can be calculated. Since no wage rate is observed for women who do not work (and who presumably are less skilled than women who do work), the reported average wage overstates the average *potential* wage of all women in both groups. However, the overstatement is almost certainly greater for women who are

dependent on AFDC than it is for nondependent women, since a much smaller propor-tion of AFDC recipients is at work.

4. Wages are measured in constant 1991 dollars using a deflator that reflects average wage growth among production workers in the private, nonfarm economy. This is different from the CPI-U deflator, which is ordinarily used to measure changes in real purchasing power. I have used a wage deflator rather than a price deflator because I am mainly interested in comparing women's earnings capacity in a consistent way over a period spanning more than a decade. If I had used the CPI-U deflator rather than the hourly wage deflator, real wage gains for both groups would have appeared smaller. In fact, AFDC-dependent women would have been seen to experience wage *losses* through 1990, because prices rose faster than economy-wide hourly earnings over the period.

5. The trend in hourly wages received by AFDC recipients at selected points in the wage distribution is shown in appendix figure 4A. For purposes of comparison, trends in hourly wages at the same points of the wage distribution are shown for *all* young women with reported wages in the lower panel of figure 4A.

6. The sample in figure 4.4 is once again restricted to women who were at least 18 years old when they were interviewed in the 1979 survey.

7. Hourly wage trends among AFDC recipients who received *less* than the median wage are shown in the top panel of figure 4A.

8. Real earnings are calculated in figures 4.6 and 4.7 by deflating workers' nominal earnings with the CPI-UX1 consumer price deflator. Note that this deflator shows a faster rate of inflation than the wage deflator used in Figures 4.1–4.5. For example, the CPI-UX1 deflator rose 68 percent between 1979 and 1989, while hourly wages in the private sector rose just 57 percent.

9. See Levy and Murnane (1992) and Burtless (1993) for recent surveys.

10. For example, in the MDRC's Arkansas experiment, only 3 percent of welfare recipients who were enrolled in the experimental treatment actually participated in a workfare job. The comparable percentage in the Illinois experiment was 7 percent; in the Virginia experiment, 10 percent; and in the San Diego experiment, 20 percent.

Appendix Figure 4A TRENDS IN REAL WAGE DISTRIBUTION, 1979–1990

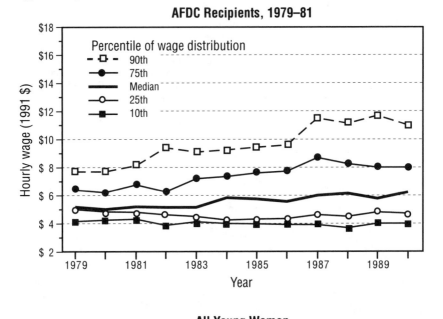

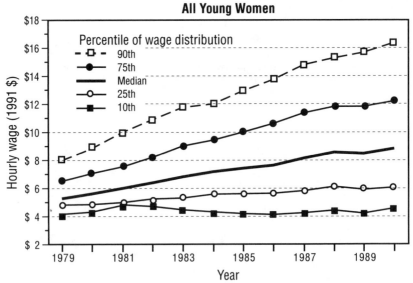

Source: Author's tabulations of NLSY.

References

Baker, Paula C., and Frank L. Mott. 1989. "NLSY Child Handbook, 1989. A Guide and Resource Document for the National Longitudinal Survey of Youth 1986 Child Data." Mimeo. Columbus, Ohio: Center for Human Resource Research, Ohio State University.

Board of Directors, Manpower Demonstration Research Corporation. 1980. *Summary and Findings of the National Supported Work Demonstration.* Cambridge, Mass.: Ballinger.

Borjas, George J., Richard B. Freeman, and Lawrence F. Katz. 1991. "On the Labor Market Effects of Immigration and Trade," NBER Working Paper 3761. Cambridge, Mass.: National Bureau of Economic Research.

Burtless, Gary. 1989. "The Effect of Reform on Employment, Earnings, and Income." In *Welfare Policy for the 1990s,* edited by Phoebe H. Cottingham and David T. Ellwood. Cambridge, Mass.: Harvard University Press.

_____. 1994. "Rising Wage Inequality and the Future of Work in America." In *Widening Earnings Inequality: Why and Why Now?,* edited by Janet Norwood. Urban Institute Monograph, Washington, D.C.

Congressional Budget Office. 1987. *Work-Related Programs for Welfare Recipients.* Washington, D.C.: U.S. General Accounting Office.

Enns, John H., Kathleen L. Flanagan, and Stephen H. Bell. 1986. *AFDC Homemaker–Home Health Aide Demonstrations: Trainee Employment and Earnings.* Cambridge, Mass.: Abt Associates, June.

Friedlander, Daniel, and Gary Burtless. 1994. *Five Years After: The Long-Term Effects of Welfare-to-Work Programs.* New York: Russell Sage Foundation.

General Accounting Office. 1987. *Work and Welfare: Current AFDC Work Programs and Implications for Federal Policy.* Washington, D.C.: Author, January.

Greenberg, David H., and Michael Wiseman. 1991. "What Did the OBRA Demonstrations Do?" In *Evaluating Welfare and Training Programs,* edited by Charles F. Manski and Irwin Garfinkel. Cambridge, Mass.: Harvard University Press.

Gueron, Judith M., and Edward Pauly. 1991. *From Welfare to Work.* New York: Russell Sage.

Karoly, Lynn A. 1993. "The Trend in Inequality among Families, Individuals, and Workers in the United States: A Twenty-Five Year Perspective." In *Uneven Tides: Rising Inequality in America,* edited by Sheldon Danziger and Peter Gottschalk (19–97). New York: Russell Sage Foundation.

Levy, Frank, and Richard J. Murnane. 1992. "U.S. Earnings Levels and Earnings Inequality: A Review of Recent Trends and Proposed Explanations." *Journal of Economic Literature* (September): 1333–81.

Nightingale, Demetra Smith, and Lynn C. Burbridge. 1987. *The Status of State Work–Welfare Programs in 1986: Implications for Welfare Reform.* Washington, D.C.: Urban Institute.

Orr, Larry L. 1986. *AFDC Homemaker–Home Health Aide Demonstrations: Benefits and Costs.* Cambridge, Mass.: Abt Associates, June.

Part Two

THE SEARCH FOR SOLUTIONS

Chapter Five

SUBSIDIZED EMPLOYMENT AND NON–LABOR MARKET ALTERNATIVES FOR WELFARE RECIPIENTS

Rebecca A. Maynard

Our success in changing the culture of poverty hinges on the ability of the reformed welfare system to establish clear expectations for individuals in need of public support, guidelines regarding the obligations of public programs to provide support and oversight, and consequences of either the welfare recipient's or the system's failure to fulfill their obligations. Moreover, a sense of fairness is critical to the system—of equity among welfare recipients and of limited opportunities for the system to ignore their needs.

A policy of time-limiting welfare could lead to higher, rather than lower, welfare caseloads if we are not precise about to whom the time limits apply, about when the clock is running, and about what alternative requirements and service options pertain to those *incapable* of making the transition to unsubsidized employment within the time limit. If there are loopholes or ambiguities in the system, some welfare recipients who could exit welfare in a timely manner may capitalize on a new sense of entitlement to a minimum period (equal to the time limit) of education, training, and support services. Others may decide to avoid the time limits altogether, by highlighting their "barriers" or failing to pursue their strengths. Still others will be labeled *exempt* by caseworkers who judge the risks of failure among certain groups of welfare recipients to be too high and/or the support service requirements (and costs) too great.

We saw evidence of the tendency of some welfare recipients to capitalize on the income support and service opportunities in a "mandatory" welfare system under the early California GAIN program, which legitimized welfare for single parents attending college. The current Job Opportunities and Basic Skills (JOBS) programs also illustrate the propensities of the welfare system to grant liberal exemptions from work requirements and, more importantly, to skew these exemptions toward recipients who present the greatest challenges (Lurie and Hagen 1993; Nathan 1993).

An underlying theme of many current welfare reform proposals is that of promoting greater equity in the system—to ensure that all welfare recipients have opportunities to contribute to their own support and to the support of their children to the extent of their abilities, and to expect them to do so. Indeed, most proposals contain elements designed to support this objective by changing the nature of the obligations on recipients and the services available to meet their individual needs.

An extreme version of welfare reform would promote a concept of equity in which some form of activity requirement would apply to *all* welfare recipients, and the system would be obligated to provide the necessary support services to enable recipients to meet these requirements. The challenge under such a model is addressing the diversity in the ability of welfare recipients to train for and work in various types of jobs. It is widely recognized that significant numbers of welfare recipients will be *unable* to make the transition to unsubsidized employment within the two-year time limit proposed in several key welfare reform proposals, including that unveiled by President Clinton on June 14, 1994. For many welfare recipients, the feasibility of their working in an unsubsidized job depends heavily on the level of resources available for training, placement, and/or employment support. At some cost, most welfare recipients could work in unsubsidized employment or could contribute to their own support through a subsidized employment opportunity. A major public policy challenge is to determine the efficient level of investment in promoting unsubsidized employment and the types of subsidized employment and non-labor market alternatives that ought to be available for those who cannot succeed in the regular labor market with "reasonable" levels of support.

This chapter lays the foundation for policy discussions about the role of subsidized employment and non-labor market alternatives for welfare recipients who do not make the transition to regular employment within the time limits established under a reformed welfare system. We begin by discussing the limits to the potential of traditional employment and training programs to move welfare recipients into permanent or semi-permanent unsubsidized jobs. I then discuss strategies for moving recipients into the work force, thereby minimizing the "residual" group for whom alternatives to unsubsidized employment may be warranted. Finally, I present two alternatives to unsubsidized employment for those who cannot temporarily or permanently make the transition.

The discussion of the alternatives to unsubsidized employment is framed by two controversial assumptions that contrast sharply with current welfare policy: first, that the social and economic prosperity of the nation will be enhanced if all members of society are expected and given opportunities to contribute to their social and economic welfare; and, second, that society has an obligation to maintain regular contact with and be ready to assist those in need. Presently, the welfare recipients in greatest need tend to receive the least attention from the social service system. They are likely to be exempt from the JOBS program. Moreover, in the vast majority of cases, the system offers no other routine points of contact to assist them in times of crisis. In practice, economic constraints will dictate policies that lie somewhere between our current laissez faire policy toward work requirements for welfare recipients and a policy that promotes a maximum contribution from each welfare recipient—albeit subsidized employment or non–labor market alternatives for sizable numbers.

LIMITS OF TRADITIONAL EMPLOYMENT AND TRAINING PROGRAMS

Among relatively recent welfare recipients, more than three-fourths have had some employment, and over 41 percent will have worked two or more years (figure 5.1). Yet, even the best designed and implemented time-limited welfare program will inevitably leave a sizeable number of mothers without unsubsidized jobs. On the one hand, a time-limited system would prompt substantially higher employment rates than typically have been achieved under even the best JOBS programs, in large part due to the episodic nature of the intervention. For example, whereas over two-thirds of the participants in the Riverside GAIN program—widely heralded as the most successful JOBS-type program—were employed at some time during the first three years after enrollment, less than half were employed at the end of three years (Friedlander, Freedman, and Riccio 1993). Under other "well-implemented" programs the employment rates are even lower (Burtless 1984; Gueron and Pauly 1991; Maynard 1993b; Nathan 1993; Nightingale et al. 1991).

On the other hand, sizable numbers of those who never get employed under the current JOBS programs also would not make the transition under a time-limited system. Furthermore, the added incentives and services under a time-limited welfare system would

Figure 5.1 WORK EXPERIENCE OF AFDC RECIPIENTS IN LAST FIVE YEARS
(1983–1987)

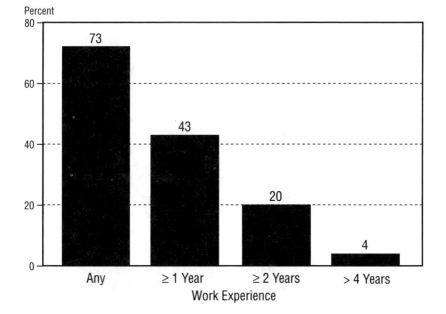

Source: Adapted from Zill et al. (1991, table 8).

be insufficient to promote stable unsubsidized employment by many who are able to make the initial transition.

The potential of a time-limited welfare system to move welfare recipients to unsubsidized employment and the nature of the "residual" pool will be conditioned by the characteristics of the population, the nature and intensity of program services, the program participation requirements and the vigor with which they are applied, and weaknesses in the local labor markets. Under a national time-limited program, participation requirements would presumably be more vigorously applied than they have been in all but a few prior welfare programs, and the services would be richer and more universally available. Potentially, this could promote employment among many of the 85 percent of the caseload who currently are not brought into the welfare work (JOBS) programs and among those who falter in these programs.

This optimism may be especially warranted among many of the 30 to 40 percent of JOBS participants whose participation requirements are deferred. For example, of the 33 percent deferred from participation in the Riverside GAIN program, just over half were

Figure 5.2 REASONS FOR DEFERRAL FROM JOBS:
RIVERSIDE GAIN PROGRAM

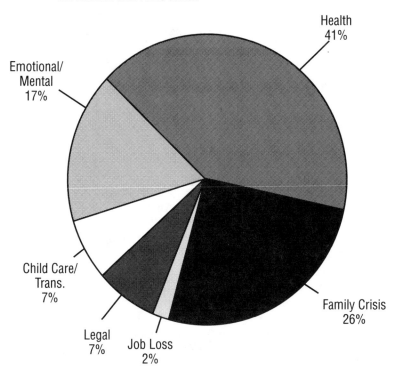

Source: Adapted from Hamilton (1993).

deferred for *potentially* insolvable reasons, such as serious health problems (some of which undoubtedly were temporary) and emotional or mental problems, including substance addiction (figure 5.2).[1] The remaining cases were deferred for reasons that should not apply under welfare reform. Seven percent were for reasons related to child care, and 35 percent were for problems that could be addressed through social service intervention, such as legal issues (7 percent), job loss (2 percent), or family crises (26 percent).

Even if we succeed in minimizing these work-limiting forces, some individuals will fail in the unsubsidized labor market for a wide variety of reasons that are specific to individual circumstances and often are difficult to predict (Friedlander 1988; Maynard et al. 1992). Some welfare recipients simply will be unwilling to work; some will have difficulty locating and/or retaining a job, due to labor market conditions and/or lack of job search and work skills; some will be geographically isolated; and others will have serious personal barriers, including chronic mental and physical handicaps and extraordinary family responsibilities (Finkel, Kulik, and Paulin 1990; Golden 1992; Herr and Halpern 1991; Olson, Berg, and Conrad 1990).

Insurmountable Barriers to Employment in Regular Labor Market

Under a reformed welfare system that includes serious attention to employment-related services, strong incentives for recipients to work toward unsubsidized employment, and a two-year time limit on employment preparation services, a sizable portion of the welfare caseload at any point in time would consist of individuals who have insurmountable barriers to employment. Whereas I estimate that only about 20 percent of the new entrants to AFDC will face such barriers, over time this group may constitute as much as one-third of the recipients, due to their longer-than-average lengths of stay on welfare.[2]

By more aggressive attempts to break down the barriers to unsubsidized employment, welfare reform can increase the proportion who leave AFDC for employment, as well as the pace at which transitions off welfare occur. Under a well-functioning reformed system, those remaining on AFDC longer than two years should consist of a small group who are victims of the natural unemployment rate and a portion of those who have serious work-limiting conditions.

Under the current welfare system, only about one-third of welfare recipients remain on AFDC for as long as two years (U.S. Congress 1993; Ellwood 1986). Nearly half of those who leave do so for reasons related to unsubsidized employment (Gleason, Rangarajan, and Schochet 1994; Pavetti 1992). Others leave due to changes in family structure or noncompliance with program regulations. For example, in Kenosha, Wisconsin, of the 54 percent of JOBS participants who left AFDC within two years, only 60 percent did so because of employment; 13 percent left because of changing living arrangements, 4 percent for noncooperation with JOBS, and the remaining 23 percent for other reasons (Kenosha County Job Center 1992). Of those still on AFDC after two years, 16 percent were employed and 15 percent were still in the JOBS program. Factoring in modest impacts of welfare reform on the proportion who leave welfare for unsubsidized employment and the rates of those transitions, I estimate that as many as 20 percent of first-time welfare recipients will not succeed in making the transition to regular employment even under a new welfare system where work pays and where employment support programs offer skills training, job placement assistance, and ongoing support.

An underlying assumption of the proposed time limit on welfare is that many recipients currently forgo employment for fear that this may jeopardize their long-run economic security. Under the current system, for example, many will lose health benefits by making the transition to a low-paying job—a situation that may change with the implementation of health care reform. Others will jeopardize their ability to return to welfare if the job does not work out—a reality for the majority of those entering employment (Gleason et al. 1994; Olson et al. 1990).

The implementation of a time limit on welfare eligibility will create strong incentives for all recipients who can make the transition to unsubsidized employment to do so, provided we do not allow liberal exemptions. There are three questions for policymakers as they work to design a welfare reform plan that will replace the current system of "hand-outs" with a system of "hand-ups." The first relates to the proportion of the caseload we can reasonably expect to make this transition with the implementation of a strong JOBS-type program—a question that can be answered in part by looking at the "natural employment" rates within this population, the incidence of absolute barriers, and evidence on the effects of JOBS-type programs on these rates. The second question relates to what can be done to strengthen the effectiveness of the JOBS program so as to minimize both the incidence and consequences of work-limiting conditions. And the third question relates to who will constitute the "residual" group.

NATURAL EMPLOYMENT RATES

There is considerable evidence that as many as 50 percent of AFDC recipients have, at most, transitory problems preventing them from participating in the labor market. For example, as noted previously, nearly three-fourths of welfare recipients have worked in the previous five years, and over 40 percent have worked for more than a year during that time (Zill, Moore, and Stief 1991). Moreover, evidence from the various JOBS-type programs run by states in recent years indicates that, with *no* intervention, about one-third of new welfare recipients will be employed within 12 months of first receiving benefits, and 40 percent will be employed within three years of first receiving welfare (Gueron and Pauly 1991). Less than 10 percent report being unable to find work, and another 20 percent cite personal reasons for not working.

WORK-LIMITING CONDITIONS

Welfare recipients themselves face a wide range of barriers to employment, including locating and paying for child care, lack of transportation, weak job skills, and chronic health conditions. Abstracting from issues of cost, only those barriers related to work-limiting health conditions and low basic skills linked to limited mental capacity, which together affect relatively modest fractions of the welfare population, pose serious policy and programmatic challenges.

Work-limiting health conditions are the most intractable problems keeping welfare recipients from gaining unsubsidized employment. However, they also affect only a modest number of cases. Only about 10 percent of welfare recipients have health conditions that preclude their working or limit the amount of work they can do, and another 4 percent may have serious mental problems (Zill et al. 1991).

Low basic skills are common among welfare recipients and certainly contribute to low employment levels and wages. Yet, they are an insurmountable barrier to employment for only a small portion of this group. In most cases, the questions are: what level of investment in skills improvement is necessary to meet labor market demands, and are we as a society willing to make that investment?

Welfare recipients have reading and math skills about the level of the typical eighth grader (Goodison 1982; Martinson and Friedlander 1994; Maynard, Nicholson, and Rangarajan 1992) and few possess the higher-order thinking and analytic skills generally demanded by today's employers (Kirsch and Jungblut 1986; Rangarajan, Kisker, and Maynard 1992; Strain and Kisker 1989; Zill and Nord 1994). By one measure, 30 percent of welfare recipients have basic skills below those of the *minimum* of all women in the lowest occupation skill areas (manual operatives) (Zill et al. 1991) (figure 5.3). Another study has estimated that as many as 25 percent to 40 percent of AFDC recipients may have learning disabilities, some of which pose challenges in upgrading recipients' basic skills levels (Nightingale et al. 1991). However, there also is evidence that most learning-disabled individuals can master the basic skills necessary to hold a competitive job, if instructional methods are tailored to specific learning styles (Burghardt and Gordon 1990; Edgar 1988; Kohaska and Skolnik 1986; Nightingale et al. 1991).

Comparisons of employment rates of low-skilled males and females also suggest that low basic skills, themselves, generally do not preclude access to unsubsidized jobs, however. For example, nearly 90 percent of young males with lower-than-average reading skills are

Figure 5.3 PERCENTAGE OF AFDC RECIPIENTS NOT MEETING MINIMUM
SKILLS REQUIREMENTS

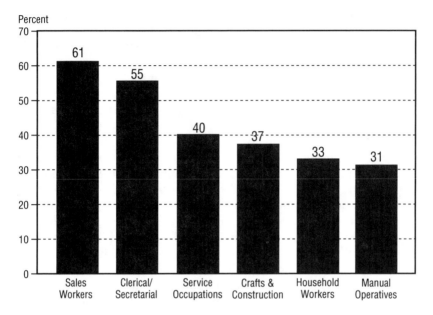

Source: Adapted from Zill et al. (1991, Table 5)

employed, compared with only half of similarly skilled females. In contrast, the employment rate differential between lower-skilled and higher-skilled young single female parents is only 6 percentage points—49 percent versus 55 percent (Strain and Kisker 1989). Moreover, while there are strong correlations between measured skills of welfare recipients and their success in the labor market, a sizable portion of those who gain employment have low measured skills (Burghardt and Gordon 1990; Maynard et al. 1992; Rangarajan et al. 1992). Overall, these employment patterns suggest that cultural factors and employment alternatives may be more critical factors in determining the employment rates of low-skilled individuals than are basic skill levels themselves. In fact, a recent survey of employers suggested that social skills and work habits are more important than basic reading and math skills for low-end jobs (Maxfield 1988).

Nonetheless, it would be helpful to minimize the degree of mismatch between the skills of welfare recipients and those demanded by employers. Employers could be encouraged to rethink their job structure to accommodate lower-skilled individuals (Berryman

1988), as occurred among some employers during the relatively tight labor markets of the mid-1980s. In essence, this also was the strategy in the supported work demonstrations where, through transitional support, job redefinition, and natural time trends, over 70 percent of long-term welfare recipients were able to hold unsubsidized jobs (Hollister, Kemper, and Maynard 1984). The most serious limitation of this strategy is that it tends to rationalize the low wages paid to those at the bottom of the queue, thereby promoting an expanded class of working poor. This strategy also would impose ccsts of job restructuring on employers, which could adversely affect the economy and hence aggregate employment opportunities.

A second approach to the problem is to offer job-specific training. Several examples of employment programs now have succeeded in compensating for nominal skills barriers through job redefinition, job-specific job training, and/or extensive employment support. For example, the Center for Employment Training experienced notable success in training and placing low-skilled individuals—many of whom have not only limited basic skills but limited English proficiency—in jobs paying well above minimum wage (Burghardt and Gordon 1990; Cave et al. 1993). In contrast, there is mounting evidence that our current adult education system is not effective in improving the employability of low-skilled individuals (Cohen et al. 1994; Granger 1994; Layzer 1994; Maynard 1994).

"Residual" Group under a Reformed System

By themselves, modest employment-training initiatives are often able to increase employment rates by 5 to 10 percentage points. The combination of stringently applied requirements for welfare recipients to engage in employment-directed activities, coupled with time-limits on their welfare eligibility, likely would increase the number who attain employment or otherwise leave welfare by another 10 to 20 percentage points. Moreover, the implementation of richer and more responsive transitional and posttransitional support programs could increase the employment rates still further. For example, there are clear programmatic solutions to barriers such as transportation and child care, and there are policy and program options to address issues such as addiction and many physical and mental limitations (see further discussion below).

A well-structured welfare reform plan could eliminate the majority of the perceived barriers to employment—that is, many of the per-

Figure 5.4 REASONS AFDC RECIPIENTS WERE NOT WORKING

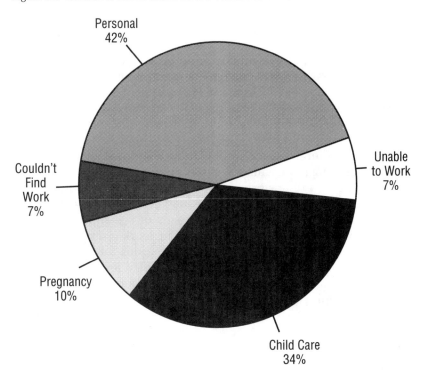

Source: Adapted from Zill et al. (1991, Tables 8 and 18). The numbers are weighted averages. They exclude AFDC recipients who were in school or who did not want to work.

sonal barriers and most of the child care barriers (figure 5.4). Over 40 percent of those welfare recipients not working attribute their nonemployment to one of a variety of personal reasons such as lack of interest in working (15 percent), housing problems, transportation problems, and extraordinary responsibilities for other family members. Some of these reasons for nonemployment would disappear as a result of stricter work requirements, and others could be addressed through a strong social support system.

Over one-third of unemployed welfare recipients indicate that they are not working because they lack child care. In fact, given the nature of the child care market, it should be feasible to eliminate this barrier for all but a handful of cases who may have unusual needs (Gilbert, Berrick, and Meyers 1992; Kisker, Maynard, and Strain 1989; Schochet and Kisker 1992). In creating the necessary child care services to support the employment of low-income workers, we also would create a substantial number of low-to-moderate skill jobs, thereby also incrementally expanding the labor market opportunities for this population.

A reformed welfare system also would address the needs of those who are temporarily incapacitated. For example, at any point in time, as many as 7 percent of the caseload (10 percent of those not working) may be unable to work due to pregnancy. We need explicit policies to deal with pregnancies in ways that promote and/or preserve employment opportunities.

Piecing together data from the few strong employment and training programs serving representative subsets of new AFDC cases, as well as information on the reasons for long-term welfare receipt, we estimate that as many as half of those not making the transition to unsubsidized employment or other means of self-support under a reformed welfare system will have chronic, work-prohibiting health conditions. For the other half, the major reasons for their inability to get and hold a job will relate to low ability levels and serious personality disorders. I could add to this figure some portion of those marginally employable individuals living in remote areas for whom it is not practical to develop and maintain employment opportunities—a portion of the 7 percent who report not working because they cannot find work.

STRATEGIES TO REDUCE "RESIDUAL" GROUP

Several strategies that can be incorporated into welfare reform to reduce the size of the residual group unable to enter the work force within the time-limit on welfare. Some of these strategies also could have important influences on the welfare of the next generation, and all would help change the culture of welfare (i.e., from being based on a system of entitlements to one of reciprocal obligations between welfare clients and social welfare agencies).

Geographic Barriers

About three-fourths of poor families reside in metropolitan areas (U.S. Department of Commerce 1992). For these families, transportation may be costly, but need not be an insurmountable barrier to employment. Even in more rural areas, geographic barriers are addressable at some cost. We simply need to make a commitment to bring jobs to people or people to jobs. The most effective strategy for addressing geographic isolation might entail a combination of job development initiatives that bring employment opportunities to these remote areas and van pools to transport workers to town centers. Even under aggressive strategies on both fronts, we would expect lower success rates in rural areas due to remoteness pushing some marginally employable individuals into the "residual" group. For example, some individuals with health limitations and/or extenuating family responsibilities who could hold down a local job may not be able to sustain the added stresses of a lengthy commute.

Dependent-Care Policies

As noted, child care is a common reason cited for nonparticipation in the labor force. The child care needs of most welfare recipients can be addressed through a combination of financial supports and resource and referral assistance (Schochet and Kisker 1992). However, a few have very challenging dependent-care needs—for example, children with serious, chronic illnesses or incapacitated adults in the household requiring extensive and ongoing care. Again, from a policy perspective, the question is not whether we can address all of these needs, but at what point the welfare recipient and society are better off having significant dependent care support to allow the recipient to enter the work force as opposed to continuing to fully support the family through welfare. The answer will differ based on individual circumstances.

Many welfare mothers, including many with infants, find it rewarding to engage in out-of-home activities, whether employment or other activities. For example, young mothers who were required to engage in out-of-home activities to maintain their welfare eligibility under a federally sponsored demonstration program, as well as those who volunteered for similar services on their own, were almost universally enthusiastic about getting out and doing something on a regular basis (Hershey and Maynard 1992a; Polit 1992; Quint, Musick, and Ladner 1994).

Expanding and Redefining Employment Opportunities

For as much as 10 percent of the welfare population, lack of employment opportunities may be the primary factor keeping them on welfare. There are three possible solutions to this problem. First, we could institute policies to physically locate the people to the jobs. Counseling and financial support could be made available to promote relocation. A small-scale experiment with such a policy in Chicago has met with some success. However, in other settings—for example, as part of programs to expedite the reemployment of dislocated workers—relocation programs have generally not been widely used by unemployed workers (Corson and Maynard 1984; Kulik et al. 1978).

A second strategy entails bringing the jobs to the people through community development. A number of nationally sponsored initiatives are aimed at promoting local job development in economically depressed areas of the country. Whereas such initiatives may be an important piece to the solution of our welfare problem, past experience suggests that, in the short run, this approach will have a relatively small impact, at best.

A third strategy entails redefining jobs to meet the skills of the potential workers. Much of the rhetoric around the welfare problem refers to the increasing skill requirements of the work force as contrasted with the low education and skill levels of the welfare population. Both job analysis research and job training experience suggest that some of the skills gap could be eliminated through redefinition of selected jobs, and some could be eliminated through targeted job training (Berryman 1988; Burghardt and Gordon 1990; Cave et al. 1993).

A fourth strategy would entail rigorous policies and programs of employment support aimed at preventing job loss and expediting reemployment when job losses occur. In one recent study, 25 percent of those who left AFDC returned within two months; 50 percent had returned within a year; and 70 percent had returned within three years (Rangarajan et al. 1994). While the highest recidivism rates were among those leaving for reasons other than living arrangements or jobs, still about two-thirds of those exiting for employment returned to welfare within three years. The encouraging fact is that most of the reasons welfare recipients lose their jobs and return to welfare relate to either transitory events and/or ones that could be addressed through some type of social intervention (table 5.1).

In addition, there is a growing body of research pointing to the potential of even low-skilled individuals and individuals with physical handicapping conditions to participate effectively in the labor market. For example, in a recent demonstration of transitional employment for SSI recipients, 50 percent to 60 percent of the trainees were employed in each of the six years following the intervention, compared with only about 40 percent to 50 percent of the control group (Decker and Thornton 1993). Moreover, program-related gains in employment rates were especially strong for those who had only borderline retardation—a group more like the lowest-performing AFDC recipients. Similar results have been found in a large number of other programs for populations with disabilities, including but not limited to those with mental retardation (Gerry and McWhorter n.d.; Kerachsky et al. 1985; Konig and Schalock 1991; Kregel, Wehman, Banks 1989).

An aggressive welfare reform plan might offer clear incentives to states to work actively with employers to redefine jobs to meet the skills and abilities of some low-skilled workers. States could also provide additional supports to workers and employers to create and sustain worker-job matches. The success of such efforts would depend in large part on the willingness of states to commit the necessary resources and their dedication to the mission. Experience suggests that the average employment support costs (exclusive of child care) can easily exceed $5,000 a year (Brock et al. 1993). An important policy question is that of where to draw the line between supporting a welfare recipient in a job and providing full income support, with or without an alternative activity requirement.

SUBSIDIZED EMPLOYMENT AND NON–LABOR MARKET ALTERNATIVES

Subsidized employment and nonmarket alternatives to employment could contribute to meeting the goals of welfare reform in two ways. First, the surest way to minimize the number who fail to make the transition to unsubsidized employment is to require all welfare recipients to engage in some out-of-home activity pursuant to a better life for themselves and their children. Under a welfare system with universal activity requirements—a system with no exemptions—the system will be challenged to continuously monitor the needs of all dependent families and to intervene early. There will be strong incentives to move people as quickly as possible into the work force, thus minimizing service costs as well as cash transfers. At the same time, welfare recipients will receive more active encouragement and incentives to seek help with their problems and to take risks associated with entering the work force.

Second, a universal system of obligations and services would afford

Table 5.1 REASONS FOR WELFARE RECIPIENTS' JOB LOSS REPORTED IN PREVIOUS STUDIES

Study	Reasons Associated with Job Held	Reasons Associated with Individual Recipient/ Job Holder	Reasons Associated with Social System in Which Participant Lives
Chicago Project Match (Herr and Halpern 1991; Kennedy 1992; Olson et al. 1990)	• Work not what they expected it to be; unfamiliar situation • Difficulty dealing with mostly white bosses and customers	• Chronically late • Didn't understand work rules (e.g., calling in if sick) • Couldn't handle transition from being free all day to having to budget their time • Didn't understand what it meant to have a boss (resented being given direction) • Refused to do things outside job description • Upsetting events (such as sick child) disrupted lives	• Pressured by family and friends not to change their lives • Children, friends, and boyfriends resented job obligations
New Jersey REACH (Thornton and Hershey 1990)	• Laid off or fired (39%) • Low wages (6%) • Did not like job (4%) • Pursued other job (3%) • Other (too many hours, bad location, no fringe benefits) (5%)	• Health problem (13%) • Moved away • In jail	• Child care problem (11%) • Family problem (5%) • Inadequate transportation • End of Medicaid coverage
Minority Female Single Parent (MFSP) (Burghardt and Gordon 1990)[a]	• Lack of experience or skills (6.8%)	• In school or training (20.4%) • Illness/disability (5.3%) • Pregnant (4.0%) • Did not want to work (2.1%)	• Child care responsibilities or could not find child care (21.2%) • Other family responsibilities (1.8%)

Study				
Teenage Parent Demonstration—Chicago site (Maynard et al. 1993a)	• Job ended (20.3%) • Laid off (9.8%) • Fired (5.0%)	• Quit (20.7%) • Maternity leave (9.3%) • Returned to school (6.1%) • Health problems (3.9%)	• Personal problems (includes drug problems, death in the family, landlord problems) (1.3%)	• Lack of transportation • Not wanting to lose benefits • Waiting for opening in a training program
Massachusetts ET Choices (Nightingale et al. 1990)	• Low wages • Poor benefits (especially lack of health insurance) • Inconvenient hours • Laid off (10.9%) • Fired (3.2%)		• Personal reasons (health problems, personal problems, pregnancy, going to school, moved) (48%)	• Child care difficulties (9.3%) • Transportation problems (3.9%) • Parental pressure (2.3%)
New Chance (Quint et al. 1994)	• Low pay • Poor supervision • At bottom of occupational hierarchy • Relational problems with supervisors and/or co-workers • Differential treatment		• Attitudes young women bring to the workplace (immaturity and inexperience) • Perception of arbitrary work-place rules	• Child care problems (14.3%) • Transportation problems (4.8%) • Cut in welfare benefits (1%)

Source: Reproduced by permission of John M. Love, Mathematica Policy Research, Inc., Princeton, NJ.

Note: If no percentages are given, either the study did not provide them or the reasons have been disaggregated from an "other" category, for which percentages for the individual reasons were not provided.

a. Sample members were asked about reasons for not working, regardless of whether they had had a job. Thus, reasons are not directly comparable with those found in other studies.

welfare recipients more dignity. The recipients will benefit from preparing for or contributing to the support of their families. Society will benefit from both the labor of those welfare recipients in subsidized employment and their satisfaction in knowing that other recipients are preparing to contribute to the support of their families in the future. The AFDC Homemaker–Home Health Aide Demonstration, which trained welfare recipients to work in a socially important labor shortage area (home health), is a good example of a subsidized employment opportunity that subsequently led to unsubsidized employment for many participants (Bell and Orr 1994). More importantly, both the recipients and society benefited greatly from this special employment opportunity.

In a world unconstrained by fiscal concerns, all welfare recipients who could do some type of productive work, but who could not succeed in the unsubsidized labor market, might be given subsidized employment opportunities. However, practical and financial considerations will likely limit such opportunities to subsets of those unable to gain unsubsidized employment. Based on a simulation of dynamics of the welfare caseloads under a full-scale time-limited welfare program that targets first-time recipients, I estimate that over a 10-year period, the demand for subsidized employment or alternative nonlabor market activity options could easily exceed 1 million cases at any one time. Thus, large numbers of both types of alternatives will be necessary to significantly impact the size and life courses of the "residual" pool.

Subsidized Employment Alternatives

Subsidized employment has been an important part of our welfare and employment policy off and on since the Great Depression. Over the years, we have had several large-scale public service employment programs, some of which have elements that mirror or could be adapted to a subsidized employment context.

HISTORICAL PERSPECTIVE

The first such programs—the federal work programs of the Great Depression—employed over 4 million persons a year (3 percent of the population). Although costly (accounting for 10 percent of the federal budget), this effort substantially strengthened our economic infrastructure—roads, bridges, dams, schools, and so forth (Kesselman 1978; U.S. Department of Labor 1993). Since much of the work entailed primarily physical labor, the similarity between this and subsidized employment depends on one's valuation of the product.

More recently, we have experienced various subsidized employment programs under the Comprehensive Employment and Training Act (CETA), which reached a peak of nearly 800,000 public service jobs in 1978. Under CETA, the majority of the jobs were held by unemployed "workers" rather than disadvantaged persons or welfare recipients. Moreover, most of the jobs entailed work valued and rewarded at well above minimum wage. Nonetheless, a limited number of jobs in public service were targeted for welfare recipients and for those with limited work skills. This latter group of jobs, which constituted less than 10 percent of public service employment slots, resembled subsidized employment in so far as the estimates of the value of product fell below the wages paid and performance expectations were often below market norms.

More recently, community work experience (unpaid) programs have been important, but relatively small, components of state welfare employment programs. Experiments with such programs during the 1970s most often entailed placements in public agencies—jobs that generally involved a considerable subsidy above the value of the work produced. However, sometimes they involved private-sector placements with partial or full wage subsidies to employers who agreed to work with welfare recipients whose productivity was valued at or near market wage (Brock et al. 1993).

A NEW VISION

The best available evidence suggests that subsidized work experience may be preferable to nonmarket alternatives or idleness for many welfare recipients who are unable to meet the demands of the unsubsidized labor market. Individuals involved in any form of work, whether on a voluntary or mandatory basis, generally feel good about what they are doing. Moreover, with sufficient supports and incentives, most of the residual welfare recipients ought to be able to perform adequately in unsubsidized employment eventually, even if not immediately. It is, however, both costly and challenging to create subsidized employment options that do not compete with unsubsidized jobs.

A subsidized employment program should more closely resemble the programs of the Great Depression era than those of the CETA years, when many public service jobs were thought to be displacing work that would have been funded by private sources. From the perspectives of both satisfaction to the worker and benefit to the nation, the most desirable jobs would contribute to national welfare— jobs that enhance our economic and/or social welfare, while not competing with the regular labor market. Examples might include providing service in schools and child care centers to enable richer and/or greater access to services by those currently underserved due to resource constraints. Finally, certain community works projects— parks, roads, and crime control, for example—would benefit society. We also could strengthen other community services, particularly for disadvantaged families, the homeless, and the elderly, without seriously interfering with local economies. However, public service and subsidized jobs inevitably will be perceived by some (often justifiably so) as displacing workers in unsubsidized jobs.

The goal would be to find useful jobs for all welfare recipients who are judged capable of working, but who cannot meet the productivity or other demands of regular jobs. In a world of scarcity, society will benefit from creating and supporting such jobs up to the point where more resources are required to create and support the positions than the total value of the work performed—factoring in potential social benefits in terms of the greater satisfaction the public derives from supporting those who contribute to the welfare of the country and to their families and the greater sense of dignity that welfare recipients feel.

CHALLENGES IN ADMINISTERING SUBSIDIZED EMPLOYMENT

Creating and managing a subsidized employment program poses numerous challenges. First, there will be opposition from organized labor, unless the jobs are clearly confined to areas judged to be noncompetitive with private sector jobs. Second, such programs require extensive administrative and supervisory support. This is particularly true in situations where jobs are dispersed throughout the community, as many would be in any large-scale initiative. For example, the community work experience jobs are estimated to cost an average of $2,200 per person per year, in addition to wages and other benefits paid to the workers (Maynard 1993a). Employment supports, such as child care, transportation, and job search assistance, together are estimated to more than double these direct job-related costs. Moreover, there also will be some costs associated with displacement of workers in unsubsidized jobs.

Wages in subsidized jobs could take the form of continued welfare eligibility or direct payment of a wage. The latter has the advantage of explicitly recognizing the work performed by the welfare recipient. In any event, the wage should be set at or near the minimum wage for two reasons. One is to discourage dependency on subsidized employment by those capable of regular employment. The other relates to the true value of the product, which is expected to be relatively low, due to both the employment barriers of the workers and the nature of the jobs, particularly if one factors in the added costs of supervision. The higher the wages and benefits paid in subsidized jobs, the more likely that some welfare recipients who are capable of unsubsidized employment will be attracted to the lower risks of this alternative in terms of job security and the economic insurance of welfare.

For a small portion of the welfare population, advancing to subsidized employment at any stage will require a substantial employment support, much like that provided to mentally and physically impaired populations. Depending on state and local funding limits, it may be necessary to restrict access to those without unusually high support service needs.

Non–Labor Market Alternatives

Those who are not yet ready for even subsidized employment (and possibly, those for whom subsidized employment opportunities are not available) could be referred to group activities aimed at promoting progressively greater responsibility for one's family and making greater contributions to community welfare. There are numerous models for such alternatives, including Project Match, which provides social and employment support to welfare mothers in public housing projects; the Parents as Teachers (PATS) and Parent and Child Education (PACE) programs, which emphasize empowerment through family literacy; the Head Start Family Service Centers, which offer one-stop health, education, and social service centers for low-income families of preschoolers; and numerous volunteer programs to help teenage mothers and tutor school children (Golden 1992). Depending on local need and interest, single or multiple service options could be created within a community, and recipients could be given some choice in their group activities.

Of greatest importance is that there be some structured and support-oriented activity that welfare recipients would participate in on a regular basis—for example, at least twice a week. Especially for mothers of young children, the activities could involve their children for all or part of the time. They also should incorporate "simulated" or real work assignments. For example, in addition to attending their scheduled activity, recipients could be required to do volunteer work for their group or for some other community organization on a regular schedule—for example, twice a month.

This type of alternative activity requirement for the unemployable welfare recipient would have numerous benefits. First, such opportunities could be used to promote improved parenting, health care, and self-esteem. The activities could also serve as opportunities to improve deficient social skills that interfere with and sometimes preclude job holding—skills like keeping appointments, budgeting time, getting along with authority figures, flexibility, and following codes of behavior, such as calling in sick rather than simply not showing up. These are all reasons why welfare recipients lose jobs and/or fail to get them in the first place (Herr and Halpern 1991; Kennedy 1992; Olson, Berg, and Conrad 1990; Polit 1992; Quint, Ladner, and Musick 1994). The routine contact between welfare recipients and a welfare system that is responsible for promoting self-sufficiency should lead to earlier detection of and quicker response to crises and other problems that arise.

The cost of creating and maintaining these types of family support programs could range from modest to high, depending on the extensiveness of the services and the level of professional support. At the low end of the service range, we might expect the cost to be between $700 and $1,000 a year per participant, inclusive of transportation and child care costs. At the upper end, the costs could exceed $2,000 per participant per year.[3] However, some of the costs of these services would be offset by the creation of regular and/or subsidized employment opportunities for other welfare recipients.

CONCLUSIONS

There are clear benefits to avoiding a leaky boat in the welfare work requirements. It is both fair and productive to expect all welfare recipients to participate in some structured activity. Priority ought to be given to moving welfare recipients into regular employment as quickly as possible. When this is not a realistic option, efforts should be made to place individuals in subsidized jobs, preferably ones that build marketable skills. However, any work experience is preferable to none in terms of building basic work skills. It would be desirable for those who are far from being work-ready and/or for whom subsidized opportunities are not available to participate in some community or welfare-based group activity designed to build personal skills that can improve home management, childrearing, and possibly, in the long run, job readiness.

In deciding how much to invest in these alternatives to unsubsidized employment, policymakers should factor in the anticipated benefits of mutual obligations on both the welfare system and welfare recipients in changing the culture of welfare. The single most important lesson from the few truly mandatory JOBS programs run by states is that the "culture shift" comes only when there are substantial costs to the welfare system of failing to work with all recipients to try to overcome whatever employment barriers they have—including recipients who may be far from the ultimate goal of employment. The hard fact is that we have extremely limited ability to predict who can succeed in the labor market, let alone the degree of preparation and support necessary to achieve and maintain employment of particular individuals. Thus, we need to create a system of support that is at once comprehensive and responsive to the varied and changing needs of individual welfare recipients.

Notes

Meredith Kelsey provided research assistance for this chapter.

1. Only 4 percent of cases were deferred because of substance addiction.

2. This estimate assumes that AFDC cases that do not find unsubsidized employment and do not exit AFDC for non-employment reasons by the end of two years will not be dropped from the rolls entirely. If they were, the entire caseload with durations of receipt in excess of the time limit would consist of those unable to work in an unsubsidized job.

3. These estimates are based on unit costs for child care, transportation, and case management presented in Maynard (1993a).

References

Bell, Stephen, and Larry Orr. 1994. "Is Subsidized Employment Cost Effective for Welfare Recipients? Experimental Evidence From Seven State Demonstrations." *The Journal of Human Resources* 29: 42–61.

Berryman, Susan. 1988. *Literacy and the Marketplace: Improving the Literacy of Low Income Single Mothers.* New York: The Rockefeller Foundation.

Brock, Thomas, David Butler, and David Long. 1993. *Unpaid Work Experience for Welfare Recipients: Findings and Lessons from MDRC Research.* New York: Manpower Demonstration Research Corporation.

Burghardt, John, and Anne Gordon. 1990. *More Jobs and Higher Pay: How an Integrated Program Compares with Traditional Programs.* New York: The Rockefeller Foundation.

Burtless, Gary. "Manpower Policies for the Disadvantaged: What Works?" *Brookings Review* 3: 18–22.

Cave, George, Hans Bos, Fred Doolittle, and Cyril Toussaint. 1993. *JOBSTART: Final Report on a Program for School Dropouts.* New York: Manpower Demonstration Research Corporation.

Cohen, Elena, Susan Golonka, Rebecca Maynard, Theodora Ooms, and Todd Owen. 1994. "Welfare Reform and Literacy: Are We Making the Connection?" Washington, DC: Family Impact Seminar and National Center on Adult Literacy, June 10.

Corson, Walter, and Rebecca Maynard. 1984. *Implementation and Process Evaluation of the National Dislocated Worker Demonstration.* Princeton: Mathematica Policy Research, Inc.

Decker, Paul, and Craig V. D. Thornton. 1993. *The Long-Term Effects of the Transitional Employment Training Demonstration.* Princeton: Mathematica Policy Research, Inc.

Edgar, Eugene. 1988. "Employment as an Outcome for Mildly Handicapped Students: Current Status and Future Directions." *Focus on Exceptional Children* 21(1, September): 1–8.

Ellwood, David. 1986. *Targeting Strategies for Welfare Recipients.* Princeton: Mathematica Policy Research, Inc.

Finkel, Meryl, Jane Kulik, and Helena Paulin. 1990. *Final Report of the Single Point of Contact Program Evaluation.* Cambridge: Abt Associates.

Friedlander, Daniel. 1988. *Subgroup Impacts and Performance Indicators for Selected Welfare Employment Programs.* New York: Manpower Demonstration Research Corporation.

Friedlander, Daniel, Stephen Freedman, and James Riccio. 1993. *GAIN: Two-Year Impacts in Six Counties.* New York: Manpower Demonstration Research Corporation.

Gerry, Martin, and C. McWhorter. n.d. "A Comprehensive Analysis of Federal Statutes and Programs for Persons with Severe Disabilities."

Gilbert, N., J. Berrick, and M. Meyers. 1992. *GAIN Family Life and Child Care Study.* Berkeley: Family Welfare Research Group.

Gleason, Philip, Anu Rangarajan, and Peter Schochet. 1994. *The Dynamics of AFDC Spells among Teenage Parents.* Paper presented at the Econometrics Society Meeting, Boston, January.

Golden, Olivia. 1992. *Poor Children and Welfare Reform.* Westport: The Auburn House.

Goodison, Marlene. 1982. *Testing Literacy Levels in the WIN Population.* Princeton: Educational Testing Service, March.

Granger, Robert. 1994. "New Chance: Interim Findings on a Comprehensive Program for Disadvantaged Young Mothers and Their Children." Talking points for a seminar in Programs for Unwed Teen Mothers. American Enterprise Institute. Washington, D.C., June 9.

Gueron, Judith M., and Edward Pauly. 1991. *From Welfare to Work.* New York: Russell Sage Foundation.

Hamilton, Gayle. 1993. *Welfare Dynamics Analysis: Additional Tables on Welfare Patterns in GAIN.* New York: Manpower Demonstration Research Corporation, August 13.

Haveman, Robert, and John Palmer, eds. 1983. *Jobs for Disadvantaged Workers: The Economics of Employment Subsidies.* Washington, D.C.: The Brookings Institution.

Herr, Toby, and Robert Halpern. 1991. *Changing What Counts: Re-Thinking the Journey Out of Welfare.* Evanston: Center for Urban Affairs and Policy Research, Northwestern University, April.

Hershey, Alan, and Rebecca Maynard. 1992. "Designing and Implementing Services for Welfare Dependent Teenage Parents: Lessons from the DHHS/OFA-Sponsored Teenage Parent Demonstration." Statement before the House Committee on Ways and Means, March 6.

Hershey, Alan, and Rebecca Maynard. 1992. *Designing Services for Welfare Dependent Teenage Parents.* Princeton: Mathematica Policy Research, Inc. Also testimony before the Senate Finance Committee, April.

Hollister, Robinson, Peter Kemper, and Rebecca A. Maynard. 1984. *The National Supported Work Demonstration.* Madison: University of Wisconsin Press.

Kennedy, David M. 1992. *The Ladder and the Scale: Commitment and Accountability at Project Match.* Cambridge: The John F. Kennedy School of Government, Harvard University.

Kenosha County JOBS Center. 1992. "Annual Report of the Kenosha County JOBS Program." Kenosha, WI: Author.

Kerachsky, Stuart H., Craig V.D. Thornton, Anne Bloomenthal, Rebecca Maynard, and Susan Stephens. 1985. *The Impacts of Transitional Employment for Mentally Retarded Young Adults.* New York: Manpower Demonstration Research Corporation.

Kesselman, Jonathan R. 1978. "Work Relief Programs During the Great Depression." In *Creating Jobs: Public Employment Programs and Wage Subsidies,* edited by John L. Palmer. Washington, DC: The Brookings Institution.

Kirsch, Irwin, and Ann Jungblut. 1986. *Literacy Profiles of America's Young Adults.* Princeton: Educational Testing Service.

Kisker, Ellen, Rebecca A. Maynard, and Margaret Strain. 1989. "The Child Care Challenge: What Parents Need and What is Available in Three Metropolitan Areas." Princeton: Mathematica Policy Research, Inc.

Kohaska, Charles, and Jill Skolnik. 1986. "Employment Suggestions for Learning Disabled Adults." *Academic Therapy* 21(5, May): 573–79.

Konig, A., and Schalock, R. 1991. "Supported Employment: Equal Opportunities for Severely Disabled Men and Women. *International Labour Review* 130(1): 21–37.

Kregel, J., P. Wehman, and D. Banks. 1989. "The Effects of Consumer Characteristics and Type of Employment Model on Individual Outcomes in Supported Employment." *Journal of Applied Behavior Analysis* 22: 407–15.

Kulik, Jane, D. Alton Smith, and Ernst Stromsdorfer. 1978. *The Downriver Dislocated Worker Demonstration Evaluation.* Cambridge: Abt Associates.

Layzer, Jeanne. 1994. "Even Start and the Comprehensive Child Development Program: Lessons for Welfare Reform." Talking points for a seminar on programs for unwed teen mothers. American Enterprise Institute: Washington, D.C., June 9.

Lurie, Irene, and Jan Hagen. 1993. *Implementing JOBS: The Initial Design and Structure of Local Programs.* Albany: The Nelson A. Rockefeller Institute of Government, State University of New York.

Martinson, Karen, and Daniel Friedlander. 1994. *GAIN: Basic Education in a Welfare-to Work Program.* New York: Manpower Demonstration Research Corporation.

Maxfield, Myles. 1988. "Characteristics Employers Prefer in Unskilled Job Applicants." Washington, D.C.: Greater Washington Research Center.

Maynard, Rebecca A. 1993a. *Building Self-Sufficiency Among Welfare-Dependent Teenage Parents.* Princeton: Mathematica Policy Research, Inc., June.

Maynard, Rebecca A. 1993b. *Costs of Employment Support Under Welfare Reform.* Washington, D.C.: U.S. Department of Health and Human Services.

Maynard, Rebecca A. 1994. *Welfare Reform and Young Unwed Mothers: Lessons from the Federal Welfare Reform Demonstration.* Talking points for a seminar on programs for teenage parents. American Enterprise Institute: Washington, D.C., June 9.

Maynard, Rebecca, Walter Nicholson, and Anu Rangarajan. 1992. *Breaking the Cycle of Poverty: The Effectiveness of Mandatory Services for Welfare-Dependent Teenage Parents.* Princeton: Mathematica Policy Research, Inc.

Nathan, Richard. 1993. *Turning Promises into Performance.* New York: Columbia University Press.

Nightingale, Demetra, Regina Yudd, Stacey Anderson, and Burt Barnow.

1991. *The Learning Disabled in Employment and Training Programs.* Washington, D.C.: U.S. Department of Labor.

Nightingale, Demetra S., Douglas A. Wissoker, Lynn C. Burbridge, D. Lee Bawden, and Neal Jeffries. 1990. *Evaluation of the Massachusetts Employment and Training (ET) Choices Program.* Washington, D.C.: The Urban Institute Press.

Olson, L., L. Berg, and A. Conrad. 1990. *High Job Turnover Among the Urban Poor: The Project Match Experience.* Evanston: Center for Urban Affairs and Policy Research, Northwestern University.

Pavetti, La Donna A. 1992. *The Dynamics of Welfare And Work: Exploring the Process by Which Young Women Work Their Way Off Welfare.* Cambridge: Malcolm Wiener Center for Social Policy, John F. Kennedy School of Government, Harvard University, October 29.

Polit, Denise F. 1992. *Barriers to Self-Sufficiency and Avenues to Success Among Teenage Mothers.* Princeton: Mathematica Policy Research, Inc.

Quint, Janet, Judith Musick, and Joyce Ladner. 1994. *Lives of Promise, Lives of Pain: Young Mothers After New Chance.* New York: Manpower Demonstration Research Corporation.

Rangarajan, Anu, David Myers, Harold Beebout, and Rebecca Maynard. 1994. "Life Prospects for Teenage Parents." Talking points for a seminar on the *Causes and Costs of Teenage Pregnancy and Parenting.* American Enterprise Institute: Washington, D.C., April 5.

Rangarajan, Anu, Ellen Eliason Kisker, and Rebecca Maynard. 1992. *Selecting Basic Skills Tests for Program and Evaluation Purposes.* Princeton: Mathematica Policy Research, Inc.

Schochet, Peter Z., and Ellen Eliason Kisker. 1992. *Meeting the Child Care Needs of Disadvantaged Teenage Mothers: Lessons from the Teenage Parent Demonstration.* Princeton: Mathematica Policy Research, Inc.

Strain, Margaret, and Ellen Eliason Kisker. 1989. *Literacy and the Disadvantaged: Analysis of Data from the National Assessment of Educational Progress.* Princeton: Mathematica Policy Research, Inc., August.

Thornton, Craig V. D., and Alan Hershey. 1990. *After REACH: Experiences of AFDC Recipients Who Leave Welfare with a Job.* Princeton: Mathematica Policy Research, Inc.

U.S. Congress. House. Committee on Ways and Means. 1992. *1992 Green Book.* Washington, D.C.: U.S. Government Printing Office.

U.S. Department of Commerce. 1992. *Census of the United States*, Pub. no. P160.85. Washington, D.C.: Economics and Statistics Administration, Bureau of the Census.

U.S. Department of Labor. 1993. *Work and Welfare.* Washington, DC: Employment and Training Administration, June.

Zill, Nicholas, and Christine W. Nord. 1994. *Characteristics of Teen Mothers.*

Paper presented at "The Causes and Costs of Teenage Motherhood." American Enterprise Institute: Washington, D.C., April 5.

Zill, Nicholas, Kristin Moore, and T. Stief. 1991. *Welfare Mothers as Potential Employees: A Statistical Profile Based on National Survey Data.* Washington, D.C.: Child Trends, Inc.

Chapter Six

STIMULATING EMPLOYMENT AND INCREASING OPPORTUNITY FOR THE CURRENT WORK FORCE

Laurie J. Bassi

Welfare provides minimal income to families that have virtually no other means of financial support. A variety of problems lead families to seek public assistance, including poor health, the loss of a wage earner, and inability or unwillingness to find suitable work. At its simplest level, an absence of suitable work can take one of two forms. Either the labor market does not generate enough work, or it does not generate a high enough wage rate to make it in an individual's interest to accept the work. The latter case may be of particular significance to many welfare recipients. Whereas such individuals might be willing to accept employment at $6.00 per hour, they might not perceive it as in their best interest to accept $4.25 per hour (i.e., the minimum wage). If labor market outcomes for low-wage workers could be improved, fewer people would resort to welfare. Consequently, labor market policies designed to improve the employment and earnings prospects of workers could serve as an important adjunct to welfare policy.

This chapter describes the range of active labor market policies that might be used to achieve these purposes. Such policies can be sorted into one of three categories—those that affect the supply of labor, those that affect the demand for labor, and those that affect the process of matching the supply of workers with the demand for them. Some of these policies would not directly affect the welfare population. All of these policies, however, could potentially affect the overall operation of the labor market, which would have indirect effects on the employment and earnings prospects of all prospective workers.

POLICIES AFFECTING SUPPLY OF LABOR

Reemployment Bonuses

A reemployment bonus is a payment made to an unemployed individual when he or she accepts a job offer. The purpose of the bonus is to encourage more rapid reemployment, thereby lowering the overall unemployment rate. One way to design a reemployment bonus is to make the payment for which an unemployed individual is eligible a declining function of the length of time that an individual is unemployed. The idea is that by increasing the implicit cost of postponing acceptance of a job, the unemployed person has an incentive both to search for work more intensively and to accept jobs that he or she might otherwise refuse. Alternatively, the bonus could be paid as a fixed amount (a design that would be more appropriate for the welfare population).

The appeal of the reemployment bonus concept is obvious: the bonuses essentially pay people to leave the condition of unemployment. In effect, they provide a mechanism for distinguishing individuals who are in some sense voluntarily unemployed from those who are involuntarily unemployed. If a fairly modest payment could induce an individual to search more intensively for work and/or to accept a job offer that might otherwise be declined, that individual could be regarded as being voluntarily unemployed. However, if the payment is inadequate to induce such a response, the likelihood increases that the individual is involuntarily unemployed.

Over the past decade, a number of social experiments have been conducted on the reemployment bonus concept (McMurrer 1993). In these experiments, unemployment insurance (UI) recipients were randomly assigned either to a "treatment" group, which was eligible for a reemployment bonus as an alternative to their normal UI benefits, or they were assigned to a "control" group, which received only their normal UI benefits.[1] Both groups of individuals were then followed to assess the effect of the reemployment bonus offer on the speed with which they found jobs, as well as the wage rate of the jobs that were ultimately accepted (McMurrer 1993).

The results from these experiments indicate that reemployment bonuses do, indeed, have the expected effect (McMurrer 1993).[2] Although only 7 percent to 22 percent of those who were potentially eligible for the bonuses actually received them, the average length of unemployment among the *entire* group was reduced from between one-half week to slightly more than a week. The experiments produced no evidence that the bonuses resulted in any reduction in the wage rate of the job that was ultimately accepted. Taken together, these findings indicate that the bonuses operate primarily by increasing the intensity of individuals' job search efforts, rather than by inducing the unemployed to accept lower-paying jobs. However, the low rate of bonus receipt among those who were offered the opportunity indicates that only a minority of the group engaged in an extensive and ultimately effective job search strategy.

There was considerable variation from one reemployment bonus experiment to the next, but the experimental results generally indicate that reemployment bonuses can be a cost-effective means for increasing employment by a modest amount among those offered the bonus. However, these experiments have been unable to assess the effects of employment displacement resulting from the bonuses. To the extent that reemployment bonuses simply result in a reordering of the unemployment queue, the experiments overstate the benefits of the bonuses.

Davidson and Woodbury (1993) have done simulations indicating that the displacement resulting from reemployment bonuses can be substantial, thereby reducing the overall increase in employment that results from bonuses. If the estimated benefit-cost ratios from the experiments are adjusted to incorporate the possibility of substantial displacement effects, the bonuses appear to reduce overall social welfare, rather than increase it (McMurrer 1993: 6). This is particularly likely to be the case during periods of high unemployment when displacement effects are apt to be the largest.

In sum, the findings from reemployment bonus experiments along with the ensuing literature indicate that the effects of such incentives are marginal, at best. These findings are consistent with the interpretation that most UI recipients are involuntarily unemployed.[3] Paying them to find jobs more quickly will have little effect if there aren't jobs for them to find.

It is possible, though, that this type of bonus plan could have a somewhat greater effect on welfare recipients. This would be the case if the primary problem that welfare recipients face in the labor market is low wages (rather than insufficient hours of work).

Wage Subsidies

Wage subsidies represent another potential vehicle for encouraging unemployed individuals to accept jobs more quickly, thereby reducing the length of their unemployment spell as well as the overall rate of unemployment. The idea behind wage subsidies is that by supplementing the wages that an individual receives, some unemployed workers may be willing to accept job offers that they otherwise would not accept.[4] In that sense, the subsidies are similar to reemployment bonuses, except that they are paid to workers over time, rather than in a lump-sum form.

Like reemployment bonuses, the potential effectiveness of wage subsidies depends on the extent to which: (1) a wage subsidy will entice an individual to accept a lower-paying job, (2) the subsidy encourages more intensive job search, and (3) jobs actually exist. The first of these factors is a function of the "elasticity of labor supply," which is a measure of the responsiveness of workers' choices about how much to work in reaction to changes in their wages. Since wage subsidies increase the effective wages that a worker receives (the effective wage is the actual wage plus the subsidy), wage subsidies should increase the supply of labor.[5] A large body of empirical literature indicates that because labor supply is fairly unresponsive to changes in wages (i.e., inelastic), it would take a large increase in wages to induce a substantial labor supply response (Mroz, 1987). The inelastic nature of labor supply indicates that, in general, wage subsidies to workers are likely to be an expensive method for increasing employment levels. However, to the extent that welfare recipients' labor supply is more elastic than that of the general population, wage subsidies targeted at this group would be more effective than untargeted subsidies.

Another limitation to the employment-enhancing potential of wage subsidies to workers is that workers must not only be willing to work, but they must be able to find work. If the supply of workers exceeds the demand for workers, then a wage subsidy that increases supply (even if by a small amount) may result in an increase, rather than a decrease, in unemployment. That is, if there is insufficient demand for workers, wage subsidies to workers may compound the unemployment problem rather than ameliorate it.

Economists have considered a variety of aspects of the operation of the labor market that tend to prevent wages from falling in response to an excess supply of workers.[6] To the extent that these factors create a downward rigidity in wages, wage subsidies targeted at workers with the intent of encouraging them to accept jobs at lower wages will fail to produce the intended results.

Although there are no experiments on the effects of wage subsidies to workers, the results from the reemployment experiments provide useful insights into the overall extent of the labor supply responses that might be expected from offering subsidies. This evidence indicates that subsidizing workers' wages could be expected to have a modest effect on the length of unemployment for those to whom the subsidy was offered, but the effect would be offset by some displacement. During periods of high unemployment, the displacement effects might be so large as to render the policy counterproductive. For reasons discussed earlier, wage subsidies targeted at welfare recipients are less prone to these shortcomings than are untargeted subsidies.

Self-employment Subsidies

An alternative to finding a job with an existing employer is for unemployed individuals to start their own businesses. Insufficient access to start-up capital is, however, often a constraint. For those who are eligible for benefits, the unemployment insurance system could also be a constraint, since UI recipients must be available to accept a job offer in order to continue to be eligible to receive benefits. An individual who has just started a business would be ineligible for UI on these grounds, although the individual may be earning very little (if anything) during the start-up phase of the business.[7]

Great Britain and France have implemented self-employment projects within their unemployment insurance system, and in recent years two demonstration projects in the United States have relaxed the UI rules to provide more help to unemployed workers interested in starting their own businesses.[8] Evidence on the effects of the British and French projects is fairly consistent with early findings from the U.S. demonstration projects. When offered the opportunity, only 2 percent to 4 percent of UI recipients avail themselves of the self-employment option. These individuals tend both to be more highly educated than the average UI recipient and to have higher earnings prior to becoming unemployed.[9] Within one to two years of starting up, a high percentage of their businesses fail, although the failure rate is comparable to that for small, start-up firms in general. Observers of Great Britain's program report that the program results in some displacement; that is to say, some proportion of the businesses would have started up in the absence of the UI program (see Bendick and Egan 1987: 531).

Overall, the results from the demonstration projects in the United States, as well as the programs in France and Great Britain, indicate that modest benefits result from allowing UI recipients the flexibility to start up businesses while receiving assistance (either in the form of living stipends or a lump-sum payment) through the UI system. For the vast majority of UI recipients, however, self-employment does not appear to be a viable option.

Education and Training for Unemployed Workers

A substantial body of empirical evidence indicates that one of the best ways to prevent unemployment is education. Individuals with higher education levels are not only less likely to be unemployed, but they are also less likely to experience a long spell of unemployment should they become unemployed (Advisory Council on Unemployment Compensation 1994: 48). Furthermore, individuals with high levels of education are more likely to receive training from their employers than are those with lower levels of education.[10] Not only does this firm-provided training result in higher earnings for the individual, but it also reduces the likelihood that the individual will be laid off by the firm in response to a temporary economic downturn.

The research evidence is much less clear, however, on the extent to which public policies that provide individuals with additional education and/or training can generate these outcomes. Over the past three decades, the federal government has funded a variety of programs to educate and/or train dislocated workers and economically disadvantaged individuals. By and large, the evaluations of these initiatives are not encouraging.

The results consistently indicate that there are virtually no employment or earnings gains from participating in government-provided education and/or training programs for youth or men.[11] The findings tend to be somewhat more encouraging for women, particularly those women with limited job experience. Even for women, however, the impacts are fairly modest[12] (Barnow 1987, Bloom et al. 1994). The largest gains that result from participating in government-provided education and/or training programs seem to accrue to those individuals who receive on-the-job training, while some of the smallest gains accrue to those individuals who participate in classroom training programs (Barnow et al. 1987).

In contrast, however, those individuals who participate in education and/or training programs that are sponsored by employers (as opposed to government programs) typically enjoy fairly substantial increases in their earnings (see, for example, Lynch 1992; Moore and Blake 1992). And as already mentioned, these individuals are less likely to be laid off by their employers during economic downturns. This suggests that to the extent that government-financed education and training initiatives are used to reduce unemployment and expand economic opportunity, those initiatives should be as closely linked to the private sector as is possible. It appears that, in general, government programs are either ineffective at providing education and training, or they provide participants with information and skills that are not in high demand by employers.

POLICIES AFFECTING DEMAND FOR LABOR

The preceding discussion offers a fairly pessimistic assessment of the efficacy of labor market policies that are designed to influence the supply of labor. It appears that these policies do have the capacity to encourage somewhat more rapid reemployment among a minority of the unemployed, although the impacts could be somewhat larger if the policies were focused on welfare recipients. Some of these gains, however, may come at the expense of other unemployed individuals. This displacement, which amounts to a reordering of the job queue, is likely to be particularly problematic during times of relatively high unemployment. It is precisely at those times when active labor market policy that influences the demand for labor, as opposed to the supply of labor, is likely to be most efficacious.[13]

Employment Tax Credits

The demand-side analog to paying workers to leave unemployment (i.e., reemployment bonuses) is to pay employers to hire unemployed workers. Offering tax credits to employers who hire unemployed individuals represents a fairly simple mechanism for the government to increase the demand for labor, thereby increasing employment levels and lowering unemployment.[14]

In practice, however, accomplishing this goal is anything but simple. First, a long list of design questions must be addressed, foremost among which is determining the conditions under which employers would be eligible for a tax credit. Presumably, only employers who increased their employment levels over the level prevailing in some previous period would be eligible for a credit.[15] In addition, consideration would have to be given to the types of employment increases that would qualify an employer for the tax credit. For example, a restriction might be made that the new workers hired must have been unemployed or economically disadvantaged in order to count toward increasing the level of employment for the purpose of calculating the tax credit.

The more restrictions that are applied to the conditions that qualify the firm for a tax credit, the smaller will be the employment gain resulting from it. However, these are precisely the conditions that minimize the cost to the government per job created.[16] The reason for this is as follows. The only way to entice firms to hire more workers than they otherwise would is to make it profitable for them to do so. That is, the larger the windfall profits to the firm, the greater will be both the increase in employment and the cost per new job created.

Therein lies the fundamental political problem with employer tax credits. If the tax credits are successful in creating jobs, that success is inevitably the result of a redistribution of income that favors the already privileged (the owners of capital). To the extent that the tax credit is narrowly focused on a particular category of workers (e.g., the economically disadvantaged), the dual problem of large windfalls to firms and high cost per job created is ameliorated. However, concerns then arise about the extent to which those individuals who qualify the firm for the tax credit will simply displace other individuals who do not qualify for the credit. The extent to which such displacement actually occurs is a function of the ease with which firms can substitute one type of worker for another in response to changes in their relative wages resulting from the tax credit.[17]

The U.S. experience with employment tax credits has been limited to the New Jobs Tax Credit (NJTC) and the Targeted Jobs Tax Credit (TJTC).[18] The NJTC, available only in 1977 and 1978, was intended to provide counter cyclical stimulus. The TJTC, as the name implies, was intended to stimulate employment of certain categories of workers, and has been continuously available (with some modifications) since 1978.[19]

Evaluating the impact of these two employment tax credits has proven to be difficult, and the literature arrives at somewhat mixed conclusions about the overall effectiveness of this approach to stimulating employment (Barnow et al. 1990). There does appear to be a consensus, however, that the effectiveness of both the TJTC and the NJTC has been restricted by the complexity of the rules governing the credit. Furthermore, the impact of the credits has been limited by the fact that many employers have not known of their existence. In addition, there is some evidence that the TJTC has stigmatized those individuals who were eligible for it, reducing employers' willingness to hire them (Burtless 1985). On the other hand, especially with the NJTC, there seem to have been considerable windfalls among some of the employers who did avail themselves of the credit.

The bottom line emerging from the research on these programs is that carefully designed, well-publicized employment credits may have the capacity to stimulate employment (either in general, or for a targeted category), although some windfall profit is created for employers (Barnow et al. 1990).

Training Tax Credits or Grants

An alternative to providing financial incentives to employers to hire additional workers is to provide incentives for firm-sponsored education and/or training. As previously mentioned, employer-provided training represents one of the best ways to prevent unemployment, as well as to promote wage growth for workers who receive it.

In recent years, a growing number of state governments have been offering training tax credits or grants to employers, either as an incentive to entice prospective employers to settle within the state or to enhance the earnings of the states' citizens. As of 1990, 46 states had at least one state-financed training program (Barnow et al. 1990). Although a few of these programs have been in existence for decades, the majority of them were created in the late 1980s in response to a growing perception that the private sector was providing less than the optimal amount of training.

As with employment tax credits, careful consideration must be given to the design of these programs so that additional training is created without leading to excessive windfall profits to firms by subsidizing them to provide training they would have provided anyway. The states have addressed this problem in a variety of ways, including limiting the types of firms that are eligible for the training programs (e.g., financially distressed firms) and/or limiting the types of training that the program will subsidize (e.g., basic skills training rather than job-specific training). States have funded the programs in a variety of ways, ranging from general revenues, to lottery funds, to earmarked payroll taxes that have typically been diverted from the UI trust funds. The level of funding of these programs has ranged from $50,000 in Vermont to $55 million in California (Barnow et al. 1990: 15).

There are very few formal evaluations of these state-sponsored programs. Several evaluations have found that state training grants often serve as a catalyst to encourage firms to embark on training programs and ultimately to invest more of their own resources in training (see Bassi 1994; Creticos and Sheets 1989). While the findings from these studies must be considered preliminary, they provide no evidence that state-financed training initiatives are simply displacing private spending that would otherwise occur. The finding of minimal (or no) displacement is undoubtedly at least partially the result of the targeting mechanisms that states use, which attempt to identify those firms (e.g., small and/or financially distressed) that are least likely to provide training.

Two studies have attempted to identify the effect of such programs on the workers themselves, using data from California's Employment Training Panel (ETP) Program (see Moore and Blake 1992; Moore, Wilms, and Bolus 1988).[20] Both studies found that workers who completed courses of training provided through the ETP Program enjoyed significantly higher earnings and lower unemployment over the course of a follow-up period that lasted several years. What these studies are unable to determine, however, is the extent to which these findings are merely the result of "self-selection."[21] Nonetheless, the gains to workers in these programs do appear to be larger than those accruing to participants in postsecondary vocational training (taught, for example, at a community college) (Moore and Blake 1992: iii). Once again, although preliminary, these findings are consistent with the interpretation that education and/or training for adult workers is most valuable when it takes place within firms.

In sum, the preliminary evidence from state-sponsored education and training programs is promising. There is little (or no) evidence that displacement is a serious problem, and the gains to the workers in these firms may be large.

Economic Development Initiatives

Training tax credits and grants are often one component of a larger financial package consisting of other tax incentives and/or infrastructure improvements that states offer firms either to encourage them to expand or to entice additional firms to locate within the state. In some cases, these packages are offered only in specially designated "enterprise zones" that have persistently high unemployment rates.

In general, the evaluation literature on the effectiveness of these economic development initiatives has been less than optimistic. A consensus seems to be emerging that state (and local) governments often give away more in benefits to firms than the residents recoup in return.[22] Furthermore, states (and localities) may be involved in a "zero-sum" game where they bid for a fixed number of employers (and jobs); when one state wins, another loses. In this situation, the primary beneficiaries of economic development initiatives are firms and their stockholders.

The evidence on enterprise zones is only slightly more optimistic, with some authors cautiously concluding that even though enterprise zones are no panacea, notable improvements in economic activity have occurred in some cases.[23] However, there appears to be no research on the cost-effectiveness of using enterprise zones for job creation.[24] Moreover, whatever the job-creation potential of enterprise zones, it must be kept in mind that at least some of the new jobs created will undoubtedly be at the expense of jobs that would have been created elsewhere.

Short-Time Compensation Programs

When firms experience downturns in demand, an alternative to laying off workers is to implement a "work-sharing" program that reduces the number of hours of work among a broader group of workers. By adjusting hours of work instead of the number of workers, the cost of unemployment (both financial and otherwise) is broadly shared, rather than being borne by a relatively small proportion of workers. At the same time, a participating firm is able to retain its skilled workers and avoid the costs of hiring new workers when demand is restored to its previous level.

The unemployment insurance system may, however, represent an impediment to work-sharing. Since even a modest level of earnings is sufficient to disqualify individuals from receiving UI, workers as a group may prefer layoff of some among them (who could then collect UI), rather than having to share the entire income loss without any offsetting compensation from the UI system.

Short-time Compensation (STC) programs represent an innovation within the UI system that can be used to encourage work-sharing as an alternative to unemployment. By relaxing the earnings disqualification, it is possible to use the UI system to compensate workers for some portion of the earnings that they lose due to work-sharing. A number of European countries, most notably Germany, have relied on STC programs for many years as a means of alleviating the hardship associated with unemployment.[25] The first STC program in the United States was introduced in California in 1978. Since then, 16 other states have implemented similar programs. In a typical STC program, workers work four days a week and receive UI benefits for the fifth day of each week. On average, UI benefits replace about 35 percent of lost earnings (Advisory Council on Unemployment Compensation 1994: 25).

As with most labor market policies, it is very difficult to isolate the impact of STC programs. In general, however, the evaluations of STC programs are quite positive, indicating that the benefits of the programs outweigh the costs, and that under some circumstances (and assumptions), the net benefits of the programs can be substantial. The programs are not, however, cost-saving from the government's perspective. That is to say, they result in larger outlays from the UI trust funds than would occur if layoffs were used as the alternative.

Despite their apparent benefits, the utilization of STC programs in those states that allow them has been low, and much lower than utilization rates in other countries.[26] There are a number of possible explanations for this, including: (1) employers do not know about the program; (2) fringe benefits represent an impediment to STC;[27] (3) the application and certification processes are burdensome; (4) the experience rating of the U.S. unemployment insurance system acts as a deterrent.

As it now stands, the minimal utilization of STC programs in the United States limits their potential for reducing unemployment. If some of the problems just outlined could be overcome, the evaluation literature indicates that STC may represent a viable alternative for relieving some of the worst suffering that unemployment causes. It is important to note, however, that such programs can, at best, deal with the symptoms of unemployment, not its underlying causes. If the programs are mistaken as a real cure, it is possible they could do more harm than good.

MATCHING SUPPLY OF LABOR WITH DEMAND FOR LABOR

Economists have long been interested in the processes by which unemployed workers find job vacancies and, in turn, by which employers find appropriate job applicants. Whereas some of the time spent in these search processes is productive for the unemployed individual, in that it can lead to a better matching of worker skills and preferences with employer needs, too much time spent in search is wasteful. There is a clear role for public policies that reduce these inefficiencies by providing useful, cost-effective information about the labor market. Unemployed individuals need information about what types of jobs are available, where the jobs are to be found, what they pay, and the skills they require. Similarly, employers need information about the availability of workers who have the necessary skills.

Providing Labor Market Information

Relative to the other developed nations, the United States spends a low percentage of its gross domestic product on the provision of labor market information that could help smooth the matching of workers' skills with employers' requirements (Organization for Economic Cooperation and Development 1990). The U.S. Employment

Service (ES), the only public facility charged with providing information either to job seekers or prospective employers, has experienced
substantial cuts in its budget over the past decade. In inflation-
adjusted dollars, ES funding fell by 20 percent between 1979 and
1993 (Jacobson 1994). In per capita terms, the 1993 expenditures
amounted to about $6 per member of the labor force.

For many years, the predominant view, both inside and outside
of the federal government, has been that the ES doesn't work. Some
critics have gone so far as to suggest that the ES should be abolished,
while others believe that its functions should be privatized (Kulik,
1994). There are at least two possible explanations for the widespread
disenchantment with the ES: first, that it is a badly functioning system; and, second, that it is an underfunded system. These two explanations are, of course, not mutually exclusive. It is entirely possible
that the ES functions badly *because* it is underfunded. Furthermore,
by law the ES is required to provide employment assistance to anyone
who seeks it. The evidence is clear that those who rely on the ES
are among the least advantaged of the labor force, and so the ES must
help to find jobs for some of the least employable people. As a result,
it compares badly to private-sector employment agencies that are
able to screen out difficult-to-place individuals.

The fact that those who avail themselves of the ES are, on average,
substantially more disadvantaged than other job seekers makes it
difficult to isolate the effect of the ES. Two recent reviews of the
research literature on the ES, however, both conclude that the ES
does represent a cost-effective means of helping unemployed individuals find jobs more quickly than they otherwise would (Jacobson
1994; Kulik 1994). It appears that the ES is more effective in helping
women find employment than it is for men, and there is considerable
variation in the effectiveness of the ES both between and within
states.

Whereas the evaluation literature indicates there is considerable
room for improvement both in the quantity and quality of services
that the ES delivers, it is encouraging that the ES appears to have
accomplished as much as it has, given the limited resources at its
disposal. Given the explosion in low-cost information technology,
additional funding to install up-to-date equipment in more Employment Service offices could represent a wise expenditure.

In addition, incentives could be provided for more employers to
list their job openings with the ES. Because the job openings listed
at the ES tend to be predominantly low-skill, low-wage jobs, workers
with high skills tend not to use the Employment Service. As a result,

employers tend not to list their better jobs with the ES. This downward spiral in the quality of job listings will, admittedly, be difficult to reverse. But the increasing availability of technology that makes large volumes of information simultaneously available to large numbers of individuals (and employers) argues that this is the time to attempt to upgrade the ES.

Providing Relocation Assistance

Another mechanism for facilitating a better match between job openings and unemployed workers is to provide relocation assistance to the unemployed. There are at least two justifications for such assistance. First, moving is expensive, and the unemployed are the least likely to be able to incur the expenses of relocation. Second, pockets of unemployment can persist for extended periods. For example, during the past decade the unemployment rate in West Virginia has remained at least 50 percent above the national rate, and at times has been twice that. For many individuals in such depressed labor markets, it is likely that the only way they will be able to find jobs is to relocate. This obvious need has led the federal government to experiment with a number of relocation demonstration projects, in which workers have been provided with financial assistance for moving expenses should they find a job outside their current geographic area. Results from the literature evaluating the effectiveness of these relocation demonstration projects and experiments, however, are not encouraging (Cook et al. 1994).

A recent experiment in New Jersey, for example, indicated that providing unemployed individuals with job search *and* relocation assistance did not result in any better reemployment outcomes than resulted from simply providing individuals with job search assistance alone. The only conditions under which relocation assistance appears to be remotely effective are in labor markets that are the most profoundly depressed, and even then the assistance only seems effective for some of the youngest members of the labor force. In most other situations, relocation assistance does not appear to be a cost-effective mechanism for assisting the unemployed in finding new jobs (Cook et al. 1994).

SUMMARY AND CONCLUSIONS

Active labor market policy designed to improve the employment and earnings opportunities of workers can take one of three forms. One category of policy attempts to affect labor supply either by creating incentives for the unemployed to search more intensively for work, or by reducing the wage rate at which unemployed workers are willing to accept employment.[28] The results from the reemployment bonus literature indicate that this type of policy can have, at best, a marginal effect on employment. During times of high unemployment, however, such policies might actually be counterproductive. In essence, encouraging the unemployed to accept jobs does not improve the situation if the constraining factor is the demand for labor, rather than the supply of it. The pessimism of this conclusion should, however, be moderated for supply-side policies targeted at welfare recipients. To the extent that low wages—rather than low demand for labor—represent the primary problem for this group, then targeted supply-side policies might be more beneficial than untargeted policies.

Investing in the employment and training of unemployed individuals is intended to affect the quality of labor, rather than the quantity of it. Although this sounds like a reasonable strategy, a mounting body of empirical evidence suggests that such efforts are generally not cost-effective when provided by the government. Firm-provided education and training, on the other hand, appears quite effective in increasing an individual's earnings and lowering his or her probability of unemployment. This suggests that future publicly financed education and training efforts should be more closely linked to the private sector than has been the case in the past.

The second category of labor market policy attempts to affect the demand for labor. Although there is evidence that demand is typically more of a constraint in the labor market than is supply, the United States has experimented in a limited manner with policies that focus on increasing the demand for labor. These efforts (TJTC and NJTC) have not met with resounding success. There appears to be some hope, however, that well-structured, well-publicized, demand-enhancing initiatives could be effective. If these initiatives could be tied to efforts that promote firm-provided education and training for workers, there is reason to believe that the long-run employment and earnings prospects of workers could be improved.

A potentially worthwhile strategy might be to offer low-income, unemployed individuals a time-limited voucher that could be used in one of two ways. The individual could cash in the voucher upon accepting a job (i.e., a reemployment bonus), or the individual could turn the voucher over to an employer who could then cash it in (i.e., a wage subsidy to the firm). The advantage of this approach is that it would encourage more intensive job search by the unemployed (i.e., affect labor supply), but at the same time would have the capacity to stimulate the demand for labor in cases where that is the constraining factor. An alternative, but undoubtedly more expensive, policy would be to offer *both* wage subsidies to low-income individuals and employment subsidies to employers who hired such individuals. The effectiveness of both approaches would be enhanced by combining them with state (or federal) programs to stimulate firm-financed education and training. The combination holds the promise of creating both long-term and short-term improvements in employment and earnings.

Finally, providing better labor market information to the unemployed—the third category of labor market policy—is likely to be a cost-effective method for reducing the length of time it takes for the unemployed to find jobs.

The evidence in this chapter makes clear that there is no silver bullet. Policies that stimulate the supply of labor without affecting the demand for it are likely to enjoy limited success. On the other hand, active labor market policy that stimulates the demand for employment, encourages employers to provide more education and training to workers, and provides the unemployed with better labor market information would represent steps in the right direction.

In the end, there is no substitute for a strong labor market. Active labor market policy can serve as a complement to macroeconomic policy, but it cannot be a substitute for it. Both are needed if the employment and earnings prospects of low-wage workers are to improve.

Notes

This chapter is based heavily on work done by the author for the Advisory Council on Unemployment Compensation. Portions of it will be included in the council's 1995 report and appear here with permission of the Advisory Council on Unemployment Compensation.

1. The bonuses ranged from twice the weekly UI benefit to one-half of the remaining UI payments for which an individual would be eligible before exhausting all benefits.

2. This summary of results from the reemployment bonuses is based on McMurrer's (1993) synthesis of four reemployment experiments.

3. Abraham's (1983) findings support this interpretation. She reported that the number of workers looking for jobs generally is substantially in excess of the number of job

vacancies. During the late 1970s, for example, she estimated a ratio of 5.0 between job seekers and job vacancies.

4. Wage subsidies could either be permanent or temporary. Since permanent wage subsidies are, for all intents and purposes, a form of income redistribution rather than a tool for active labor market policy, they are not considered.

5. Consistent with the findings of the empirical literature, this statement is based on the assumption that there is a non-negative elasticity of labor supply (i.e., that the substitution effect outweighs the income effect).

6. Some of the sources of downward rigidity in wages considered by economists include imperfect information, the existence of contracts (either implicit or explicit), and minimum wage legislation. See Davidson (1990) for an excellent review of many of these issues.

7. A recent legislative change in the United States allows states the option of incorporating a self-employment option into their UI programs.

8. One demonstration project (in the state of Washington) provided lump-sum payments to UI recipients, in lieu of their regular UI benefits. Another demonstration (in New Jersey) provided regular UI benefits to individuals who were starting up their own businesses, even though these individuals were unavailable for work should they receive a job offer.

9. Since UI recipients are, on average, more highly educated than welfare recipients, this suggests that self-employment programs would be helpful to an even smaller fraction of the latter group.

10. See, for example, Brown (1989) for a review of the literature on this issue.

11. See, for example, Barnow (1987) for a review of the evaluation literature, and Bloom et al. (1993, 1994) for recent evidence from the JTPA experiment.

12. Those positive outcomes that do exist for women seem to be primarily attributable to an increase in the number of hours that women work, rather than to an increase in their hourly wage rate.

13. An alternative to active labor market policy is expansionary macroeconomic policy, discussion of which is beyond the scope of this chapter.

14. Alternatively, unemployed workers could be given vouchers that would enable employers who hire them to get an immediate rebate, rather than waiting until they file taxes.

15. Otherwise, the tax credit would generate very large windfall profits to firms relative to the number of jobs created.

16. This point is demonstrated by Bassi (1985).

17. The magnitude of the displacement would tend to be offset to the extent that the tax credit generated an overall increase in economic activity, thereby increasing the demand for all categories of workers (including those subject to displacement).

18. Other similar tax credits have been for research (the Research and Experimentation Tax Credit) and investment (the Investment Tax Credit). A recent literature review by Barnow et al. (1990) indicates that the lessons learned from the evaluations of these two alternative types of credits are essentially analogous to those from the NJTC and the TJTC.

In addition, the Illinois reemployment bonus experiment included a subcomponent that experimented with bonuses to employers (see Woodbury and Spiegelman 1987). (Since bonuses are equivalent to subsidies, except that they are paid in lump-sum form, the results from the Illinois experiment are relevant to this discussion.) Essentially, the findings were consistent with those from the evaluations of the tax credits. Bonuses to employers had marginal effects, and the effects seemed to result almost entirely from increased hiring of women.

19. The credit is only available to certain categories of economically disadvantaged and/or handicapped individuals.

20. Funds for these programs are generated through an earmarked payroll tax. In essence, this payroll tax represents a diversion of UI trust funds, since at the inception of the program, the UI payroll tax was reduced by the amount of the training payroll tax so as to hold employers harmless.

21. If it is the most able and/or most motivated individuals who enroll in and complete such programs, the fact that these individuals have higher earnings and lower unemployment after the program may be caused by their greater ability, rather than by the program itself.

22. See, for example, Milward and Newman (1989) for a review of the research on this issue.

23. See Rubin (1990) for a review of the empirical literature on enterprise zones.

24. Rubin (1990) did attempt a cost-effectiveness study for enterprise zones in New Jersey. Her analysis, however, was simply based on returns to state expenditures, rather than focusing on job creation.

25. Most of the material in the remainder of this section is based on a 1993 literature review of STC programs by KRA Corporation (Cook, Brinsko, and Tan 1993).

26. In states with programs, the average usage has been about 0.2 percent of UI claimants, whereas in Germany the usage rate has ranged from 10 percent to 17 percent.

27. Most states do not require the ongoing payment of fringe benefits in order for a firm and its employees to qualify for an STC program. Nevertheless, most participating firms do continue to provide fringe benefits.

28. This latter option could include self-employment as an alternative to accepting a job offer from an existing firm.

References

Abraham, Katherine. 1983. "Structural/Frictional vs. Deficient Demand Unemployment." *American Economic Review* 73(4): 708–24.

Advisory Council on Unemployment Compensation. 1994. *Report and Recommendations.* Transmitted to the president and Congress. Washington, D.C.

Bailey, Martin Neil, Gary Burtless, and Robert E. Litan. 1993. *Growth with Equity.* Washington, D.C.: Brookings Institution.

Barnow, Burt S. 1987. "The Impact of CETA Programs on Earnings." *Journal of Human Resources* 22(2): 158–93.

Barnow, Burt S., Amy B. Chasanov, and Abhay Pande. 1990. "Financial Incentives for Employer-Provided Worker Training: A Review of Relevant Experience in the U.S. and Abroad." Prepared for U.S. Department of Labor, Employment and Training Administration, Washington, D.C. Photocopy.

Bassi, Laurie J. 1985. "Evaluating Alternative Job Creation Strategies." *Economic Inquiry* 23: 671–90.

_____. 1994. "Workplace Education for Hourly Workers." *Journal of Policy Analysis and Management* 13(1): 55–74.

Bendick, Marc, Jr., and Mary Lou Egan. 1987. "Transfer Payment Diversion for Small Business Development: British and French Experience." *Industrial and Labor Relation Review* 40(4): 528–42.

Benus, Jacob M., Michelle L. Wood, and Christopher J. Napierala. 1992. "Self-Employment Programs for Unemployed Workers." Unemployment Insurance Occasional Paper 92-2. Washington, D.C.: U.S. Department of Labor, Employment and Training Administration.

Bishop, John H., and Mark Montgomery. 1993. "Does the Targeted Jobs Tax Credit Create Jobs at Subsidized Firms?" *Industrial Relations* 32(3): 289–306.

Bloom, Howard S., Larry L. Orr, George Cave, Stephen H. Bell, and Fred Doolittle. 1993. "Title IIA Impacts on Earnings and Employment at 18 Months." In *The National JTPA Study.* Bethesda: Abt Associates.

Bloom, Howard S., Larry L. Orr, George Cave, Stephen H. Bell, Fred Doolittle, and Winston Lin. 1994. "Overview: Impacts, Benefits, and Costs of Title II-A." In *The National JTPA Study.* Bethesda: Abt Associates.

Brown, Charles. 1989. "Empirical Evidence on Private Training." In *Labor Economics and Public Policy*, edited by Laurie Bassi and David Crawford. Greenwich: JAI Press.

Burtless, Gary. 1985. "Are Targeted Wage Subsidies Harmful? Evidence from a Wage Voucher Experiment." *Industrial and Labor Relations Review* 39(1): 105–14.

Cook, Robert F., Anthony Brinsko, and Alexandra Tan. 1993. *Short-Time Compensation: A Literature Review.* KRA Corporation report prepared for Advisory Council on Unemployment Compensation, Silver Spring: KRA Corporation.

Cook, Robert F., Tony Brinsko, Jenifer Elmas, and Alexandra G. Tan. 1994. *"Government-Funded Relocation Assistance."* KRA Corporation report prepared for Advisory Council on Unemployment Compensation. Silver Spring: KRA Corporation.

Creticos, Peter A., and Robert G. Sheets. 1989. *State-Financed, Workplace-Based Retraining Programs: A Joint Study of the National Commission for Employment Policy and the National Governors' Association.* Washington, D.C.: National Commission for Employment Policy.

Davidson, Carl. 1990. *Recent Developments in the Theory of Involuntary Unemployment.* Kalamazoo: Upjohn Institute.

Davidson, Carl, and Stephen A. Woodbury. 1993. "The Displacement Effects of Reemployment Bonus Programs." *Journal of Labor Economics* 11(4): 575–605.

Devine, Theresa, and Nicholas M. Kiefer. 1991. *Empirical Labor Economics: The Search Approach.* New York: Oxford University Press.

Jacobson, Louis. 1994. "The Effectiveness of the U.S. Employment Service." Report prepared for the Advisory Commission on Unemployment Compensation, U.S. Department of Labor, Washington, D.C. Draft.

Johnson, Terry R., and Janice J. Leonard. 1992. "Self-Employment Programs for Unemployed Workers." Unemployment Insurance Occasional Paper 92-2. Washington, D.C.: U.S. Department of Labor, Employment and Training Administration.

Kulik, Jane. 1994. *The Evolution of the U.S. Employment Service and A Review of Evidence Concerning Its Operations and Effectiveness.* Report prepared for the Advisory Council on Unemployment Compensation. Washington, D.C.: U.S. Department of Labor.

Lynch, Lisa M. 1992. "Private-Sector Training and the Earnings of Young Workers." *American Economic Review* 82(1):299–312.

McMurrer, Daniel. 1993. "Reemployment Bonuses: Summary." Report prepared for the Advisory Council on Unemployment Compensation. U.S. Department of Labor, Washington, D.C. Draft.

Milward, H. Brinton, and Heidi Hosbach Newman. 1989. "State Incentive Packages and the Industrial Location Decision." *Economic Development Quarterly* 3(3): 203–22.

Moore, Richard W., and Daniel Blake. 1992. *Does ETP Training Work? An Analysis of the Economic Outcomes of California Employment Training Panel Programs.* Northridge: California State University, Northridge School of Business Administration and Economics.

Moore, Richard W., Wellford W. Wilms, and Roger E. Bolus. 1988. *Training for Change: An Analysis of the Outcomes of California Employment Training Panel Programs.* Santa Monica: Training Research Corporation.

Mroz, Thomas A. 1987. "The Sensitivity of an Empirical Model of Married Women's Hours of Work to Economic and Statistical Assumptions." *Econometrica* 55(4): 765–99.

Organization for Economic Cooperation and Development. 1990. *Labor Market Policies for the 1990s.* Paris: Author.

Rubin, Marilyn. 1990. "Urban Enterprise Zones: Do They Work? Evidence from New Jersey." *Public Budgeting and Finance* 10(4): 3–16.

Storey, James R., and Jennifer A. Neisner. 1992. *Unemployment Compensation in the Group of Seven Nations: An International Comparison.* Washington, D.C.: U.S. Congressional Research Service.

Woodbury, Stephen A., and Robert G. Spiegelman. 1987. "Bonsues to Workers and Employers to Reduce Unemployment Randomized Trials in Illinois." *American Economic Review* 77(4): 513–30.

Chapter Seven

OUT-OF-WELFARE STRATEGIES FOR WELFARE-BOUND YOUTH

Hillard Pouncy and Ronald B. Mincy

To deliver on the president's popular campaign promise to "end welfare as we know it," the Clinton administration's welfare reform bill proposes radical changes inside and outside the welfare system. Changes inside the welfare system would increase participation in a more effective JOBS program. Changes outside the welfare system would provide enough cash and noncash assistance to enable a single parent, working full-time and full-year, to raise family income above the poverty level. That assistance includes: increases in the Earned Income Tax Credit, which passed in the 1993 Omnibus Budget Reconciliation Act; expanded health care coverage, which is before the Congress; and increases in child support payments, through a set of initiatives that are part of the current welfare reform effort.

Other outside-of-welfare programs can help welfare-bound youth avoid the welfare system entirely. Although it is hard to predict which young people will become welfare recipients, welfare-bound youth certainly include young women who have out-of-wedlock births before completing school or acquiring work experience. The term *welfare-bound youth* also should include young men whose early sexual activity, school performance, and work experience make it likely that they will become unwed fathers, unable to support their children. Given the higher rates of welfare enrollment, school failure, dropping out, teenage pregnancy, and joblessness among inner-city youth, this chapter focuses on the inner-city segment of the welfare-bound population. We also focus on school-to-work and training tax policies, two major outside-of-welfare ideas that could, with the modifications discussed, substantially reduce future poverty and welfare use among inner-city poor.

More specifically, we review three barriers—a "spatial mismatch," a "hard skills" gap, and a "soft skills" problem—that limit the effectiveness of the School to Work Opportunities Act for welfare-bound youth. The administration's efforts to prevent future welfare enrollments depend on this robust training program and others like it. We note initiatives that could surmount the spatial mismatch and the hard skills gap in school-to-work programs. We also review a demand-side training tax that helps address the spatial mismatch and hard skills gap through training programs for out-of-school welfare-bound youth. We then suggest that mediators and advocates be made available to provide youth and employers with the services needed to surmount the soft skills problem and increase retention rates in inner-city training programs. Finally, we suggest a national support structure of technical assistance groups to help local and state officials implement initiatives to increase the effectiveness of school-to-work programs for welfare-bound youth.

CRAVING FOR SKILLS

The United States economy has increasingly emphasized the need for job-related skills. In fact, a shift in the demand for labor toward experienced and college-trained workers is an important part of the rising wage inequality and "working poverty" of the previous decade (Bound and Freeman 1991; Burtless 1993; Levitan and Shapiro 1987). This shift in relative demand was broad-based, affecting all industries; shifts of employment to skill-intensive industries have played a relatively minor role (Murphy and Welch 1988). Hence, to be successful in the labor market, either young people need to leave school with job-related skills, or employers must provide such skills training, especially to those new entrants with the lowest skills. On both counts we now fail.

Because typical high school graduates lack job-related skills, they must wait up to seven years before forming a stable attachment to the labor market (Bishop 1987; Lerman 1994). Moreover, employers of younger workers rarely provide training, and when they do, the most disadvantaged young workers—women and minorities—are least likely to receive it (Lynch 1989). One important reason for the dearth of employer-provided training is the well-known poaching problem; employers are afraid that if they provide expensive, high-skill training, other firms will "poach" those workers and avoid training costs (Howard 1991).

> In a world where workers often lack skills and where no common
> institutions exist to train them, companies often rationally choose to

concentrate on low-skill forms of work organization. And because they adapt their business strategy to the low-skill environment, they perceive their 'need' for worker training as correspondingly low. (ibid.)

These firms remain extremely profitable by following a low-wage, low-skill path. However, the strategy is disastrous for the living standard of young American workers.

This broad-based craving for skills coupled with the inadequate skills and training available to most younger workers means that working poverty is a potential problem for a large share of young workers and their families (Children's Defense Fund 1991). Thus, antipoverty policy should focus on improving the skills of most non–college-bound workers.

SKILLS-BASED ANTIPOVERTY EFFORT

In the 1980s antipoverty policy discussions often divided the working from the nonworking poor. Advocates for the former asked that we "make work pay." The Bush administration responded with increases in both the minimum wage and the Earned Income Tax Credit.

Debates about antipoverty policies for the nonworking poor centered on the role of education and training versus the role of behavioral change strategies. For example, liberals advocated a substantial increase in employment training services for welfare recipients. The result was the JOBS program. Conservatives sought to control the marital, fertility, and schooling decisions of the welfare population through a number of state welfare demonstrations, such as learnfare and bridefare. At best, these policies of the 1980s tried to subsidize the earnings of those with minimal skills or to require those with marginal attachments to the labor force to acquire minimal skills and work.

Today, antipoverty policy should meet the needs of the working and nonworking poor simultaneously by focusing on the declining demand for low-skilled labor. Such a policy upgrades the skills of both the working and nonworking poor. That is, it shifts up the bottom tail of the skill distribution. This would not only have enormous economic benefits but would help diffuse divisive policy discussions about the working poor, the underclass, and racial inequality in the United States.

There are three significant barriers to the success of such a policy. The first is the "spatial mismatch" problem. The job opportunities of inner-city poor and of inner-city high school graduates are restricted by declining urban labor markets, while most of the growth in metropolitan-area employment has been occurring outside the central cities. To overcome this spatial mismatch, policymakers must provide more opportunities for inner-city high school graduates in the same growing suburban labor markets where most other noncollege youth will find employment. We term this a universal placement strategy.

The second barrier is the "hard skills" problem. The basic mathematics, reading, and higher-order thinking skills of inner-city high school graduates and many nonworking poor adults are lower than the corresponding skills of other noncollege youth. To overcome the hard skills problem, policymakers must target basic skills training to youth and nonworking poor adults in inner cities. And they must couple this targeted training strategy with the universal placement strategy just mentioned.

The third barrier is the "soft skills" problem. Inner-city youth are isolated from others in society by housing segregation. As a result, they have developed a subculture—including language, demeanor, dress codes, and patterns of interpersonal relations—that leads to ridicule and conflict in the American workplace (Bourgois 1991; Majors, with Billson 1992), and at the same time makes it difficult for these youth to value the norms of the workplace. To overcome the soft-skills problem, policymakers must supplement targeted training and universal placement strategies with mentors, mediators, and career guides to help both employers and young workers accommodate one another.

BARRIERS TO POVERTY POLICY

The Clinton administration's School to Work Opportunities Act can help upgrade the skills of the average non–college-bound youth, but as currently implemented the act is unlikely to help inner-city youth because it does not overcome the barriers just discussed. The reasons for this are discussed in the subsections following.

Spatial Mismatch

Ihlanfeldt and Sjoquist (1990) singled out Philadelphia's metropolitan region as a classic example of the spatial mismatch problem plaguing urban youth. This problem is illustrated in figure 7.1. Like its major urban counterparts on the East Coast, the industrial Midwest, and parts of the West Coast, Philadelphia (labeled *E* in the figure) is surrounded by a technology-based, high-growth suburban corridor (Hughes, with Sternberg 1992). This corridor is Route 202, running through Bucks County (*A*), Montgomery County (*B*), Chester County (*C*) and Delaware County (*D*), down to Wilmington, Del. and New Castle County (*H*). The entire Philadelphia standard metropolitan statistical area (SMSA) also includes two counties in New Jersey (Camden [*F*] and Gloucester [*G*]).

Philadelphia's metropolitan region lost 79,000 manufacturing jobs between 1977 and 1987, with the largest losses in the city proper. The region gained 97,000 retail jobs, but 93 percent of these were in the high-growth corridor. It gained 258,000 service jobs; 81 percent of these jobs were within the counties along Route 202 (Hughes 1993).

Recent data from the Philadelphia metropolitan region show how uneven job growth affects employment prospects for urban and suburban youth. Noncollege urban youth are less likely to find a full- or part-time job than their suburban counterparts (see table 7.1), although the gap is not as wide as one might initially expect. In 1988, white male suburban teenagers had an 85 percent chance of getting some type of job, while their urban counterparts had a 74.3 percent chance. Black male suburban teenagers had an 83.2 percent chance, and their urban counterparts had a 71.7 percent probability. The corresponding percentages for women were much lower: 68.7 percent for suburban white women versus 52.8 percent for urban white women; and 65.8 percent for suburban black women versus 49.5 percent for their urban counterparts.

Both urban and suburban youth had a tough time securing full-time work. Black male suburban teenagers actually had a slightly higher chance of finding a job than their white suburban counterparts (42.7 percent versus 40.9 percent, respectively), but all white and black male suburban youth had a better chance at finding a job than their city counterparts (32.6 percent versus 31 percent, respectively). The percentages were dramatically lower for women in both suburbs and city: 17.3 percent and 16.3 percent for black and white suburban women, respectively; and 12 percent and 11.2 percent for black and white urban women, respectively.

The employment prospects for suburban and urban youth who dropped out of high school were particularly dismal. The part-time employment probability for male youth was 63.9 percent (suburban blacks) and 66.9 percent (suburban whites) versus 47.4 percent (urban

Figure 7.1 CHANGE IN MANUFACTURING PRODUCTION JOBS IN PHILADELPHIA CONSOLIDATED METROPOLITAN
STATISTICAL AREA, 1977–87
(PER 100 RESIDENTS FOR COUNTIES)

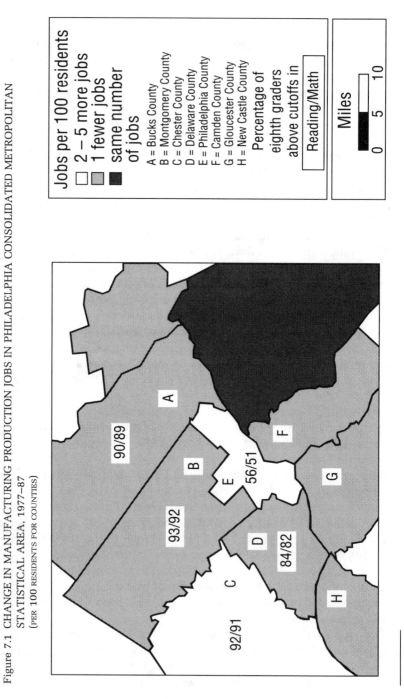

Source: Reproduced, by permission, from Mark Hughes, December 1993, "Over the Horizon: Jobs in the Suburbs of Major Metropolitan Areas. A Report to Public/Private Ventures."

Figure 7.2 CHANGE IN SERVICE JOBS IN PHILADELPHIA CONSOLIDATED METROPOLITAN STATISTICAL AREA, 1977–87
(PER 100 RESIDENTS FOR COUNTIES)

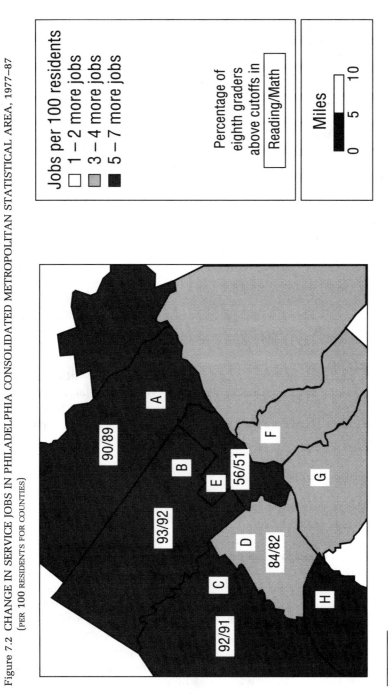

Source: Reproduced, by permission, from Mark Hughes, December 1993, "Over the Horizon: Jobs in the Suburbs of Major Metropolitan Areas. A Report to Public/Private Ventures."

Table 7.1 EMPLOYMENT PROBABILITY OF MEN AND WOMEN IN
PHILADELPHIA PRIMARY METROPOLITAN STATISTICAL AREA (AGES
16–24 IN 1988)

	Men		Women	
	Black	White	Black	White
Any employment				
High School Graduates:				
Suburban	83.2	85	65.8	68.7
City	71.7	74.3	49.5	52.8
Dropouts:				
Suburban	63.9	66.9	40.6	43.9
Urban	47.4	50.7	25.9	28.5
Full-time Employment				
High School Graduates:				
Suburban	42.7	40.9	17.3	16.3
City	32.6	31	12	11.2
Dropouts:				
Suburban	25.5	24.1	8.8	8.2
City	18.2	17.1	5.9	5.5

Source: Computations from *Work, Wages and Poverty*, 1991. Janice Madden and William Stull, Temple University–University of Pennsylvania Economic Monitoring Project, Philadelphia: University of Pennsylvania Press.

blacks) and 50.7 percent (urban whites). The probabilities for full-time work for males were 25.5 percent (suburban blacks) and 24.1 percent (suburban whites) versus 18.2 percent (suburban blacks) and 17.1 percent (suburban whites). Again, the corresponding percentages for women were dramatically lower in all categories.

Hard Skills Gap

The second barrier to an antipoverty strategy that simultaneously benefits suburban and urban youth is the hard skills problem. Urban youth may not have the hard skills needed for the main skills programs envisioned by the School to Work Opportunities Act. The main school-to-work (STW) program requires that youth have significant basic entry skills to gain the job-relevant skills for high-wage employment. As the Philadelphia data illustrate (see table 7.2), the urban/suburban skills gap is as significant as the urban/suburban employment probability and job growth gaps. In a 1990–91 statewide test for basic math and reading skills, Philadelphia fell 28 to 37 points below neighboring, suburban counties on reading scores and 31 to 41 points below suburban counties on math scores. Just over half of

Table 7.2 EIGHTH-GRADE SKILL LEVELS, PHILADELPHIA METROPOLITAN
AREA BY COUNTY

Skill (1990–91)	Philadelphia County	Bucks County	Chester County	Delaware County	Montgomery County
Eighth-Grade Reading:					
Number tested	10,079	5,049	3,464	3,326	4,500
Above the cutoff	5,676	4,558	3,189	2,817	4,169
Score	56	90	92	84	93
Mathematics:					
Number tested	10,016	5,055	3,468	3,326	5,402
Above the cutoff	5,070	4,505	3,171	2,733	4,129
Score	51	89	91	82	92

Source: Pennsylvania Department of Education, Testing for Essential Learning and
Literacy Skills (TELLS). This table summarizes the number of regular students whose
scores were above a state-established minimum level of acceptable performance in
basic reading and mathematics skills.

the city's 8th graders passed either test. At the time of this writing,
June, 1994, Philadelphia school district officials were in the middle
of 11th-grade skill assessments and chose not to release partial findings, but they expected these 8th-grade gaps to continue or to deepen
by the 11th grade.

Other national studies illustrate the implications of severe urban/
suburban hard skills gaps for STW programs. First, programs for low-
skilled youth will have difficulty fixing the minimal entry requirement. Second, programs will have difficulty retaining low-skilled
students. Jobs for the Future, for example, evaluated the impact of low
skills on a Boston-area pilot health training program that purposely
selected youth "unlikely to complete college-level training without
a supported pathway" from three nonexamination Boston-area high
schools (Kopp, Goldberger, and Morales 1944).[1] The program, entitled ProTech, required that applicants have at least a C + grade point
average with at least a B average in the core subjects—math, science,
and English—and a 90 percent attendance. The ProTech administra-
tor considered this a generous standard, but after school officials
pointed out that this standard would "cream," or select only the best
students, ProTech modified the criteria. Yet, even when standards
were modified to a C + grade point average with at least a C − average
in core subjects and a 90 percent attendance, administrators could
fill only 31 percent of the 88 available slots. They filled those slots
only after they lowered the grade standard to at least a C grade point
average, a C − in the student's last math class, and an 85 percent
attendance record.[2]

Although ProTech administrators used these modified criteria in the second year and in their opinion selected a stronger group, the program still could not fill all its slots simply by defining relevant skill levels. Stated Kopp et al. (1994:11): "Twenty-nine percent of ProTech students in the second cohort failed to earn a C average in the 10th grade. . . . A high percentage of students entered the program without basic foundation skills in math and reading as indicated by standardized test scores. . . ."

A more carefully controlled New York City study found that low-skilled youth in high schools with career training programs did not benefit as much as students entering with average skills (Thaler, Crain, and Si 1994).[3] Their performance in mathematics and their absenteeism rates were not better, and sometimes worse, than that of students randomly assigned to traditional academic comprehensive high schools.

This group is only the lowest one-sixth of New York City eighth graders in reading; the New York City school population is very disadvantaged with many recent immigrants.

The results are more positive for students whose skills are better; even those who are only at the average for New York City show improvements in reading, absenteeism, and dropout rates, but losses in mathematics.[4]

Low entry skills also mean low exit skills. Thus, a work-based education did not have an immediate impact on academic performance. In a Project ProTech evaluation, Goldberger (1993) stated: "High quality work-based learning experiences cannot substitute for needed reforms in the schools."

Soft Skills Problem

Poor soft skills are the third barrier to an antipoverty strategy benefiting suburban and urban youth. Tardiness and erratic school attendance are examples of the soft skills problem; they often indicate that youth who live in communities where job discrimination and weak labor force attachment rates are high do not learn accountable behaviors that are critical in the workplace (Majors, with Billson 1992). Kopp et al.'s (1994) study noted that once students are admitted to an attractive training program, outright quitting and expulsion among inner-city youth did not correlate strongly with entering grade point averages.[5] However, quitting and expulsion did correlate with the attendance habits that youth exhibited before entering the program (ibid.: 27).[6] Youth with low academic skills who nonetheless listen well to instructors and supervisors can survive late-stage training programs.[7]

CURRENT INITIATIVES

Several current initiatives address the spatial mismatch and hard skills issues for programs that begin in high school, that is, late-stage training programs.

One ongoing school-to-work demonstration in Pennsylvania, the Pennsylvania Youth Apprenticeship, focused on the spatial mismatch problem. It matched high-skill inner-city 11th graders with suburban employers. Program administrators selected youth who successfully completed an algebra course by the 10th grade and received a recommendation from their high school guidance counselor. The demonstration succeeded in linking Philadelphia and Pittsburgh youth with suburban manufacturing employers through van pools and public transportation systems.

Most STW programs do not have such universal placement components. As a result, racial patterns, which derive from the concentration both of minorities in urban areas and of white youth in suburban areas, emerge. Students are not evenly distributed across fields in these programs, which limits the career options available to them. In inner cities, the fields tending not to be available to youth include electronics, computer-related employment, and manufacturing.

These patterns are illustrated in table 7.3, which shows the racial composition of 10 national STW demonstrations monitored by Jobs for the Future. Note that most white youth were in manufacturing, business, and technical fields, whereas most minority youth were in health technician and teaching assistant slots, or in jobs linked to employers who cannot easily leave urban labor markets. The allied health care field has among the highest entry and exit skills requirements of all fields available. Therefore, urban youth have geographical access to this option. Unfortunately, however, the skill requirements tend to limit the number who succeed. Regarding gender composition, it should be noted that, at least in terms of Jobs for the Future demonstrations, young women are increasingly entering fields such as electronics and metalworking in which they were previously not well represented (table 7.4).

Table 7.3 RACIAL COMPOSITION OF NATIONAL YOUTH APPRENTICESHIP
INITIATIVE, 1992–94

	White (%)			Black (%)		
Demonstration Site	Site 1992	Site 1993	% in District	Site 1992	Site 1993	% in District
Careers in Education Polaroid Internship	33	40	45	33	38	34
Cornell Youth and Work Program	88	87	N.A.	5	7	N.A.
Craftsmanship 2000	71	63	57	21	33	31
Kalamazoo Health Occupations	84	74	80	10	19	16
Oakland Health and Bioscience Academy	5	4	8	66	56	55
Pasadena Graphic Arts	32	25	17	31	23	35
Pennsylvania Youth	86	50	81	12	44	12
Pickens County Youth	100	95	91	0	5	8
Project ProTech	12	8	20	54	50	48
Roosevelt Renaissance	67	67	70	12	13	15
All sites, all students	38	34	68	39	41	20
All sites, weighed equally	57	44	50	23	34	30

Table 7.3 RACIAL COMPOSITION OF NATIONAL YOUTH APPRENTICESHIP
INITIATIVE, 1992–94, *continued*

Latino (%)			Other (%)			
Site 1992	Site 1993	% in District	Site 1992	Site 1993	% in District	Occupation/Industry
21	23	13	13	0	3	Teaching (allied health careers in 1993–94)
2	2	N.A.	5	4	N.A.	Health care; administration and technology; manufacturing and engineering technology
0	0	3	7	4	9	Metalworking industries
0	0	2	5	7	2	Health careers
6	8	17	23	32	20	Health; medical; biotechnology; life sciences
35	48	43	3	4	4	Printing industry occupations
2	4	4	0	2	2	Metalworking; health care
0	0	0	0	0	1	Electronics industry; automotives; business management; industrial electricity
25	28	22	9	14	10	Health careers; financial service
6	5	4	15	15	10	Business information systems; health and human services; manufacturing technologies
12	14	8	11	11	4	
10	14	13	7	8	7	

Source: Jobs for the Future, Somerville, Mass.

Table 7.4 GENDER COMPOSITION—NATIONAL YOUTH APPRENTICESHIP INITIATIVE, 1992-94

Demonstration Site	1992-93			1993-94			Occupation/Industry
	Male (%)	Female (%)	Total Numbers (%)	Male (%)	Female (%)	Total Numbers (%)	
Careers in Education Polaroid Internship	33	67	24	30	70	40	Teaching (allied health careers in 1993-94)
Cornell Youth and Work Program	41	59	41	35	65	46	Health care; administration and technology; manufacturing and engineering technology
Craftsmanship 2000	85	14	14	79	21	24	Metalworking industries
Kalamazoo Health Occupations	18	82	77	22	78	89	Health careers
Oakland Health and Bioscience Academy	38	62	237	33	67	236	Health; medical; biotechnology; life sciences
Pasadena Graphic Arts	52	48	98	54	46	102	Printing industry occupations
Pennsylvania Youth	91	9	100	66	34	361	Metalworking; health care
Pickens County Youth	100	0	4	76	24	21	Electronics industry; automotives; business management; industrial electricity
Project ProTech	35	65	108	27	73	234	Health careers; financial service
Roosevelt Renaissance	52	48	961	53	47	1,217	Business information systems; health and human services; manufacturing technologies
All sites, all students	46	54	703	45	55	1,153	
All sites, weighed equally	55	45	N.A.	48	52	N.A.	

Source: Jobs for the Future, Somerville, Mass.

Bridging Hard Skills Gap

A number of studies point to steps that late-stage training programs can take to reduce the inner-city hard skills gap. For example, there appears to be a correlation between a program's being perceived as attractive by inner-city youth (i.e., as leading to a white-collar job) and the likelihood that these youth will succeed in the program. This finding was reported in a study of Chicago's allied health care professions (NCI Research 1992). The study noted that the allied health care field contains excellent jobs that "fulfill the role that high-wage manufacturing jobs played in past decades" (ibid.: 8). Yet, these training programs graduated youth at rates too low for the programs' clients. No program graduated more than 40 percent of its enrollees. The study concluded that inner-city youth failed to complete the programs at such significant rates that simply "raising training program completion rates could substantially reduce projected shortages in many of the allied health occupations" (ibid.: 17). A striking pattern in this high dropout rate suggests that the more the training could be associated with white-collar skills (thus enhancing its attractiveness), the more the overall dropout rate declined. In Chicago training programs for good-paying technician jobs, completion ranged from 40 percent for records technicians to only 13.9 percent for surgical technologists, the latter of which is a great name for what youth considered mundane work.

Recent work points to a second way inner-city training programs may attack the hard skills gap (Thaler et al. 1994). If students have flexibility in the kinds of careers they choose, even the poorest-performing students can succeed. Crain uncovered this finding upon reexamining the performance of the lowest-ranked students from his study of New York City magnet schools. He discovered that his findings for the lowest-ranked students were a pooled result across the city's 133 career programs. In some career magnet schools the bottom-ranked students improved significantly: their skills increased; they completed their programs; and they presumably found jobs. In other career magnet schools, however, lowest-skilled students did poorly, even more poorly than the average performance of the lowest-skilled youth in the original pooled sample.

In general, the more aggressively the high school attempted to prepare students for specific careers, the more likely students with very low reading scores were to have difficulty. Presumably, these programs demanded the highest exit-level skills. But programs which taught students career skills without insisting that they be fully trained at the end of high school seemed successful. For example, low-skilled youth in business-related programs improved their attendance and completed more courses, although reading scores did not improve as much.[8]

The Boston ProTech and Chicago allied health care experience seem to reinforce the negative point that low-skilled youth have difficulty in STW programs with high exit skill requirements. A study based on ProTech's first year showed that few youth in the demonstration improved academically, and almost half washed out (Goldberger 1993).[9]

Critics of career programs in high school are also concerned that career training will take time away from teaching hard skills; and that seems born out by small losses in mathematics scores in New York City career magnets. But the New York City study shows a surprising pattern: schools which stress career training show a more-than-offsetting gain in reading performance. This occurs even in careers seemingly unrelated to reading. For example, programs in computing, especially those that try to integrate academics and career teaching, yield especially high scores.

Finally, career academy studies consistently note the positive impact of mentors and role models, but new evidence from the New York City study points to something more dramatic (Crain, communication with authors). When career programs bring in industry leaders on even the most casual terms, students (particularly those with low reading scores) show high gains in reading and math scores in the 9th and 10th grades. Low-skilled students exposed to such leaders also show lower absenteeism and more courses passed. Researchers are uncertain how to interpret this result. Students could be inspired to perform well by industry leaders. Or, the presence of industry leaders may simply indicate that other less well-identified, but more important, activities are occurring at the school.

Lessons of Current School-to-Work Initiatives

Although some current initiatives offer promise in their ability either to match inner-city youth with suburban employers or to address the hard skills problem, they are stopgaps at best. The Pennsylvania Youth Apprenticeship model does match urban youth with suburban employers, but it reserves its slots for high-skilled youth. The New York City career magnet program restricts the number of slots available to low-skilled students. Similarly, the Boston program has an entry skills threshold. The slots for low-skilled youth in these late-stage programs are even lower when we take into account that programs requiring high exit skills have high washout rates.

Other studies make it increasingly clear that successful, large-scale skills programs for urban youth will require earlier interventions that increase academic skills before youth enroll in late-stage school-to-work programs. A ProTech study, for example, found that students from one of its three feeder schools, Brighton School, had a significantly higher retention rate (86 percent at Brighton versus 69 percent and 63 percent at the other two schools). Brighton school had a health professions magnet program beginning with ninth graders. Eighty-two percent of student participants from that school had a prior interest in a health-based career. "Consequently, students quitting because they decided that they were not interested in health care was much less likely to occur" (Kopp et al. 1994: 34).

The School to Work Opportunities Act recognizes these issues, but its funding levels—$350 million in the next two years to support school/business training partnerships in local communities—are inadequate for the panoply of services that inner-city STW programs will require in order to have the desired impact on welfare-bound youth. Within its comprehensive embrace, the act targets some $10 million for high-poverty areas for fiscal year 1994.[10] These funding levels provide too little money for the hard skills and spatial mismatch issues facing current school-to-work initiatives.

We return to the soft skills issues that none of these programs recognizes later in the chapter, but first we address the difficulties faced by welfare-bound youth and young adults who have dropped out of school.

DEMAND-SIDE TRAINING TAX: UNIVERSAL PLACEMENT

Thus far we have focused on school-to-work programs and how they affect welfare-bound youth still in school. We now briefly turn our attention to young people who have dropped out of school and cannot be reached by school-based training efforts. Inner-city dropouts, whether on welfare or not, face the same three barriers described earlier for in-school students. A targeted demand-side strategy with the characteristics discussed here may address two of those three barriers—the hard skills and universal placement barriers. We examine the soft skills barrier for both in- and out-of-school youth in the next section.

Figure 7.3 THREE PATTERNS FOR REDUCING BIAS IN EMPLOYER-FINANCED
TRAINING

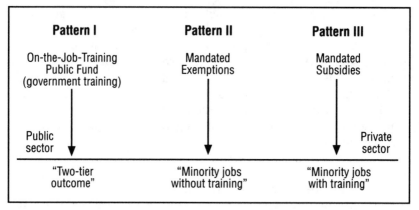

Currently, employer-financed training proposals give employers a
choice. They may spend a certain fraction of their payroll costs to
train their own low-skilled workers, or they may contribute to a
public training fund (Baily, Burtless, and Litan 1993). These options
are likely to result in a considerable increase in private on-the-job
training for low-skilled workers. At present, as mentioned earlier,
firms are reluctant to make such expenditures, out of concern that
workers may take the general skills they acquire to other firms, making it impossible for the initial firms to recoup investments in training. However, if all employers must make such investments (or pay
a training tax), it will remove any single firm's incentive to poach
another's trainees.

If current patterns continue, however, young white males will
benefit most from increased training expenditures. Among the
employed, young white workers are twice as likely to train within a
firm through either an apprenticeship or other forms of on-the-job
training (OJT) (Lynch 1989). Given that white employment rates are
higher, the actual gap in private training opportunities is undoubtedly greater than two-to-one. Three possible solutions to the problem
of bias in training opportunities are discussed next. These patterns
are outlined in figure 7.3.

Pattern I: Employer-financed training proposals could be altered
in several ways to reduce the bias in training opportunities. One
solution is to use the public fund created by firms who prefer to pay
the "training tax" to supplement current public expenditures for
"disadvantaged" employment and training programs. These pro-

grams, such as those sponsored by the Job Training Partnership Act, currently serve disproportionate numbers of minorities anyway. Unfortunately, this solution would only exacerbate the current two-tier training system in which young whites receive employer-provided training and young minorities receive government training. Not surprisingly, the former more closely matches actual employer skill requirements.

Pattern II: Another solution would be to exempt or reduce training expenditures and taxes if firms employed larger fractions of previously unemployed young workers. These workers are more likely to be minorities. However, this solution would steer minority employment to firms that provided no training.

Pattern III: A third, and preferred, solution would be to use the public training fund to subsidize training in firms that hired more previously unemployed workers, allowing the subsidy to increase as a function of the post-training wage. Thus, firms might compete for training grants based on their ability to increase the post-training wages of previously unemployed or underemployed, low-skilled workers. The result would be to increase training investments in young minority workers.

Participants in employer-financed training programs might be encouraged to train more low-skilled black workers if they received a subsidy for hiring and training the previously unemployed. This is consistent with work that suggests employers respond best to non-stigmatizing interventions (Burtless 1985; Palmer and Barth 1978) (e.g., a new jobs tax credit) and worst to highly targeted interventions (e.g., training tax subsidies for welfare recipients). Once workers are hired, however, the program will maximize training possibilities if employers and youth can be helped to recognize the difficulties they will both have in making work in a traditional employment arrangement successful.

TARGETED SOFT SKILLS TRAINING WITHIN UNIVERSAL PROGRAMS

To overcome the soft skills barrier, policymakers should establish a network of service providers who can function as mediators and advocates between inner-city youth and employers engaged in early and late training programs.

Standard STW programs are designed to "fine-tune" existing,

though weak, connections between schools and existing jobs. In high-poverty, inner-city neighborhoods, most youth are not attached to the labor market, the schools, or the adults in the community (Anderson 1992). Thus, for inner-city STWs, the 'fine-tuning' assumption does not apply.

Service providers must be identified who can assist inner-city school-to-work programs to make the missing connections between home, school and, now, work (Bourgois 1987; Majors, with Billson 1992; Mincy 1994). These service providers would use authoritative, supervisory messages to increase the ability of youth to sort through what to value and achieve on the job. The service providers would also help teach youth about acceptable workplace behavior, while instructing them in how to "code switch" between the workplace and their own neighborhoods (Bourgois 1991). Finally, the service providers would teach employers how to accommodate young inner-city employees (i.e., encouraging employers to be patient while young workers learn appropriate workplace behavior, rather than rejecting them at the first sign of street comportment; and helping employers resolve conflicts that develop because young inner-city employees are often late, absent, or unwilling to accept demeaning assignments). In some instances, service providers may intercede directly between employers and young workers. The service providers gain the license to reprimand young workers as a trusting relationship between the two evolves; or the service provider may alert employers to actions that may be detrimental to the long-term success of a placement. This mediating function is perhaps most successful when service providers increase the retention and recruitment of youth who would otherwise wash out.

The most straightforward evidence for a service provider that fits this definition comes from Project Strive. Project Strive is an employment training and placement service with sites in New York, Chicago, and Pittsburgh. It serves extremely disadvantaged youth and young adults between 18 and 30 years old. The program provides two weeks of training emphasizing attitudinal change. It locates jobs for Strive participants and conducts a two-year follow-up after the placement is made. During the postplacement phase Strive service providers are available to employees and employers to resolve problems and conflicts. An evaluation of the Strive program in New York showed that Strive placed 75 percent of all participants and achieved an 82 percent retention rate during the two-year follow-up period (Ofori-Mankata and Won 1993).

Another example of a mediating service was reported by Maynard

(1993), who examined a teenage parent population handled by case managers who combined some of these service provider roles with more authoritarian roles. The coercive intervention targeted young women already on welfare to discourage subsequent out-of-wedlock births. These young women were told that if they did not find training, education or a job, they would lose a portion of their AFDC benefits. When provided with authorities to help them be accountable for their behavior, these young women increased their participation in program activities. In a typical month, one-fourth to one-third of the target group were in school or job training or were employed, compared with 19 percent to 20 percent of the regular services group. The program had its largest impact on Hispanic women,[11] and evaluators speculate that it gave teenage women a "compelling counterargument" to their partners, who sought to restrict their mobility.

In another relevant case, Anderson (1990) made a telling observation about inner-city youth working in employment training programs. Supervisors, whose discipline was too capricious, sometimes could not tell when progress was being made. Anderson's work points to a need for guides, advocates, or mediators who can encourage mutual adjustments between inner-city youth and traditional employers in a more judicious, nurturing stratagem (Anderson 1990; Mincy 1994).

We also endorse initiating school-to-work programs far earlier in the student's schooling than in the standard model produced by the School to Work Opportunities Act. In addition, we encourage efforts that provide mobility within the urban area.

NATIONAL ANTIPOVERTY SUPPORT SYSTEM

In order for STW programs to help move welfare-bound youth into high-skill, high-wage careers, the programs must address the spatial mismatch problem, the hard skills gap, and the soft skills issue. If these programs are to carry out a welfare-prevention function, we need to develop a network of technical assistance and service providers who can assist in establishing the innovative practices already recognized as helpful to inner-city youth, as well as the soft skills practices that are not widely recognized. Jobs for the Future, with its nonprofit demonstrations,[12] is an example of a technical assistance agency that could perhaps provide services in a national support system for large cities that wish to restructure their public schools to address the hard skills problem.

Hughes, with Sternberg (1992) listed a number of groups that could be involved in a national support system of technical assistance for universal job placement efforts. The earlier-mentioned Project Strive now serves mostly out-of-school youth. A similar program could be created to provide attitudinal and postplacement service to inner-city students enrolled in school-to-work programs.

The Clinton administration's welfare reform plan hopes to meet the needs of a targeted population—welfare recipients—by linking them to as many universal programs as possible. It also attempts to link welfare-bound youth to universal career training programs. We suggest that this strategy of linking targeted groups to universal programs be extended beyond government-to-government linkages. A conduit structure providing an array of technical assistance networks and private-sector resource providers to these government efforts would expand the school-to-work initiative to incorporate welfare-bound youth.

CONCLUSION

A crucial part of the administration's proposal to reform the nation's welfare system involves preventing welfare-bound youth from joining the welfare rolls in the first place. A new generation of training programs can be so universally implemented that they capture these youth before they become enmeshed in a welfare-centered life. The 1994 School-to-Work Opportunities Act is a useful example of this new generation of training strategies.

The employment/training strategies included in the major welfare reform proposals in the mid-1990s fall short on three grounds, however. First, job opportunities are not equally distributed within metropolitan regions. Under present circumstances, even a successfully implemented national program is likely to leave black and inner-city youth blocked from high-tech, manufacturing, and other opportunities disproportionately located outside central cities. A successful prevention strategy requires a placement component that ensures reasonable inner-city access to unique suburban job opportunities.

Second, inner-city skill levels are currently too low for most youth to qualify for standard school-to-work programs. The most promising strategy for improving low skills seems to be innovative pre-apprenticeship programs that begin at middle school levels or younger.

Third, the most significant and least understood barrier is what we term the "soft skills" problem. Research continues on what the bare-bones components of programs delievering these "soft skills" should be, but it seems clear that employers and urban youth look for different qualities in the mediators, mentors, and career guides that negotiate accommodations in attitudes and behavior between them. One reasonable strategy is to make sure that local programs include teams of mediators that reflect both sides of these opposed cultures.

Finally, an employer training tax that rewards those firms most willing to hire and train previously unemployed workers is worth exploring as a strategy for minority, wefare-bound youth who are not in school. Taken as a group, efforts such as these could strengthen the Clinton administration's welfare prevention strategy. Without them, the strategy may well fail.

Notes

1. Boston's school system is considered the most rigidly tracked in the country. Twenty percent of its high school population, selected on the basis of grades and entry examination scores, attend 3 examination schools. The rest go to 13 nonexamination schools. ProTech draws its applicants from 3 of these 13 schools: English, Boston, and Brighton High Schools.

2. Hilary Pennington, President of Jobs for the Future (Somerville, Mass.), communication with the authors.

3. The study employed a randomized experimental design of New York City's 133 competitive career magnet schools. These schools select their students (16,757, estimated) based on reading scores. In a sixfold ranking, each school reserves two-thirds of its slots for average readers (those between the second to fifth ranks). It reserves another one-sixth of its slots for students from the top sixth rank, and a final one-sixth for the bottom sixth rank. In a further criterion, each school must then select half its students at each rank by lottery.

4. For technical reasons, the New York City study cannot provide results for students who are above the New York City average in school performance.

5. "Academic performance in the 10th grade did not prove a significant predictor of program retention" (Kopp et al. 1994:27).

6. "Students who entered the program with poor school attendance were more likely to quit or be terminated from the program" (Kopp et al. 1994: 27).

7. Dennis Collins, vice president of the Hospital of the University of Pennsylvania, Philadelphia, conversation with the authors, spring, 1994. Stated Collins: "We want youth who have the ability to work in teams with patients, peers, and supervisors of

very different backgrounds. Once we have someone with those attitudinal skills, we believe we can teach them the hard skills."

8. Robert Crain in a communication with the authors (summer, 1994), stated: "Secretarial programs are highly successful. We have 15 in the sample. Pooling them, they on average have significantly higher reading test scores, lower absenteeism, and the students are making more rapid progress toward their degrees. The programs are also very popular; they get a large number of applicants, and students who are admitted to these schools by lottery are less likely to quit school at the end of junior high school or [to] transfer to a private high school. The reading result is impressive because it is very difficult to get a statistically significant result on a standardized test. . . . There are 12 other programs that focus on higher-level business careers—accounting, management, etc. These programs don't show reading gains of the same magnitude, but they show extremely high impacts on attendance, and positive impacts on number of courses passed."

9. In that first-year cohort (1991–92), ProTech retained 62 percent of its students (33 of 88 dropped out) at the end of the 11th grade. Forty-seven of the 55 remaining students returned their senior year, and 38 finished. That 43 percent retention rate approximates the retention rates in Chicago's allied health care program. Also, the ProTech program is a 2 + 2 program, meaning it picks up enrollees in their junior and senior years of high school, then provides an additional two years at junior college. All 38 who finished the senior year enrolled in a junior college or a full four-year college, beginning the higher education phase of their training.

10. The School-to-Work Opportunities Act program for high-poverty areas is an excellent example of an effort that fuses skills training and poverty policy. By setting aside funds for high-poverty areas, the law ensures that some programs will be located in the inner city, specifically to meet the needs of at-risk youth in and out of school. The act mandates funding for staying in school, academic learning gains, and job placement.

11. Compared with those in the regular-services group, Hispanics in the enhanced-services group were 55 percent more likely to engage in a major activity (74 percent versus 49 percent), twice as likely to attend school (42 percent versus 21 percent), 37 percent more likely to have job training (23 percent versus 17 percent), and 68 percent more likely to have a job (42 percent versus 25 percent)" (Maynard 1993:10).

12. Jobs for the Future's newly implemented Benchmark program provides technical assistance to several major cities to initiate large-scale career training programs with pre-apprenticeship components.

References

Anderson, Elijah. 1990. "Racial Tension, Cultural Conflicts, and Problems of Employment Training Programs. In *The Nature of Work: Sociological Perspectives*, edited by Kai Erikson and Steven Peter Vallas. New Haven, Conn.: Yale University Press.
———. 1992. "Drugs and the Inner-City Family." Urban Institute Working Paper. Washington, D.C.: Urban Institute.

Baily, Martin Neil, Gary Burtless, and Robert E. Litan. 1993. *Growth with Equity: Economic Policymaking for the Next Century.* Washington, D.C.: Brookings Institution.

Bishop, John H. 1987. "Why High School Students Learn So Little and What Can Be Done about It." In *Competitiveness and the Quality of the American Workforce.* Hearings before the Subcommittee on Education and Health of the Joint Economic Committee, 100th Cong., 1st sess., October.

Bound, John, and Richard B. Freeman. 1991. "What Went Wrong? The Erosion of Relative Earnings and Employment among Young Black Men in the 1980s." Technical report. Cambridge, Mass.: National Bureau of Economic Research, July.

Bourgois, Phillippe. 1989. "In Search of Horatio Alger: Culture and Ideology in the Crack Economy." *Contemporary Drug Problems* 16 (Winter): 619–49.

———. 1991. "In Search of Respect: The New Service Economy and the Crack Alternative in Spanish Harlem." Technical report. New York: Russell Sage Foundation.

Burtless, Gary. 1985. "Are Targeted Wage Subsidies Harmful? Evidence from a Wage Voucher Experiment." *Industrial and Labor Relations Review* 39 (1, October): 105–14.

———. 1993. "Rising Wage Inequality and the Future of Work in America." Technical report. Washington, D.C.: Brookings Institution. November.

Children's Defense Fund. 1991. "The State of America's Children." Technical report. Washington, D.C.: Author.

Crain, Robert B., A. L. Heebner, Y. P. Si, W. J. Jordan, and D. R. Kiefer. 1992. "Effectiveness of New York City's Career Magnet Schools: An Evaluation of Ninth Grade Performance Using an Experimental Design." Technical report. Berkeley, Calif.: National Center for Research on Vocational Education, April.

Goldberger, Susan. 1993. "Creating an American-Style Youth Apprenticeship Program: A Formative Evaluation of Project ProTech." Technical report. Somerville, Mass.: Jobs for the Future, February.

Howard, Robert. 1991. "New Training Strategies for a High Performance Metalworking Industry." Technical report. Cambridge, Mass.: Jobs for the Future.

Hughes, Mark. 1993. "Over the Horizon: Jobs in the Suburbs of Major Metropolitan Areas. A Report to Public/Private Ventures." Philadelphia, Pa.: supported by the John D. and Catherine T. MacArthur Foundation. December.

Hughes, Mark Alan, with Julie E. Sternberg. 1992. "The New Metropolitan Reality: Where the Rubber Meets the Road in Antipoverty Policy." Washington, D.C.: Urban Institute.

Ihlanfeldt, Keith R., and David L. Sjoquist. 1990. "Job Accessibility and Racial Differences in Youth Employment Rates." *American Economic Review* 80 (March): 267–76.

Kopp, Hilary, Susan Goldberger, and Dionisia Morales. 1994. "The Evolution of a Youth Apprenticeship Model: A Second Year Evaluation of Boston's ProTech." Technical report. Somerville, Mass.: Jobs for the Future, March.

Lerman, Robert. 1994. "Building Hope, Skills, and Careers: Making a U.S. Youth Apprenticeship System." Report prepared for Social Policies for Children Conference. Princeton, N.J.: Woodrow Wilson School of Public and International Affairs, April.

Levitan, Sar A., and Isaac Shapiro. 1987. *Working but Poor: America's Contradiction.* Baltimore: Johns Hopkins University Press.

Lynch, Lisa M. 1989. "Private Sector Training and Its Impact on the Earnings of Young Workers." National Bureau of Economic Research Working Paper Series 2872. Washington, D.C.: National Bureau of Economic Research.

Majors, Richard, with Janet Billson. 1992. *Cool Pose: The Dilemmas of Black Manhood in America.* Lexington, Mass.: Lexington Press.

Mincy, Ronald B., ed. 1994. *Nurturing Young Black Males.* Washington, D.C.: Urban Institute Press.

Murphy, Kevin, and Finis Welch. 1992. "The Structure of Wages." *The Quarterly Journal of Economics* 107 (February, 285–326).

NCI Research. 1992. "Increasing Employment Opportunities in Allied Health Occupations for Inner City Residents." Technical report for Rockefeller Foundation. Evanston, Ill.: NCI Research, February.

Ofori-Mankata, Juliet, and Bo Young Won. 1993. "Strive's Results: Evaluating a Non-Profit Organization in East Harlem." Technical report. New York: New York University, Robert F. Wagner Graduate School for Public Service.

Palmer, John L., and Michael C. Barth. 1978. *The Distributional Effects of Inflation and Higher Unemployment.* Washington, D.C.: Brookings Institution.

Thaler, R., Robert L. Crain, and Y. P. Si. 1994. "The Effectiveness of New York City's Career Magnet Schools: An Evaluation Using an Experimental Design." Technical report, National Center for Research on Vocational Education. Berkeley, Ca.

Part Three

CONCLUSIONS: EXPECTATIONS AND REALITIES

Chapter Eight

THE CLINTON ALTERNATIVE TO "WELFARE AS WE KNOW IT": IS IT FEASIBLE?

Robert H. Haveman

This volume's discussions contain abundant information on current proposals for welfare reform, and suggest, as well, the pitfalls that await these proposals as they "hit the road." I endeavor in this closing chapter to synthesize these multiple perspectives, while offering some of my own reflections on the problem, the plan, and the process.[1]

DOES EVERY PRESIDENT NEED A WELFARE REFORM PLAN?

I begin with a question addressed by several contributing authors: "Why does every president need a welfare reform plan?" In particular, why does this president need a welfare reform plan? I would note that, in fact, every president since 1970 has had a welfare reform plan save George Bush, and he had Senator Daniel P. Moynihan!

Nathan Glazer, in chapter 2, asserted that the answer to this question involves neither cost nor program growth, nor any notion that we have a "welfare crisis," nor new or startling revelations of waste and inefficiency. In Glazer's view, the Clinton administration needed a welfare reform plan for symbolic reasons. Welfare, he says, is equated in people's minds with dependency, teenage out-of-wedlock births, inner cities, homelessness, crime, and ghetto poverty; people envision welfare reform as ultimately changing the behavior of the underclass.

That is clearly one answer, though a cynical one; there are other answers as well. A more political reason is that President Clinton promised welfare reform during his campaign, and his critics have not let him forget it. Moreover, having a plan has allowed the president to position himself more to the right than he is normally perceived. But while this political reason is plausible, it is overly simplistic.

An analytic reason would acknowledge that current welfare policy has failed to reduce poverty; moreover, it contains incentives that encourage undesireable behaviors. For two decades now, we have seen antipoverty expenditures rising, but poverty has not been reduced. In addition, the system in place now has visible adverse incentives and a bewildering, multiprogram patchwork that leads to well-known examples of horizontal inequity—among states, between one- and two-parent families, and between the working and nonworking poor. It discourages work, encourages family breakup, and prohibits the accumulation of assets beyond a bare minimum. An overhaul, therefore, seems in order.

Apart from these reasons, there is a more fundamental—and perhaps even more cynical—reason why we are again attending to welfare reform. The fact is, there now exists a fundamental gap between the objectives of existing programs and society's social and economic goals. At their core, existing welfare programs seek to secure for the market-income poor a level of aftertax or disposable income that exceeds some minimum standard. They do this by distributing direct cash payments and essential goods. Citizens today, on the other hand, see something quite different than the simple need for income assistance when they consider the poor population. Contrary to when the welfare system was started, we now expect that able-bodied women with children should contribute to their own well-being through work. We have also come to believe that for able-bodied people, some quid pro quo should be associated with the provision of income support. And, if those requiring help are not job-ready, we seem to believe in education and training, rather than direct cash support.

Perhaps most important, today's nonpoor citizens expect minimum standards of civil behavior and effort—and responsible decisions—from those who receive public support. While the images may be colored by stereotypes and prejudice, many Americans believe that those in the bottom tail of the income distribution are there because of irresponsible choices they have made—the choice to bear children out of wedlock as a teen, the choice not to complete high school, the decision to refuse minimum wage employment when it is available, the decision to abuse drugs and sell them, the willingness to run in gangs and to engage in crime and violence, often against other poor people. After all, the poor did not use to be like this. And while economic and social factors, urban schools, and the barriers created by racial prejudice may make these choices a rational response to the options available—and while people at some level understand this—it is also true that most Americans view these outcomes as socially costly and destructive.

If this characterization is true, the questions that people ask today about the current welfare system become more understandable. If recipients are able to engage in some productive activity, why don't we require work as a condition of providing cash and in-kind assistance? If recipients are unable to break into regular jobs because of a lack of training or a lack of child care or health care support, why don't we make sure they get these services while at the same time requiring them to work? If they are having additional children that can be supported only by taxpayer assistance, or if they are working "off the books," or drug-dealing while they should be learning, or opting not to marry in order to sustain public payments, or not requiring their kids to go to school, why should we simply provide support without attempting to change these behaviors?

Concerns like these are not addressed by the current welfare system, and it is concerns such as these—commonly expressed, albeit in diverse ways, by the authors in this volume—that have motivated the powerful reforms proposed in the Clinton plan.

BACKGROUND ON POVERTY AND WELFARE POLICY

Before examining the specifics of the Clinton plan, it is important to review some basic facts on poverty and welfare. Table 8.1 provides an overview of antipoverty programs since 1970. The years in the table correspond to peaks in the business cycle (1989–92 are included for completeness). The first two columns of the table show the number of persons with market incomes below the poverty line, before and after cash transfers. Although not shown, in 1960, 39.9 million people (22.2 percent of the population) had incomes after cash transfers below the poverty line. By 1970, this number had fallen to 25.4 million (or 12.6 percent of the population). Some combination of economic expansion, demographic changes, increased coverage and generosity of the Social Security system, and the War on Poverty/ Great Society programs caused this improvement. Since 1973, however, the poverty population has increased sharply. The gain from 1979 to 1989 is particularly distressing; contrary to earlier experience, the sustained period of economic growth from 1982 to 1990 failed to raise the economic position of the poorest among us. As a result,

Table 8.1 U.S. POVERTY POPULATION AND REAL CASH AND NEAR-CASH TRANSFER PROGRAM EXPENDITURES, SELECTED YEARS

Year	Number of Pretax, Pretransfer Poor (000s)	Persons in Official Poverty (000s)	Percentage of Population in Official Poverty	AFDC Benefits ($)[a]	Food Stamp Benefits ($)	SSI Benefits ($)[a]	Total Benefits ($)	EITC Expenditures ($)	Benefits as Percentage of GDP
1970	N.A.	25,420	12.6	15,051	N.A.	10,627	25,678	N.A.	0.70
1973	N.A.	22,973	11.1	22,382	7,186[b]	10,801	33,183	N.A.	0.78
1979	42,783	26,072	11.7	19,382	11,184	13,672	44,238	3,966	0.92
1983	52,700	35,303	15.2	17,975	16,585	13,247	47,807	2,528	1.00
1989	49,052	31,534	12.8	18,120	13,760	16,640	48,520	7,462	0.82
1990	50,851	33,585	13.5	18,529	15,717	17,277	51,523	7,437	0.87
1991	54,679	35,708	14.2	19,319	18,463	18,520	56,302	9,689	0.96
1992	57,350	36,880	14.5	20,431	21,884	21,258	63,573	11,783	1.05

Sources: Council of Economic Advisors (1994: table B-1, 268; table B-59, 335); U.S. Bureau of the Census (1993: xviii); U.S. Congress (1993: 678, 867, 1058, 1312–13, 1342, 1609).

Note: Benefits in millions of 1992 dollars.

a. Includes state and federal benefits.

b. Includes administrative costs of the program in 1973.

the common belief in the antipoverty impacts of good macroeconomic performance has been shaken.

Columns four through seven of table 8.1 show federal expenditures on the largest cash or "near-cash" means-tested programs: Aid to Families with Dependent Children (AFDC), Food Stamps, and Supplemental Security Income (SSI). Through these programs, the United States currently spends around 1 percent of its gross domestic product on families and individuals with incomes below the poverty line. Aid to Families with Dependent Children (AFDC, in column four), commonly referred to as "welfare," is the nation's largest antipoverty income support program directed at families with children. The overwhelming bulk of recipients are single mothers and their children. The real value of aggregate AFDC benefits peaked around 1973; over the next 10 years real AFDC expenditures fell by almost 20 percent, although the number of persons in families with incomes below the poverty line increased by 54 percent. Real AFDC expenditures have edged up since 1983. About 14 million people receive AFDC benefits, and two-thirds of them are children. AFDC spending accounts for about 1 percent of the federal budget, and about 2–3 percent of the budgets of most states.

The decline in AFDC benefits has been more than offset, in the aggregate, by a rapid increase in expenditures on the Food Stamp program, the nation's only antipoverty program available to all of the poor. There has been modest growth in the combined value of AFDC and Food Stamps. SSI, a federal cash assistance program for poor people who are elderly, blind, and disabled, has grown fairly steadily since the early 1970s. In addition to these cash or near-cash programs, a number of additional federal programs have significant antipoverty components, including Medicaid ($76 billion) and public housing/supplements ($22 billion).

Finally, the next to last column in table 8.1 reports on the costs of the Earned Income Tax Credit (EITC), a refundable subsidy to earned income directed primarily toward low-income workers with children. The EITC is a major antipoverty program administered on the tax side of the budget. By 1996, the program is expected to be the largest cash or near-cash program directed toward low-income families with children.

This constellation of existing tax and transfer measures contributes importantly to improving the lives of the nation's most disadvantaged citizens, and to reducing the incidence of pretax and pretransfer poverty. The full set of programs existing in 1991 removed from poverty 20 million of the 55 million pretax and pretransfer poor.

Table 8.2 MEDIAN INCOME OF PERSONS 25 AND OVER, BY EDUCATIONAL
ATTAINMENT AND GENDER, SELECTED YEARS
(1989 DOLLARS)

	Males ($)			Females ($)		
	High School		College,	High School		College,
Year	1–3 Years	4 Years	4+ years	1–3 Years	4 Years	4+ Years
1967	22,858	26,894	39,186	7,574	10,800	19,205
1970	23,442	28,034	40,527	7,629	10,866	19,735
1973	24,079	30,252	41,065	7,920	11,087	19,667
1979	18,697	26,416	36,626	6,726	9,085	16,923
1983	15,138	21,932	35,188	6,531	9,326	18,427
1989	14,439	21,650	37,553	6,752	10,439	21,659

Source: For 1967–83 figures, U.S. Bureau of the Census (1990); for 1989 figures, U.S.
Bureau of the Census (1991).

Without these programs, the nation would have had a poverty rate
of 21.8 percent, but with them, the actual poverty rate was 14 percent.
Without the programs, it would take over $160 billion (in 1991 dol-
lars) to close the poverty gap; with them, the remaining poverty gap
stands at about $52 billion.

This background on poverty and welfare provides some perspective on the Clinton proposal; what has happened in the low-wage
labor market provides additional evidence. The data in table 8.2,
which shows median incomes of men and women by their level of
educational attainment, reflect the serious increase in inequality in
the American economy. More important, they show the deterioration
at the bottom of the distribution, which has contributed to the growing gap among the rich and the poor.

In 1973, the median male with one to three years of high school
made about $24,000 in annual income (in 1989 dollars); by 1989 the
median worker with the same level of education made only $14,439
in income. The erosion of labor market opportunities for people with
low levels of education has placed an enormous strain on the nation's
antipoverty programs. Note that the fall in income has been greater
for those with little education—both male and female—but a greater
decrease has been recorded for males than for females.

CLINTON'S WELFARE REFORM PROPOSAL:
MAKING WORK PAY

The Clinton plan to "end welfare as we know it" would "make
work pay" through an expanded EITC, supplemented by child care

assistance and job training; it would make parents more responsible, in part through child support enforcement; it would make recipients experience "workfare"—including education and training—through a signed contract between recipients and government; it would force some recipients to leave welfare after some point—a limit of two years is the goal. It would discourage teenage motherhood, either by forcing teenage mothers to live with their parents, or by having the government send welfare checks to the parents. It would change the "culture" of the welfare office by transforming welfare workers from check writers to case managers who would assess capabilities and work out an individualized training/education plan designed to help each recipient achieve independence.

Administration spokespersons consistently stress that the Clinton plan aims to change the expectations of the poor and establish a new norm. The plan thus wants to threaten the loss of benefits, in part because of the change in expectations that will result. At the same time, the plan wants to make jobs and work more attractive through supplements, services, and training. The administration, moreover, clearly sees health care reform as a precursor to welfare reform. In particular, the administration's proposal embodies four broad themes.

The first theme is to "make work pay." Large steps have already been taken to achieve this goal through the major expansion of the Earned Income Tax Credit as part of the 1993 Omnibus Budget Reconciliation Act. This is rarely noted by media reports of the strategy. By 1998, the EITC is projected to cost $24.5 billion, $7 billion of which is the result of the 1993 expansion. For taxpayers with incomes in the lower earnings range of the credit, the expanded EITC can be thought of as a well-targeted increase in the minimum wage, to $6 per hour for families with two or more children, from $4.25 an hour. The expanded credit will deliver benefits to more than 6 million working taxpayers with incomes below the poverty line, will close the poverty gap by $6.4 billion, and will raise the incomes of over 1 million taxpayers to a level above the poverty line. And to reiterate: This component has already been passed into legislation.

The second theme is that parenting implies responsibility. Accordingly, paternity will be established for newborns at the hospital, absent parents will be sought, and mandatory contributions will be made to support their children through wage withholding. Such "child support enforcement" is not a new proposal—it was a central part of the 1988 Family Support Act—but the intent is to beef it up.

The third theme recognizes that education, training, and child care assistance are necessary if welfare-eligible people are to become self-sufficient in today's economy. Therefore, welfare recipients will be simultaneously assisted (indeed, required) to acquire training, education, and/or work experience; this will be the workfare experience. And, their child care while working will be subsidized.

The fourth theme is that the receipt of welfare benefits (as distinct from the EITC) cannot go on indefinitely. Those able to work will be forced to operate in a world in which income support is a temporary and transitional "help," a mechanism designed to enable people to get their lives in sufficient order to live independently, relying on the returns from their own efforts. This is the rationale for "time-limited welfare." When the proposed two-year time limit for support has been reached, recipients will be turned out to find their own way in the world of work, assisted by child care subsidies and, of course, health coverage as part of the president's health care reform proposal; if they are unable to find work, the government will guarantee them a low-paying public service job or subsidize the private sector to provide jobs. However, this provision will apply only to young recipients—those born in 1972 or after—and then only to those with children older than one year. And, in a last-minute decision, the president has determined that recipients not able to find a private-sector job will be allowed to keep their public service job indefinitely—if they play by the rules—that is, keep searching for a job and do not decline one if offered.

WAS YOGI BERRA RIGHT, OR IS THIS A NEW APPROACH?

Those of us who have long followed the course of welfare reform may indeed wonder, to borrow Yogi Berra's words, "Is this déjà vu all over again?" To be sure, several themes in the current discussion hark back to President Jimmy Carter's Program for Better Jobs and Income (PBJI), and before that to President Richard Nixon's Family Assistance Plan (FAP). Indeed, 20 years ago we worried about whether those who are able to work should be distinguished from those who are not able to work; and about whether or not we should impose stiff requirements—work requirements—on the former group. We still worry about that.

And, in the debate over the PBJI, we struggled to design the program to "make work more attractive than welfare." We were worried about whether government should serve as an employer of last resort. We asked: "Won't public service employment be too expensive or too artificial?" We again ask that question.

We disagreed then, too, over whether or not reform should be incremental, building on what we have accomplished, or whether it should be an "overhaul" (the word used then). Should we go fast, hoping for benefits from a sudden change in regime, or should we proceed slowly and surely, building on research findings and the experiences from evaluated demonstrations. The Clinton plan does what most previous welfare reform proposals did; it proceeds on the basis of belief and hope. The Family Support Act of 1988 was an exception to this procedure.

So far, this is old wine in a new welfare reform bottle; however, there are several new themes in the current plan. For example, whereas welfare reform used to be about changing benefit levels, structures, and arrangements so as to improve the lives of the poor, now it is about getting people off welfare, substituting recipients' own earnings or family help for public help—and using whatever benefits remain to change recipients' behavior. Any incremental expenditure today— all of $9.3 billion over the next five years!—will go toward enforcing work mandates, toward making regular work more possible through child care assistance and job training, and toward providing public service work or work subsidies. These aspects, then, are different.

Also, unlike prior reform debates, the term *benefit adequacy* has now been stricken from the lexicon of welfare reform debate. Today's theme is getting welfare recipients to provide for their own well-being through work; *self-sufficiency* has replaced *benefit adequacy*.

Similarly, gone is the concern with the potentially stigmatizing effect of visible transfers. Have recipients changed or have we changed? Gone, too, is the emphasis on maintaining and strengthening incentives. Contrary to the claims of some administration representaives at the April 1994 Urban Institute conference on welfare reform,[2] I believe we have virtually given up on incentives; mandates, instead, are the focus of the day.

Gone is the concern for crafting an integrated system in which program structures are well-matched and consistent. Rather, the overriding emphasis is on changes that will make work—almost any work—more attractive than welfare. Requiring recipients to obtain work is today a matter of meeting a social norm, and compulsion is entertained in a way almost unimaginable a decade ago.

Gone is the concern with extending income support to the working poor. Indeed, today's issue is the reverse: How can we accomplish withdrawal of unrestricted support from the nonworking poor?

Gone is the debate over cash versus in-kind benefits. Suddenly, no one argues for program support on the basis that it affords recipients more control over the choices they make.

Finally, to an extent I cannot recall experiencing, we have come to accept the proposition that the purpose of a legislative proposal, indeed of the legislation itself, is to change the expectations of the poor, to change their behavior, and to change their efforts. Preaching about the ills of teenage pregnancy is but one example. This is "public policy as moral suasion."

HOW DOES THE CLINTON PLAN STACK UP? A "REALITY CHECK"

How has the Clinton plan fared at the hands of this volume's analysts and practitioners? Did it pass our reality check?

In terms of the first theme mentioned earlier—to "make work pay"—the authors represented here saw the expansion of the Earned Income Tax Credit (EITC) as important and effective policy. The EITC increases the return to work for those with children and does so coherently and within the structure of the personal income tax. Improvements to the advance payment option so that families can secure work-related income support throughout the year were suggested by a number of conference participants. Gary Burtless, in chapter 4, pointed out, however, an important but overlooked aspect of the program as now structured. Within the EITC, there is a substantial "marriage penalty," which in turn provides an incentive for family breakup and a disincentive to marry. This aspect of the policy should be reduced or eliminated. The EITC also creates a work disincentive for some subsidized workers, and this feature is a cause for concern.

The second theme of the Clinton plan, that parenting implies responsibility (i.e., increasing federal effort will be made to collect an assured child support and to routinize the collection system) was generally supported by the volume's contributors. But at the conference Ronald Mincy reminded us of the family responsibility of young, especially minority men, as opposed to their financial responsibility. These two responsibilities are not the same, and depending on how policy is implemented, stringency in the latter dimension could well impede performance in the former. Like others who have studied child support enforcement and are its biggest advocates, the authors assembled here seem to agree that this effort will have no more than a marginal effect on the available income support accruing to most mothers now on welfare.

The third and fourth themes of Clinton welfare reform stress training and education through workfare-type programs, child and health care assistance, time-limited welfare, and a guaranteed public service job. In the eyes of this book's analysts, these components also provide grounds for skepticism. Whereas changing the structure of both welfare benefits and work to minimize the rewards available to dysfunctional behavior is one thing, effectively canceling income support seems quite another. Chapters 3 and 4, by Rebecca Blank and Gary Burtless, respectively, provided convincing evidence that most current recipients lack the basic capabilities to raise themselves out of poverty on their own, even if they worked full-time, full-year at the wage rate that their experience, education, and health characteristics would command.

The volume's discussants agreed, moreover, that whereas those training or welfare-to-work programs with which we are familiar may pass a benefit-cost test, they are unable to close much of the remaining poverty gap. They concluded that it is but a dream to expect that the training and remedial education programs offered by the Clinton plan will be able to make more than a handful of welfare recipients job-ready and economically-independent. Moreover, the total cost of operating a reasonable public service jobs program—perhaps in the neighborhood of $15,000 per participant year[4]—was viewed as sufficiently high to ensure that the available supply of slots would be far exceeded by the demand, given current budgetary constraints.

Let me speculate on what will, in fact, determine how the program would operate. The limited funds available will go for additional training, education, child care, and public service employment. The monies available for the latter of these—public service employment jobs—will determine how many job slots are available. The number of slots, together with some estimate of the number of welfare recipients encountering the two-year limit and who will not be able to secure private-sector jobs, will determine the number of recipients who will be made subject to the two-year-and-out provision. This figure will ultimately drive the level of exemptions to "two years and out."

These considerations lead to an inexorable—and painful—conclusion: the effectiveness of a policy of time-limited welfare, combined with child care, education, and job guarantee measures, could run the gamut from being harsh and punitive, to merely rhetorical, or, in the best of circumstances, it could offer an effective route to independence and self-sufficiency. The policy's success will depend on how time limits are implemented and, especially, on the amount of available funds and how those funds are allocated.

If a rigid, time-limited welfare program were actually implemented, the nation would be engaging in social measures more severe than any of those in other Western industrialized societies, and more severe than we have ever accepted in the past. While one might acknowledge the need for harsh treatment for some adults who have made welfare recipiency a career, the hardships imposed on them fall also on the children for whom they care. The consensus of analysts in this volume is clear: the imposition and enforcement of a time limit on welfare receipt would, *by itself*, be an overly simplistic answer to a problem whose solution requires extensive social service support for dysfunctional families; an overhaul of schools that fail to educate poor children; community-based services to combat gangs and violence; and housing initiatives to enable the poor to live in a clean and safe dwelling. Because the Clinton initiative has so far precluded much in the way of additional expenditures, time-limited welfare becomes a potentially dangerous and mean-spirited approach to the poverty problem.

On the other hand, if time limits are enacted together with a wide variety of exemptions and opportunities for delaying or avoiding their enforcement—for example, exemptions for older women, those with small children, those who cannot locate adequate child care or for whom no private or public job seems appropriate, or those who are long-term recipients with few job skills—this aspect of the program could be merely rhetorical. The long history of enacting, but failing to impose, work requirements in welfare programs makes this a real possibility, especially in the absence of funding to support the education, training, and job-guarantee measures that are necessary for a successful program.

The promise of time-limited recipiency can be realized only if the training and employment subsidies and child care support on which terminated recipients will depend do, in fact, provide the means for attaining independence and self-sufficiency. The effectiveness of these measures depends crucially on the structure of, and financial support for, these work-enabling measures. Given past experience, it is difficult to be optimistic that job training programs can lead to independence. Even the most extensive and successful of these— Supported Work and the Homemaker–Home Health Aide Demonstration —yield earnings increases of only about $500 per year, and little in the way of self-sufficiency and independence.

LOW-WAGE LABOR MARKET: THE WEAK LINK OF THE CLINTON PLAN?

Aside from these concerns, other serious reservations to the Clinton plan relate to the structure and performance of the low-wage labor market. The volume's contributors express substantial doubts about the wisdom of coercing the least-able groups of the nation's working-age population into that niche of the labor market that has performed most poorly. The low-wage end of the labor market is already struggling to absorb large and growing flows of immigrants, both legal and illegal, as well as a rapid increase in female labor force participants, many of whom have few skills and little experience. If ever there was "swimming against the tide," forcing welfare recipients into this market is it.

The implicit assumption of the plan's designers seems to be that the low-wage labor market can absorb up to 2 million additional low-skilled workers (existing welfare recipients) over the next few years without serious dislocation. Yet, this volume's authors have noted the plan's failure to adequately address the damper that the low end of the labor market places on opportunities for low-educated workers. Numerous suggestions are included throughout this book of ways to both increase the private demand for low-skilled labor and to make low-paying jobs more attractive. Indeed, these analysts seemed dismayed that more attention has not been paid by the administration to the potential of various labor market options.

After all, numerous possibilities have been studied, and some have received rather high marks. One of these, the New Jobs Tax Credit (NJTC), was in place in the nation in the 1970s, and offered a tax credit in the range of $4,000 to $7,000 (in today's dollars) to employers who increase the number of jobs they fill over some base employment level (typically the number of jobs offered during the previous year). Because the credit is a flat amount, it forms a higher percentage of the wage bill for less-skilled workers than for more highly paid workers and, as such, it tilts the hiring decision toward the lowest-wage workers.

Many observers are convinced that a nontrivial increase in jobs for low-skilled workers can be generated through such a program, and at a rather low cost to the U.S. Treasury.[5] This is especially so if the program is taken seriously by the administration, is publicized widely, and is administered efficiently. Note that I am referring here to a universal program, which would cover all marginal additions to the worker pool, and not to a targeted program that awards vouchers to individual low-wage workers and sends them into the labor market. The current Targeted Jobs Tax Credit Program is an example of this latter strategy, and evaluations of it have generally not been favorable.

A second possibility, this time on the supply side of the market, could be a wage-rate subsidy arrangement. Such a program would complement an expanded EITC, and would make work pay even more directly. A target wage rate—assume, say, $10 an hour—would be set. Any worker taking a job at less than this amount—say, $6 an hour—would be subsidized at a rate equal to 50 percent of the difference between the actual wage ($6) and the $10 target. Take-home pay in this example would thus be $8. The effect of the plan would be to simply and effectively provide all low-wage workers with a labor-market advantage. It would make regular private-sector work at low wages more attractive than it is now, and would give low-skilled workers an incentive to seek work. Again, a number of potential concerns would have to be ironed out in the program's design, and the effects of the measure on the overall level of the market wage would have to be monitored.

The combination of these programs would fundamentally alter the wage structure in private labor markets, raising the take-home pay of low-skilled workers relative to those with more secure positions in the labor market. The cost of such an arrangement would be substantially lower than providing equivalent jobs through public service employment, which is a central point of the Clinton plan.

Other measures for increasing labor demand and job opportunities are suggested in this book. These include Rebecca Maynard's (chapter 5) recommendation to subsidize work experience for welfare recipients, with required participation and no deferral; and Ronald Mincy and Hillard Pouncy's (chapter 7) advocacy of detailed case management and mentoring to assist people to develop soft skills and become job ready. Numerous programs were furthermore proposed by conference participants, including support for public service community jobs as the main thrust of policy; and advocacy of empowerment zones, community initiatives of a variety of sorts, and targeted job training programs linked to school-to-work transition measures. Without more specifics on program operation, eligibility, administration, financing, and cost-effectiveness, it is difficult to assess the potential of these proposals on a national scale. They do, however, focus on the Clinton plan's failure to tackle the constraints on work imposed by the current structure and functioning of the low-wage labor market.

THOUGHTS ON THE "REALITY CHECK"

I conclude by offering a few insights and reflections based on the conference discussions and the analyses in this volume.

First, I agree that welfare reform policy is no longer antipoverty policy. The ultimate goal of all of this activity is not to make poor people's lives better than they are now. Getting poor people to *work* is equated with making their lives better; perhaps this may happen in the long run, but certainly not in the short term for the majority of today's welfare recipients.

A second reflection stems from the remarks by William Gorham, president of the Urban Institute, at the beginning of the conference. Gorham spoke about institutions that seem no longer to work in American society—families, churches, and neighborhoods—and emphasized the difficulty that government faces in attempting to replace them. His comments triggered a thought that has often crossed my mind—namely, how difficult and expensive it is to bring a young person to a position where (in Nathan Glazer's terms) "work will work." The list of tasks in this complex process is staggering and bank-breaking. Perhaps there is a lesson in many of our own personal experiences that would be of use to the government as it sets its ambitious goals for welfare reform. First, we give them lots of education, with monitoring and advice and expectations and parental participation in schools. Then, when they finish their schooling, we support them for a time while they "get their heads together." Sometimes they engage in job search, sometimes they ski, sometimes they travel. Following this, we actively, and in a one-on-one relationship, help them with job search. We help them prepare a résumé, we put them in touch with friends and acquaintances, we help them prepare for job interviews—all so they can find their own special niche in the world of work. Finally, we often support them in moving to another location, frequently far from our home if that is where the best opportunity lies. And, think of how often, even with all of this nurturing, the process doesn't really work out too well.

The main lesson, I fear, is that performing this guidance and nurturing effectively and successfully is costly, very costly. As our own experiences have taught us, there is no way to do it "on the cheap." This truth makes more distressing our talk of making welfare recipients self-sufficient with a reform that will not violate budget neutrality.

A third reflection involves the relationship between the current welfare reform and health care reform proposals. Administration spokespersons have asserted that health care reform must occur prior to welfare reform. I am not certain I agree with this formula. From one perspective, passage of health care reform will make welfare reform easier, but from another perspective, it will make it more difficult. To be sure, if we had health care reform, we would eliminate both the "welfare lock," which is due to Medicaid provisions, and the "job lock," which is due to the large number of jobs that do not carry health care benefits. However, if we had in place a health care system that provided universal coverage and did so in part by mandating employers to pay for health benefits, the demand for low-skilled workers would be lower than it is now. The provision of health care by employers—costing from $3,000 to $5,000 per family—would form a higher share of the wages of low-skilled workers than of more highly paid workers, hence constraining the demand for just those people that we hope to make self-sufficient through employment. Considered this way, it is not clear to me that passage of that kind of health care reform will make passage of welfare reform easier or more effective.

A fourth reflection has to do with the administration of the welfare reform plan. Much has been written regarding the need for effective case management, consistent data, management information systems, institutional change within welfare agencies, the sorting of recipients, and the transforming of case workers into detailed case managers. The paths to achieving these improvements seem both ill-understood and extremely difficult. Yet it is stuff like this that makes changes in public policy either succeed or fail. I feel very chary about charging forward before we understand better how these fundamental changes in the operation of the nation's income transfer system can be accomplished.

One final reflection: I return to the dysfunctional—some would say destructive—choices and behaviors of a disproportionate number of people at the lowest income levels: teenage nonmarital childbearing, crime, acquiescence to a life of dependence, substance abuse. I am distressed that so few options appear feasible or attractive to address this special welfare-based problem. Moral suasion, the denial of benefits, punitive measures, or the status quo seem to be the main options on the table. In my view, none of these looks very appetizing, yet doing nothing is wrong as well. I am troubled by what appears to me to be a near-total lacuna concerning appropriate and effective policy in this area. Robert Woodson, of the Center for Neighborhood Enterprise, stated the problem as follows:

There are people whose poverty is due to external circumstance but who, even so, retain what are essentially middle-class values. For this group, social and economic programs may be all that is needed. But there is another group of the poor whose poverty is caused—or at least exacerbated and entrenched—by their own self-destructive attitudes and behavior. For them, social programs, day care and job training will make very little difference.

Unfortunately, Woodson did not offer a solution for this latter group.

I do not know the answer, either, but I am convinced that harsh measures, such as mandated adoption for some welfare recipients, are the wrong way to go. And I also doubt that preaching will get the job done.

Notes

1. Parts of this chapter are drawn from Robert Haveman and John Karl Scholz, "Transfers, Taxes, and Welfare Reform," *National Tax Journal*, 47 (2, June): 417–24. An outstanding synthesis of the welfare reform debate is contained in the Public Broadcasting System's documentary, *Making Work Work* (produced by Roger Weisberg and Dan Klein; narrated by Walter Cronkite).

2. This and subsequent text referrals are to the Urban Institute conference on "Self-Sufficiency and the Low-Wage Labor Market: A Reality Check for Welfare Reform," in Arlington, Va., April 12–14, 1994, from which this book's discussions are drawn.

3. Should the reform process continue, however, one must believe that issues of program design and integration will be increasingly emphasized and debated.

4. See Haveman (1980), citing Isabel Sawhill's congressional testimony regarding a study undertaken by the National Commission on Employment Policy.

5. See, for example, Bishop and Haveman (1979). Other relevant references are in Haveman (1988).

References

Bishop, John, and Robert Haveman. 1979. "Selective Employment Subsidies: Can Okun's Law Be Repealed? *American Economic Review* 69 (May): 124–30.

Council of Economic Advisers. 1994. *Economic Report of the President.* Washington, D.C.: U.S. Government Printing Office, February.

U.S. Bureau of the Census. 1990. *Current Population Reports, Series P60–167, Money Income of Households, Families and Persons in the U.S.: 1988 and 1989*. Washington, D.C.: U.S. Government Printing Office.

————. 1991. *Current Population Reports, Series P60–172, Trends in Income, by Selected Characteristics: 1947 to 1988*. Washington, D.C.: U.S. Government Printing Office.

————. 1993a. *Current Population Reports, Series P60–186RD, Measuring the Effect of Benefits and Taxes on Income and Poverty: 1992*. Washington, D.C.: U.S. Government Printing Office.

————. 1993b. *Statistical Abstract of the United States: 1993*. 113th ed. Washington, D.C.

Haveman, Robert. 1980. "Direct Job Creation." In *Employing the Unemployed*, edited by Eli Ginsberg. New York: Basic Books.

————. 1988. *Starting Even: An Equal Opportunity Program to Combat the Nation's New Poverty*. New York: Simon & Schuster.

Robert H. Haveman is John Bascom Professor of Economics and Public Affairs at the University of Wisconsin-Madison, where he also serves as Chair of the Department of Economics, and faculty member in the La Follette Institute of Public Affairs and the Institute for Research on Poverty. His research focuses on the economics of social policy, as exemplified in his 1988 book, *Starting Even: New Policy for the Nation's New Poverty* (Simon and Schuster), and on the determinants of children's attainments, published jointly with Barbara Wolfe in *Succeeding Generations: On the Effects of Investments in Children* (Russell Sage Foundation, 1994).

Demetra Smith Nightingale is director of the Welfare and Training Research Program at the Urban Institute in Washington, D.C. Her research includes a number of studies on employment and training policy, evaluations of federal and state welfare programs and welfare reform initiatives, and analyses of federal anti-poverty policies and budgets. She also directs the Urban Institute's projects tracking the implementation of the Family Support Act of 1988 and subsequent welfare reform efforts, and was co-principal investigator of the Evaluation of the Washington State Family Independence Program. She is coauthor of *Evaluation of the Massachusetts Employment and Training (ET) Choices Program* (Urban Institute Press, 1991).

ABOUT THE CONTRIBUTORS

Laurie J. Bassi is an associate professor of public policy at Georgetown University and the executive director of the Advisory Council on Unemployment Compensation. She is the author of numerous articles on policies that affect low wage individuals, including "Workplace Education for Hourly Workers" and "Employment and Welfare Participation Among Women."

Rebecca M. Blank is professor of economics at Northwestern University, a member of the research faculty at NU's Center for Urban Affairs and Policy Research and serves as co-director of its Urban Poverty Program, an interdisciplinary research and graduate training program. Her own research focuses on the interaction between the macroeconomy, government anti-poverty programs, and the behavior and well-being of low-income families. She is editor of the recent volume, *Social Protection versus Economic Flexibility: Is There a Tradeoff?*

Gary Burtless is a senior fellow in the Economic Studies program at the Brookings Institution in Washington, D.C. He does research on issues connected with public assistance, education and training programs, aging labor markets, income distribution, social insurance, and the behavioral effects of government tax and transfer policy. He is coauthor of *Growth with Equity: Economic Policymaking for the Next Century* (Brookings, 1993) and *Can America Afford to Grow Old? Paying for Social Security* (1989).

Nathan Glazer is co-editor of *The Public Interest,* and Professor of Education and Sociology, Emeritus, Harvard University. He is the author of *The Limits of Social Policy.*

Rebecca A. Maynard, is Trustee Professor of Education, Social Policy and Communication at the University of Pennsylvania and senior fellow at Mathematica Policy Research, Inc. Previously, she served

Mathematica Policy Research, Inc. as senior vice president and director of Princeton research. She has directed several evaluations of large-scale social experiments and published on a variety of topics, including employment and training policy, welfare policy, child care, and teenage pregnancy.

Ronald B. Mincy is a program officer for Employment and Welfare in the Urban Opportunity Program at the Ford Foundation. He is a nationally recognized economist and policy analyst whose principle areas of expertise are the under class, poverty, and incomes and welfare policy. He has published widely on measurement of the growth and composition of under class and concentrated poverty populations, and is the editor of *Nurturing Young Black Males: Challenges to Agencies, Programs, and Social Policy* (Urban Institute Press, 1994).

Hillard Pouncy, political scientist, is an independent researcher concerned with urban politics and policy. He has taught at Swarthmore College and Brandeis University in American Politics and African-American Studies. He has coauthored several articles on the school-to-work transition.

LIST OF CONFERENCE SPEAKERS

William F. Baker, President, Channel 13 WNET, New York City

Laurie J. Bassi, Economist, Georgetown University

Gordon Berlin, Senior Vice President, Manpower Demonstration Research Corporation

Rebecca M. Blank, Associate Professor of Economics, Northwestern University

Barbara Blum, President, The Foundation for Child Development

Susan Boyd, Director, Denver Family Opportunity Partnership

Lynn Burbridge, Associate Director, Wellesley College

Gary Burtless, Senior Fellow, The Brookings Institution

Rodolfo de la Garza, Vice President, Tomas Rivera Center and Professor of Government, University of Texas-Austin

Mark Elliott, Program Officer, The Ford Foundation

David Ellwood, Assistant Secretary for Planning and Evaluation, U.S. Department of Health and Human Services

James Gibson, Senior Associate, The Urban Institute

Nathan Glazer, Professor of Education, Harvard University

William Gorham, President, The Urban Institute

Robert H. Haveman, Professor of Economics and Public Affairs, University of Wisconsin

Toby Herr, Founder and Director, Project Match, Chicago, Illinois

James Hyman, Associate Director, The Annie E. Casey Foundation

Lawrence Jackson, Commissioner, Virginia Department of Social Services

Lawrence Katz, Chief Economist, U.S. Department of Labor

Marvin Kosters, Resident Scholar, American Enterprise Institute

Sharon Long, Senior Research Associate, The Urban Institute

Julia Lopez, Equal Opportunity Director, The Rockefeller Foundation

Rebecca A. Maynard, Professor of Education and Policy, University of Pennsylvania

Ronald B. Mincy, Program Officer, The Ford Foundation

Demetra Smith Nightingale, Senior Research Associate, The Urban Institute

Janet Norwood, Senior Fellow, The Urban Institute (former Commissioner, Bureau of Labor Statistics)

June O'Neill, Professor of Economics and Finance, Baruch College, City University of New York

Van Doorn Ooms, Senior Vice President and Director of Research, Committee for Economic Development

Hillard Pouncy, Associate Professor of Political Science, Swarthmore College

The Honorable Robert Reich, Secretary, U.S. Department of Labor

David Riemer, Chief of Staff, Mayor's Office, Milwaukee

The Honorable Rick Santorum (R-Pennsylvania), Ranking Minority Member, Human Resources Subcommittee of the House Committee on Ways and Means

Isabel V. Sawhill, Associate Director, Office of Management and Budget

Sharon Schulz, Executive Director, New Hope Project, Milwaukee

Donna Shalala, Secretary, U.S. Department of Health and Human Services

Joseph Stiglitz, Member, Council of Economic Advisers

Andrea Taylor, Media Programs Director, The Ford Foundation

Wayne Vroman, Senior Research Associate, The Urban Institute

Roger Weisberg, Television Documentary Producer, Director and Writer

INDEX